Russian Tarot of St. Petersburg

Russian Tarot
❧ of ❧
St. Petersburg

by

Cynthia Giles

Publisher
U.S. GAMES SYSTEMS, INC.
Stamford, CT 06902 USA

Library of Congress Catalog Card Number: 95-070428

ISBN 0-88079-196-9

10 9 8 7 6 5 4 3 2 1
Printed in Canada

U. S. Games Systems, Inc
179 Ludlow Street
Stamford, CT 06902 USA

Table of Contents

Preface

When I first saw the Russian Tarot of St. Petersburg, I was charmed—as most people are—by its beautiful execution and its exotic designs. But through my research on its imagery, I came to appreciate this unusual deck far more. The information I gathered on Russian history and culture made the Russian Tarot of St. Petersburg come alive, so I decided to include a lot of that information in the book. An understanding of the Russian world—through its amazing history, its luminous arts, and its powerful spirituality—is bound to enrich anyone's enjoyment of the Russian Tarot of St. Petersburg.

In the process of writing this book, I was especially surprised to discover the exceptional role that women have played in the shaping of Russian history. Although Russian women as a whole never had what we think of today as "equality," Russia had female leaders of authentic power and international influence. In fact, the whole of Russian culture had a more feminine cast—deriving from the Slavic devotion to "moist Mother Earth"—than we are accustomed to in the West.

The drama, humanity, and sheer scope of Russian history impressed me greatly. Even though I had studied Russian literature and art, I had never had a real sense of the Russian soul until I tried seriously to understand Russian history. The Russians themselves believe their history, their story as a people, is the key to their national character, and perhaps that is why Yury Shakov incorporated so many historical references into the imagery of the Russian Tarot of St. Petersburg.

There is one interesting item which I couldn't find a place for in the book, so I thought I'd mention it here. Yury Shakov created an extra card for the deck, something of a "title page," apparently, which bears an image found nowhere in the Tarot tradition. As nearly as I can tell, based on the conventions of religious iconography, the figure on the card is St. Jerome. Saints (since their true likenesses often remained unknown) were made identifiable in art by giving them certain symbolic accessories, and St. Jerome—a Christian scholar and Church Father who lived in the fourth century—was typically shown in art accompanied by an owl, a token of wisdom and solitude, befitting Jerome's life as an ascetic; and often by writing implements, signifying his importance as the translator of the Old Testament into Latin.

St. Jerome was well-loved in Russia (see the commentary in this book on the Strength card), but I don't have any idea why Yury Shakov might have chosen to give him his own card in the Russian Tarot of St. Petersburg! I can only speculate that it might have something to do with Jerome's role as a translator—perhaps a parallel with Shakov's own undertaking, to "translate" the Tarot into Russian imagery.

Gratitude is due to Yury Shakov's widow Ludmilla and his daughter Olga (an editor and a writer respectively), who graciously shared materials concerning the artist's life and work. Shakov was evidently a most unusual man, whose talent surfaced at an early age. Born in 1937, in Azerbajdzhan, the young Shakov was soon sketching classical sculptures and making studies of Renaissance paintings. He attended a special school for gifted children, and then continued his art while completing three years of medical school *and* playing championship tennis! Ultimately, art prevailed over his other interests, and Yury Shakov became a successful photo journalist in his hometown of Baku before moving to Moscow; there, he began designing books, and soon became interested in the Palekh style of miniature painting.

This very special art form proved to be Yury Shakov's true calling, and he began to build a brilliant career as a miniaturist. But after his brother emigrated to the United States, Shakov found himself penalized by the Soviet establishment, and finally decided to leave Russia. He and his family were permitted to join their relatives in America, but the Soviet officials would not allow Shakov to take a single piece of his art, save a portrait of his wife. So the artist had to start his new life and his new career almost literally from nothing—yet he was soon recognized as one of the most gifted miniature painters of our time.

It was a great good fortune for the Tarot that Yury Shakov applied his talent and insight to the creation of the Russian Tarot of St. Petersburg, even though he did not live to complete the project. It seems unlikely that anyone else could have given us a collection of images which so successfully merges the rich Russian culture with the equally rich tradition of the Tarot. The Russian Tarot of St. Petersburg clearly reflects both a great talent and a humane spirit at work.

In closing, my thanks to Stuart Kaplan for asking me to do this book. I've learned a great deal in the process. Thanks are also due to my son, Chris Giles, for sharing his prodigious knowledge of history and his keen perception of artistic symbolism, as well as to Robert Alexander for his helpful comments on the manuscript. As always, I'd like to extend my appreciation to family and friends for the many ways in which they deepen my understanding of life, and to my Tarot colleagues for the insights they have shared with me.

Introduction:
The Unique Russian Tarot of St. Petersburg

THE RUSSIAN TAROT OF ST. PETERSBURG

*T*he Russian Tarot of St. Petersburg is strikingly handsome. Its brilliant colors and delicate gold borders stand out against the night-black background, combining the richness of Russian fairy tales, the passionate artistry of the Russian *icon*, and the luxuriant detail of medieval illumination. Vivid images, drawn from Russian history and from the tradition of the Tarot, engage the viewer and bring an added dimension of aesthetic pleasure to the process of working with the cards.

But the Russian Tarot of St. Petersburg is more than just another pretty deck. It is also a fascinating example of how the traditional Tarot images may be refracted through the prism of a particular culture, to reveal and elaborate the essential qualities of those images. The Russian Tarot of St. Petersburg provides an opportunity to explore the fascinations of a little-known world, while at the same time enriching your acquaintance with the Tarot.

This unique deck came to life in a suitably unusual way. In 1987, Stuart Kaplan—chairman of the Tarot publishing company U.S. Games Systems, Inc., author of *The Encyclopedia of Tarot,* and enthusiastic Tarot collector—happened to see some artwork created by Yury Shakov for use on lacquered boxes. Shakov was at that time already recognized as the foremost miniaturist in America, even though he had emigrated to this country only a few years before. His works, which included precious jewelry, intricately decorated Easter eggs, and marvelously detailed miniature icons, were eagerly sought after by collectors, and were acquired by museums.

Fascinated by the precise technique and the exotic character of Shakov's designs, Stuart Kaplan immediately thought of a Tarot done in this distinctive Russian style. But even after locating Shakov, Kaplan still had to wait several months before the artist would agree to try painting a Tarot. Since Yury Shakov was completely unfamiliar with the Tarot, he would have to undertake the process of becoming acquainted with the cards, as well as making the huge commitment of creating seventy-eight original miniature paintings. The miniaturist's art is extremely demanding (miniature painters often use a brace to steady the arm as they wield brushes so fine some are made of only a single hair), and even though Shakov is said by his family to have loved his work so much that he sometimes worked sixteen hours a day, both Shakov and Kaplan knew the project would take a long time to complete.

Over the next two years, Shakov created the master designs for the whole deck, and completed nearly half of the paintings. Using several Tarot decks (in particular, the Classic Tarot, the Tarot of Marseilles, and the Waite deck), the artist developed concepts and then discussed them with Stuart Kaplan and George Bennett, who was at that time art director for U.S. Games Systems. This three-way dialog brought together in the preparation of the Russian Tarot of St. Petersburg both in-depth knowledge of the Tarot tradition, and a marvelously creative imagination, steeped in Russian art and folklore.

The fact that Yury Shakov came to the Tarot without preconceptions and without a metaphysical agenda makes his creation, the Russian Tarot of St. Petersburg, all the more interesting. In many instances, Tarot decks are created by artists to illustrate their ideas or beliefs about what the cards "mean." But Shakov's designs are the product of an intuitive response to the *visual imagery* of the Tarot. The themes and implications which abound in the deck were not put there intentionally; rather, they emerged from the fertile ground of Russian myth and history, in the very process of Shakov's artistic work.

Unfortunately, Yury Shakov was not able to complete the Russian Tarot of St. Petersburg. His sudden death in March of 1989 saddened those who knew him, and deprived the world of one of its few great miniaturists. However, the deck was by then fully conceptualized. The trumps and the suit of Cups were complete, and notes and sketches documented Shakov's overall vision of the Russian Tarot of St. Petersburg. So Stuart Kaplan decided to commission a second artist to complete the remaining three suits. A broker was retained to find an artist in Russia who could continue the deck in Shakov's style, and the new artist worked from Shakov's materials to prepare the additional drawings.

It will never be known, however, just how much of the imagery in the suits of Swords, Clubs, and Coins was conceived by Shakov, and how much was created by the second artist. As the second artist began work, a new and tumultuous chapter in Russian history was unfolding—one which would lead to the fall of Communism and bring increasing economic and social chaos. Although the rest of the art was in due course completed, and the Russian Tarot of St. Petersburg became a reality, the identity of the second artist was never revealed by the broker. It may be a long time before the Russian people will finally be free of the habit of secrecy acquired under decades of Communist rule.

The completion of this book was actually delayed for several months, in an attempt to find out something about the second artist and the process by which he or she worked; although we know that the artist used the Waite Tarot (probably the Universal Waite, a version of the deck re-colored by Mary Hanson Roberts in a softer palette than the original) along with Yury Shakov's notes and sketches as a guide, we don't know whether the artist had other knowledge of the Tarot. And since Shakov's notes and sketches were lost in the process, there's no way of telling what, if anything, the second artist may have contributed to the final design of the Swords, Clubs, and Coins cards.

It's a great shame not to be able to give credit to the second artist for the fine craftsmanship which not only complements the style of Yury Shakov, but also adds its own charm to the overall effect of the Russian Tarot of St. Petersburg. Perhaps this book will someday find its way to the unknown artist, and let him or her know the work is appreciated.

Later, there will be more information about the art and artistry of the Russian Tarot of St. Petersburg. There will also be a detailed guide to understanding the elements of the deck and the imagery of the individual cards. But first it's important to consider some things about the nature of the Tarot, its connection with culture and imagination, and the ways in which the special character of the Russian tradition may illuminate the special character of the Tarot.

THE TAROT: ARCHETYPES AND CULTURE

In the five centuries (more or less) since the Tarot images first appeared in Western history, many hundreds of decks have been created. Most of the decks were quite similar to one another, based on fundamental designs that changed little over the years. These designs depicted characters, costumes, settings, and symbols generally associated with the early Renaissance in Italy, where the twenty-two Tarot trumps first appeared and were evidently joined with an existing four-suited card deck. Interest in the Tarot spread throughout Europe, and decks were devised which gave a French, German, or Dutch cast to the images; but the essential "core" images, and their general style, remained the same. For the most part, the Tarot cards were used in a popular game called Triumphs, and there was little information—and less interest—concerning the origin of the images.

In the late eighteenth century, however, an entirely new phase in the life of the Tarot began when amateur anthropologist and occult enthusiast Antoine Court de Gébelin discovered the Tarot trumps and became rapturously convinced that they represented a lost "book" of old Egypt. In Court de Gébelin's day, little was known about the ancient Egyptians, and many Europeans with metaphysical interests believed that Egyptian hieroglyphics, then undeciphered, depicted the wisdom of the ages. So it is not surprising that when Court de Gébelin (who was not familiar with the game of Triumphs) came upon the exotic images of the Tarot, he jumped to the conclusion that they had esoteric significance and must derive from the great Egyptian civilization.

Court de Gébelin was surely right in recognizing that the Tarot images had special properties, but he was quite wrong in attributing them to old Egypt; within a few years after Court de Gébelin's death, the riddles of Egyptian language and culture began to be unraveled, revealing absolutely nothing which would support a connection with the Tarot. Nevertheless, Court de Gébelin's idea took up a life of its own. Over the next century, his theory was elaborated by enthusiasts such as Eliphas Lévi and Papus, whose book *The Tarot of the Bohemians* supposed a connection between the Tarot and the Gypsies (then thought to be descendants of the Egyptians).

Lévi and his followers developed theories relating the Tarot images to ritual magic, and toward the turn of the nineteenth century, the Tarot became an important component in the activities of the Hermetic Order of the Golden Dawn, a group which sought to integrate magic and art through an exploration of the creative imagination. The great poet William Butler Yeats was active in the Golden Dawn, as was the infamous magical practitioner Aleister Crowley, creator of the strange and luminous Thoth Tarot. Another member was the scholarly Arthur Edward Waite, who gave the twentieth century its most popular deck, the Rider-Waite. It was Waite who added a new dimension to the Tarot by designing images for the minor arcana cards, which previously had only suit signs and numbers.

The high point of the Golden Dawn group coincided with a very active period of cultural change that produced Picasso, Stravinsky, Einstein, Jung, and a whole new direction in the arts and sciences. During the first half of the twentieth century, the world was almost completely transformed, and for a time, metaphysical interests such as the Tarot were eclipsed by the rapid pace of political events and technological developments. But over the past twenty-five years, a renewed interest in the imagination has brought about many new types of Tarot activity. One of the most important developments has been the recognition, based on the psychology of

C.G. Jung, that the Tarot trumps are representations of images deeply embedded in the human psyche. These images, which Jung called "archetypes," are common to all cultures, but they are expressed differently according to the traditions and perceptions of different peoples.

Archetypes are the essential elements of all stories, from Shakespeare to soap opera, from myths to movies. Although details may change endlessly, at the deepest level, all tales of human life reflect a few basic patterns. Our perennial fascination with the Tarot derives from its ability to reveal to us this fundamental architecture, and to create links between the archetypal realm and our own experience. When we look at the images of the Tarot trumps, we are able to see in a depersonalized or objective form the hopes and fears, the emotions and ideas, the characters and processes which make up the stories of all our lives.

In this broad sense, it is nearly irrelevant what style is given to the Tarot images. The Tarot images as we know them were apparently created originally in the style of the late Middle Ages/early Renaissance, and they are basically European in character. But the archetypes they represent are by no means limited to that time and place. The same archetypal images and structures were just as present in the lives of the pre-Columbian Americans, the ancient Sumerians, the farmers and warriors of feudal Japan. They are with us today, whether we live in small towns or urban ghettos, on Navaho reservations, in the rain forests of Brazil, or the monasteries of Sri Lanka. Accordingly, they can be translated into the styles of many different cultures.

The numerous translations of the Tarot which have taken place in recent years not only give us wonderful visual variety in the cards, but also demonstrate the many faces of the Tarot. Some of these contemporary decks, such as the Native American Tarot and the Celtic Tarot, have been created to express special ethnic and historical perspectives. Others, like the Tarot of the Cat People and the Voyager Tarot Deck, create entirely new worlds, where our fantasies are made visible. The Haindl Tarot and the Tarot of the Ages are among those decks which bring together images from different cultures, while decks as diverse as the Dali Tarot and the Enchanted Tarot reveal the intimate relationship between the esoteric power of the Tarot images and the creative imagination of the artist. In all of these various "realizations" of the Tarot, aspects of its essential character are given new visibility, meaning, and depth.

Amazingly enough, though Tarot decks have proliferated in recent years, the richness of the images never seems to be exhausted. Each new deck brings to light more facets of the Tarot and offers new possibilities to the Tarot reader. In this same way, the Russian Tarot of St. Petersburg offers fresh insight by casting the traditional Tarot images in the shapes and colors of a now-vanished way of life.

RUSSIAN HISTORY, ART, AND FOLK LIFE

Most people outside of Russia know very little about the Russian culture. For centuries, the vast distances and the hardships of travel in the Russian empire discouraged casual visitors, and more recently, Russia has been politically isolated from our own world. The average American today views Russia through the lens of the Cold War. We know the history of Russia mainly as a tale of brutality, from Ivan the Terrible to Stalin; we see the culture of Russia as the product first of feudal oppression, then of Communist collectivization. For most of our lives, we have been accustomed to thinking of Russia as a barbaric land and an implacable enemy.

It is now only a short time since the collapse of Communism and the dissolution of the Soviet Union. As I am writing this, there is still much violence and uncertainty amongst those who once made up the great Soviet state. But even so, the advent of *glasnost* (or "openness") has already made Russian society far more visible to us. With a freer flow of information, we are learning more about the true nature of the Russian people, and about the complex historical forces which led to the rise and fall of the Soviet Union. Now that our fear is lessened, we can see more clearly that Russia, like all countries, has always been a mixture of many things: beauty and cruelty, generosity and injustice, sublime art and crushing hardship.

Today, by placing the good in proportion to the bad, we can begin
to appreciate the strength and diversity of Russian culture.

Suzanne Massie, in her book *Land of the Firebird*, has portrayed
in wonderful detail the almost-forgotten beauty of Old Russia. As
she explains in her introduction:

> Russian culture has much to offer us. The Russians
> know the darker side of humanity, but they also
> understand the extraordinary capacity of the human soul
> for sacrifice and love, and they have the ability to accept
> both sides of man with greater equanimity than we in the
> West. They know how to take a long view, something we
> have all but forgotten in our anxious desire for immediate
> gratification...They have approached God in a spirit of
> meekness; they have loved nature. They have revered poets
> and poetry with a passion equaled by few other
> peoples...Their knowledge of suffering and their
> understanding of human weakness have made their 19th-
> century novels probably the greatest in world literature.
> They gave depth and feeling to formal movements and
> *divertissements* intended only for the aristocracy of Europe
> and turned ballet into an uplifting and popular
> art...Their music has stirred hearts all over the world.

For all these reasons, Russian culture deserves to be better
understood by us, and the Russian Tarot of St. Petersburg offers a
special opportunity to explore the uniqueness of Russian life and art,
while appreciating the creative new energy they bring to the Tarot
tradition. As Massie points out, the "manifestations of beauty which
Old Russia produced so brilliantly, permeated by the spiritual
qualities of the Russian people, are perhaps what we most need to
rediscover now, to offset the coldness and impersonality of an
increasingly heartless, technological and materialistic modern
world." It may not be altogether coincidental that we value the Tarot
as a means to that same end.

The Russian Tarot of St. Petersburg does not merely
superimpose quaint Russian scenes on the Tarot. Although the card
images are fundamentally those which have been established over

several centuries of Tarot history, they are not just "dressed up" in a Russian style; rather, they are re-visioned and re-presented through the medium of a Russian artistic tradition which is deeply imbued with the spirit of symbolism and mysticism. In fact, the Tarot and the culture of Old Russia share something profoundly in common: a reliance on the psychological power of the visual image.

In Old Russia, the Russian Orthodox Church was the heart of the country, and the *icon* (a devotional painting) was the soul of the Church. Every church (and there might be thousands of churches in a single city) was filled with images in the forms of painted icons, frescoes, murals, and embroideries. Walls, ceilings, windows, doors, vestments, and furnishings depicted the life of Christ, the stories of the saints, the events of the Bible, the feasts of the church, and so on. In fact, the creation of icons was a major industry in Old Russia, for not only did churches require endless numbers of icons in every size, but private homes, also, were furnished with icons. Even the lowliest peasant house had its "beautiful corner," graced with the best icon the family could afford.

It is very difficult for us, as Westerners, to appreciate the passionate veneration which the Russians felt for their icons; our religions, like most aspects of our culture, are firmly grounded in *words*. Pictures are, for us, valuable primarily as illustrations which can clarify language or convey basic information more quickly than language. When pictures are viewed for their own sake, rather than as an accompaniment to language, we expect them to be "decorative" or "artistic" or "innovative"; in other words, to have visual or intellectual interest. It is only in a very few instances—and the Tarot is one of them—that we respond to pictures in a direct, *emotional* way.

This quality of eliciting direct response is, of course, the reason why (a) the Tarot makes a good tool for divination, and (b) the Tarot images cannot be neatly explained in language. The multi-layered and mysterious nature of the images speaks directly to the unconscious and resists reduction into logical, linear statements. In much the same way, the Russian icon reached out to its viewers and communicated the mysteries of faith and grace, good and evil, and life and death, *without any kind of explanation.*

From a theological standpoint, an icon actually participates in the divine essence and serves as an instrument of "sacred communication." The Byzantine (or Greek Orthodox) Church, from which the Russian Orthodox Church took its traditions, including that of icon-painting, regarded the icon as a "door to heaven," revealing to the pious meditator the nature of God. In the same way, the Tarot images might be described as "doors" to the unconscious, to a superpersonal dimension of reality, even to mystical experience. Through reading the cards and/or meditating on the Tarot images, we can discover aspects of ourselves, as well as aspects *beyond* ourselves, which are hidden from us in ordinary perception.

It is actually accurate to say that the Tarot images are, in a general sense, themselves icons. The word *icon* (from the Greek *eikon*) simply means "image," but it has come to be used in a special way to mean an image which partakes of the kind of deep symbolism just described. Although we most commonly use the word *icon* to describe a stylized painting of a religious subject, done in tempera on wood, an icon need not necessarily be a picture at all; in Orthodox theology, the Church, for example, is regarded as an icon of the cosmos, and the priest an icon of Christ. But among the Russians, the icons served their most immediate purpose as pictures, for they provided a means of conveying to the illiterate masses the stories of Christ's life and Passion, the miracles and martyrdom of the saints, and the precepts of the Church. "Icons," wrote John of Damascus, "are open books to remind us of God. The icon is a song of triumph and a revelation…an enduring monument to the victory of saints and the disgrace of demons."

Here again, the tradition of the icon may shed light on the mystery of Tarot. For a long time, it has been speculated that the Tarot trumps, whose origins are still unknown, may have been devised originally as memory aids or teaching materials that illustrate the doctrines of a Gnostic or heretical Christian sect. Some Tarot scholars have suggested that a group facing persecution for their religious ideas may have wished to preserve the ideas in an unwritten form, and so encoded them in the images we now know as the Tarot trumps. In the form of individual cards, the images would have been portable (preachers of these banned sects are thought to have traveled from group to group and to have taught their doctrines secretly), and easy to rearrange for a variety of purposes.

It's unlikely that we will ever know whether this scenario, or any other, accurately accounts for the origin of the Tarot cards. But there is a noteworthy parallel to be found in the tradition of the Russian Orthodox Church itself, where sets of small icons (not much larger than the earliest known Tarot cards, hand-painted for the Renaissance nobility) called *tabletka* were used as illustrations for various lessons and scriptural readings. The icons were given card-like form so that they could be conveniently stored in boxes, and groups of them could be selected to suit particular purposes. Like most icons (and like the Tarot images), these *tabletka* were created anonymously, in accordance with the tradition that the icon painter expressed not his own individuality, but the will of God.

There is no mention at all of the Tarot in Russian history, and no reason to think that the Tarot images we know were ever known there. Yet there is surely much resonance between the dense symbolism that for so long permeated Russian culture, and the richly symbolic nature of the Tarot. The Russian Tarot of St. Petersburg reveals and enhances that resonance. For this reason, an understanding of Russian history, art, and folk life will not only increase your enjoyment of this particular deck, but also expand your appreciation of the Tarot's depth and breadth.

RESOURCES FOR EXPLORING RUSSIAN CULTURE

This book will help you discover the special character of the Russian Tarot of St. Petersburg. Part I provides an overview of Russian history and culture, but as you continue to work with the deck, you may want to understand even more about traditional Russian life and art. The bibliography at the end of this book lists some of the works which provided the information contained here; although I used many more references, I've included only those which are readily available and interesting enough for enjoyable reading.

If you would like to acquire a few of the best books about Russia, I'd recommend the following three works, from which were taken the many colorful details and quotations which I've used throughout the present book to bring Russian history and culture to life.

The Horizon Book of Russia presents the history of Russia in a clear and enthralling way. Helpful illustrations and just the right amount of detail make this a very satisfying one-volume overview of Russia from prehistory through the 1960s.

James Billington's classic *The Icon and the Axe* offers a thorough examination of Russia's intellectual history, a subject which is treated only lightly in most other works. This is a somewhat scholarly book, and it assumes a general knowledge of Russian history, but it is reasonably accessible and frequently fascinating.

By far the most ravishing book about Russia (and perhaps about any country!) is *Land of the Firebird: The Beauty of Old Russia* by Suzanne Massie. Massie, who helped in the research for *Nicholas and Alexandra*, her husband's best-selling study of Russia's last imperial family, is clearly in love with Old Russia. Anyone who reads *Land of the Firebird* will share her enthusiasm for Russia's rich cultural heritage, and her sorrow at its destruction under Communism.

Not a book, but a terrific source of information about Russian spirituality, past and present, is the Spring 1994 issue of *Gnosis* magazine. It contains a number of interesting items, including essays on "Esoteric Russia," by Stephan A. Hoeller (author of the Tarot classic *The Royal Road*) and "The Eastern European Conception of Suffering," by Valentin Tomberg (better known as "Anonymous," author of *Meditations on the Tarot*). Also in this issue—which can probably be obtained by writing to *Gnosis*, P.O. Box 14217, San Francisco, CA 94114—are articles on Slavic shamanism, post-Soviet religious movements, and Baltic Gnosticism.

While non-fiction materials are great resources, it's difficult to get a real sense of another culture merely through reading *about* it. I found that it was very helpful to read some of the great works of Russian literature and poetry, to listen to the music of Russia, to look at Russian art, and to watch some of the films which provide glimpses into Russian culture. Here is a list of the best of those resources.

Russian Literature

For centuries, literature in Russia was made up of church writings on the one hand, and legends, myths, and folk tales on the other. Since only a very few people, and most of them in the church, could read or write, the bulk of Russia's story-telling was carried out orally. Many of these stories were gathered, written down, and published in the nineteenth century, and have become among the most beloved in the world. For a wonderful sampling, try to find Janet Higonnet-Schnopper's *Tales From Atop a Russian Stove.*

Although serious Russian literature may have been late in getting started, in the nineteenth century Russia produced a body of works which are among the greatest in the world. There is no better way to get a feeling for the passion of the Russian soul than reading Pushkin, Tolstoy, Gogol, Dostoevsky, Chekov, and Turgenev.

Several of the greatest Russian novels actually illuminate directly some of the Tarot archetypes. Dostoevsky's *The Idiot*, which explores the uniquely Russian character of the "holy fool," offers insight into the nature of the Tarot's Fool; while *The Brothers Karamazov*, which explores the relationship of good and evil, depicts from the Russian point of view the tension between Temperance and the Devil. Turgenev's *Fathers and Sons* examines the confrontation of youth and authority (the Fool and the Emperor), change and tradition (the Magician and the Hierophant), within the tumultuous cultural upheaval of Russia in the nineteenth century .

For a wonderful one-volume sampling of Russia's remarkable writers, try *The Portable Nineteenth-Century Russian Reader*, edited by George Gibian and published by Penguin Books (1993). It contains a selection of poems by the great Pushkin, as well as several of Russia's most famous short stories, including "The Overcoat" (Gogol), "The Death of Ivan Illych" (Tolstoy), and "The Lady with the Dog" (Chekhov). Also included are excerpts from the great novels *Obolomov* (Goncharov) and *The Brothers Karamozov* (Dostoevsky); the full text of "Uncle Vanya," Chekhov's drama about Russian life; and quite a few essays and observations by various Russian literary figures.

Russian Music

There are many great Russian classical composers from the nineteenth and early twentieth centuries, the most important of whom are Peter Tchaikowsky, Nikolai Rimsky-Korsakov, Alexander Borodin, Modest Mussorgsky, Sergei Prokofiev, Mikhail Glinka, Alexander Scriabin, and Igor Stravinsky. Of special interest are the several well-known compositions which musically depict great events and characters from Russian history. Among these are Mussorgsky's "Boris Godunov" and Prokofiev's "Alexander Nevsky."

Russian classical music, however, draws significantly from Western European musical forms, and gives only limited insight into Russian history and folk life. On the other hand, there are several recordings of traditional Russian music which offer a real sense of the Russian people's heart and soul. Look for *Dark Eyes: Russian Folk Songs* from Philips and *Balalaika Favorites* from Mercury Living Presence.

Russian Art

Many city art museums will have a few examples of Russian icon-painting and liturgical textiles. Larger libraries and bookstores will have books on Russian art. Generally speaking, however, it is difficult for most people to see much in the way of Russian art. One strategy may be to find out if there is a Russian Orthodox church nearby. The Russian Orthodox religion still maintains its emphasis on visual beauty and instruction, so almost every church, however small, will have its icons, murals, and embroideries.

The Horizon Book of the Arts of Russia is a wonderful introduction to the great artistic heritage of Old Russia, covering not only the visual arts, but music and literature as well. For a compact and informative survey of painting, architecture, and the decorative arts in Russia, *Art Treasures in Russia*, from the McGraw-Hill Art Treasures series, is an excellent choice.

To learn more about the particular style of art reflected in the Russian Tarot of St. Petersburg, be sure to see *The Fine Art of Russian Lacquered Miniatures* by Vladimir Guiliayev (Chronicle Books). This richly illustrated book offers a good deal of historical background concerning lacquerware and miniature painting, as well as profiles of Palekh, Mstera, and the other villages famous for this craft.

Films and Videos

You can use your VCR to get a sight-and-sound orientation to Russia. There are several travel videos designed to give you a virtual tour of Russian life and culture. For example, the Rand-McNally Video Trip series includes a "Guide to Moscow," in which you can take an imaginary stroll through the city, stopping (briefly) at Red Square and St. Basil's, the Kremlin, the Bolshoi Theater, the Moscow Circus, and a number of other tourist attractions. Other video travel series include similar tours of Moscow and Leningrad (which, don't forget, was the Communist name for St. Petersburg).

Audio-Forum (1-800-243-1234) and Audio Editions (1-800-231-4261) offer learning tapes if you would like to have a browse through the Russian language. Audio-Forum also has a video guide called "Russian Journey," as well as "Russian Folk Song and Dance," and a video tour of the Kremlin.

A charming look at the countryside and folklife of Russia's Georgian region is found in a short film called *The Falcon*. This joint Russian-American project tells a classic Russian story of a maiden who leaves her indulgent father and two spoiled sisters to rescue her true love, who comes to her in the guise of a magical bird. Although the sets and costumes are not lavish, you will get a real feeling for the wry wit and exotic fantasy of the Russian fairy tale. The film is produced by Palmer/Fenster Productions, 4027 Eastern Avenue North, Seattle, WA, 98103.

There are also quite a few movies readily available on video cassette which offer glimpses into the Russian culture. For a good understanding of the Russian contribution to early film-making, as well as an intensive view of Russian history as seen through Russian eyes, take a look at Sergei Eisenstein's great films, *Potemkin* (silent, 1925), *Alexander Nevsky* (1938), and *Ivan the Terrible,* Parts I and II (1944/1946).

Hollywood director Joseph von Sternberg offered an outrageously surreal picture of Catherine the Great in *The Scarlet Empress* (1934) and produced a more realistic treatment of Dostoevsky's *Crime and Punishment* (1935). *The Scarlet Empress,* if you can find it (probably on cable—it is not currently available on video) is well worth watching, for its strange excessiveness seems to capture something of the extremism which characterized Imperial Russia.

There are two film versions of Tolstoy's epic *War and Peace* available, both of interest. The American version, with Audrey Hepburn and Mel Ferrar, is very pretty and quite manageable to watch; the French version is even prettier, but very, very long.

For something completely different, Woody Allen offers a comic treatment of Russian melancholy in *Love and Death.* This very funny film is most enjoyable if you have read at least a couple of Russian novels or plays, for it does a great job of satirizing Russian literature's preoccupation with cosmic questions such as the nature of good and evil. Comic director Mel Brooks offers a more slapstick version of Old Russia in *The Twelve Chairs,* a hilarious picture of the resourcefulness for which the Russian peasant is justly famous.

A fairly new film, *The Russia House* is primarily about post-Cold War goings-on in the former Soviet Union, but it was filmed in Russia and offers some of the most wonderful views of Russian scenery available. In the city scenes, observe the interiors, where the sparse modern trappings do little to conceal the Imperial grandeur of the old buildings. The scene in the forest cottage, or *dacha,* where Sean Connery attends a traditional vodka-fueled political discussion, provides a nearly timeless example of Russian life.

The epic musical *Fiddler on the Roof* offers a surprisingly detailed and realistic view of country life in pre-Revolutionary Russia. Since the story is primarily about Jewish life, the customs, dress, and ceremony portrayed in the film are more characteristic of Eastern European Jewish communities in general than of Russian life among the Orthodox majority, but the film shows very well how work was done and life was lived in the Russian countryside. Notice the inside of the butcher's house when Tevya visits him, and you will see a very typical merchant-class dwelling, complete with samovar and tile stove.

Torrents of Spring is based on a Turgenev novel, and is an absolutely ravishing film. It has the look and feel of a European art film, but it is in English, and it portrays very effectively the absurd wealth and the confused despair of the Russian aristocracy in the nineteenth century. Watch for the wonderful scene at the Gypsy encampment.

Doctor Zhivago, perhaps the best-known of all movies about Russia, focuses so much on specific political and personal events that it does not offer much insight into larger issues of Russian culture. However, no film conveys more convincingly those qualities of the Russian landscape and culture which have played such a large role in the shaping of Russian life. You will feel the cold of the Russian winter and the vastness of the Russian steppe.

Many of the these films can be found at a good-sized video store, or even through your local or state library system. But if you are especially interested in seeing a film you can't find, you may want to try Critic's Choice Video. Call 1-800-367-7766 for information about the Video Search Line. There is a charge for the service, but they will track down most titles for you and give you information about price and ordering.

Part I

The History and Mystery of Russia

Chapter 1

The Story of Russia

A Russian proverb says, "The past is not a bad witness." This wisdom certainly applies to understanding their own vast, troubled, brilliant land. So for anyone who wishes to gain insight into the nature of Russian thought and culture, there is no better way than to explore the lavish drama of their history. And to fully appreciate that history, it is necessary above all to have a sense of the Russian landscape, for it has shaped every facet of Russian life.

THE RUSSIAN LAND AND LANGUAGE

Most of us grew up with maps and geography books that depicted not the country of Russia, but a collection of states known as "the Soviet Union." When we heard the term *Russia* in history class and on the news, it was used more or less interchangeably with the terms *U.S.S.R.* or *Soviet Union.* But actually, the historical country called "Russia" was only one part, and not the largest, of the Soviet Union. Strictly speaking, the term *Russia* applies historically to a country which existed from the middle of the ninth century to the year 1917. During those thousand years, that country grew in size from a loosely allied group of settlements scattered across the so-called *steppes* (from the Russian word for "lowlands"), to an empire which comprised one-sixth of the earth's land mass—a staggering 8,500,000 square miles.

Russia was always a vast and varied land. Its geographical centerpiece is an enormous plain, once the floor of an ocean that stretched from the Arctic to the Black and Caspian Seas. At its southerly edge, the plain gives way to some of the earth's mightiest mountains—the Caucasus, the Hindu Kush, the Pamirs, the Tien Shan, the Altai—but the broad expanse of the plain is interrupted only once by a north-south mountain chain, and that one, the Urals, is no more forbidding than our own gentle Adirondacks. Thus, no real barriers interrupt the east-west passage across Russia, a fact which long forced the Russians to be on constant guard against invasion from both directions.

Among the most extraordinary features of the great Russian plain is its drainage. In the European part, all the main streams originate around a slight central elevation (roughly the present site of Moscow), and from there, they wind their way to five great seas: in the north, the White and the Baltic, and in the south, the Black, the Azov, and the Caspian. In the Asian part of Russia, five huge river systems flow across the continent from south to north, from the heart of Asia all the way into the Arctic.

This amazing water network provides Russia with its famous rivers—the Don, the Volga, the Dneiper, and many others—and also with some of the most fertile land on earth, called in Russian *chernaya zemlya*, "black earth." North of this rich agricultural zone, sweeping from Finland four thousand miles to the east, is the *taiga*, a vast belt of forest, once almost unbroken, and densely populated with fur-bearing animals such as ermine and sable. When this seemingly inexhaustible forest bounty was combined with the far-reaching Russian river system, the result was the foundation of a powerful trade empire.

But Russia is by no means a geographical paradise. It also has large swampy areas, as well as sandy, barren expanses and vast frozen wastelands. The climate is harsh, featuring in most regions bitter-cold winters and sweltering summers. And everywhere, the enormity of the country, the sheer *difficulty* of it, is overwhelming. Yet these very hardships have played an important part in shaping the Russian culture. Historian Vasili Klyuchevsky speculated that the vast flatness of the steppes and the thickness of the spreading forests brought about in the Russian people "a ghastly feeling of imperturbable calm and deep sleep, of loneliness conducive to abstract, sad musing without any clearly defined thought."

Perhaps because of the country's unique and powerful landscape, Russians have always had a strong sense of place. In a way which is probably difficult for most non-Russians to understand, the Russian people were profoundly connected with and affected by their land. Over time, their sense of place merged with their sense of purpose, and the image of "Holy Mother Russia," a land of great fruitfulness and great suffering, came to burn in the hearts and minds of all Russians with a romantic passion that far exceeds what we normally think of as "patriotism" or "nationalism."

In fact, it is this idea or attitude of "Russianness" which defines Russia more clearly than its geographical boundaries, since the physical size and shape of the country has waxed and waned over many centuries through conquest and colonization. Mostly, however, Russia always grew bigger, and more diverse. On the eve of World War I, the Russian empire was made up of four huge regions: Russia proper (sometimes called European Russia), which then included all of Finland and most of Poland; the Caucasus (made up of many regions, including Georgia and Armenia); all of northern Asia (Siberia); and Russian Central Asia (which is mainly Turkestan). Although European Russia was populated primarily by people of Slavic descent, whose religion was Orthodox Christianity, the other regions were composed of many different ethnic groups and religious practices.

Furthermore, European Russia itself was not a single entity, but was made up of different groups which were formed when populations dispersed during the Mongol occupation; in that period, the Velkorussians or "Great Russians" came to live in the northern area around Novgorod and Suzdal. Malorussians or "Little Russians" settled to the southwest of them in the area surrounding Kiev, later called Ukraine. Byelorussians or "White Russians" came to the northwest in Byelorussia, where they lived among Polish and Lithuanian settlers.

Each of these groups developed its own special character, expressed not only in dress and custom, but also in a distinctive dialect of the Russian language. Yet even so, the Russian language has always been a uniting factor among the peoples of Russia. Russian is a Slavic language, based on an alphabet of 36 characters which represent all the possible sounds of the language. There are no sounds represented by two or more characters, as in the English "ou" or "th." The Russian language shares few roots with English, and it both looks and sounds quite different. It is not difficult to pronounce Russian words, however, for they are spoken much as they would be in English.

Words are arranged and accented very freely in Russian, allowing for a great variety of poetic cadences and effects. For this reason, such widely different works as those of Homer, Shakespeare, Rimbaud, and Hemingway can all be translated into Russian with exceptional faithfulness to the form and spirit of the originals. The flexibility and fertility of the Russian language—which has a famous capacity for forming compounds and derivatives—made possible the rich tradition of Russian literature that eventually yielded some of the greatest novels and plays of modern times.

For hundreds of years, however, there was *no* Russian literature and little, even, of literacy in Russia. There was no Russian writing until the Cyrillic alphabet was introduced in the tenth century (though probably not by St. Cyril, as was long believed), and for centuries afterward, writing was used almost entirely for ecclesiastical purposes. Even after secular literature such as history, biography, and fiction began to be written in Russian, most of Russia's lore continued for the most part to be preserved and passed on orally. It is mainly from the rich heritage left us by those long-ago storytellers that we know anything at all about the earliest history of Russia.

OLD RUSSIA

To understand what is truly "Russian" about Russia, we must look all the way back to its beginnings, when complex historical forces created the old Russia and sowed the seeds of the Russia we know today. The story of old Russia is filled with beauty and daring as well as tragedy and terror, and its course is marked with events of almost unimaginable scope. During that tumultuous time we call the "Dark Ages," the essential nature of Russian culture took on the shape that would carry it first to heights of grandeur, then near the brink of ruin.

The Earliest Russians

Since the earliest inhabitants of the land had no writing, little is known in detail about the history of Russia before the ninth century AD. But we can piece together the general outlines of primitive Russia from accounts of the Greeks and Romans and from modern archaeology.

About 800 BC, Scythians from Persia (now Iran) began to roam the south Russian steppes. The nomadic Scythians were regarded by the Greeks as barbarians, but they had their own subtleties, including great artistry with gold. Like the many other nomadic tribes of Asia, the Scythians were expert horsemen and savage warriors, shooting bronze-tipped arrows from their short, double-curved bows with swift accuracy at distances of several hundred feet. Once they had seized territory, they allowed the inhabitants to continue farming and trading, but levied tribute, which they used to fund their continuing usurpations. However, unlike other early barbarians, the Scythians took an interest in the Greek culture, which they encountered in the Greek colonies established along the shores of the Black Sea. One of their princes, Anacharsis, was even said to have gone to Athens to study with the great Greek statesman Solon.

By around the third century BC, however, the Scythians were supplanted in Russia by a very similar group, the Sarmatians. The Sarmatians, in turn, were overrun by the Goths, a warrior tribe from Scandinavia. Invasions and counter-invasions surged back and forth across the south Eurasian steppes, with the Goths soon displaced by the Huns from the east, the Huns later routed by a Tatar people called the Avars. The Avars were pushed out by the Magyars (early Hungarians) and the Khazars, a Turkic people, who established in the seventh century AD a kingdom which reached all the way to the Dneiper River and south to the Caucasus and the Crimea.

The chief influence on the development of Russian culture, however, was provided by the Slavs, who were not very much like their nomadic predecessors. Their origin is unknown, but it appears they traveled on foot, lived in forest settlements, and were more interested in farming and trade than in battle. Because they didn't expend all their energy and progeny in the constant pursuit of war, the Slavs were able to increase their population and their holdings steadily. By the sixth century they had expanded from the forest along the rivers and across the steppes of Russia. The settlements they established became the foundations for early Russian cities such as Novgorod and Kiev.

By the eighth century, the mostly peaceful expansion of the Slavs began to be threatened by the arrival of the Vikings (sea-faring Scandinavian adventurers, called "Varangians" by the Slavs), whose swift raids endangered the orderly flow of commerce which had developed along the Russian trade routes. The unwarlike Slavs must have seemed easy prey to the marauding Vikings, but the collision of these two cultures turned out in an unexpected way. The Viking raiders, who were few in number, found themselves seduced by the relatively prosperous and comfortable trade culture which had grown up in Russia. By the same token, the Slavs—who had little inclination toward government organization or military strategy—were attracted to the idea of the Vikings as protectors. Before long, the Vikings had begun to settle along the river highways and intermarry with the Slavs, eventually becoming almost completely absorbed by the Slavic culture. Their legacy lives on, however, because it seems likely that the word *Russia* itself came from the term *Rus* (thought to be the Finnish word for "rowers") which was applied to the Scandinavian swashbucklers.

In fact, the first ruler of a Russian state was actually a Viking prince named Rurik. Supposedly the Slavs of a large settlement called Novgorod at first drove out Rurik and his band, but then they fell into contention among themselves and realized they were unable to bring about order on their own. So, around 862, they invited Rurik to return as their leader, and he became the founder of the first Russian ruling dynasty. An eleventh-century history called the *Primary Chronicle* tells us that Rurik soon dispatched his lieutenants Askold and Dir (possibly his brothers) to take over the far more strategically-located Kiev, and it was there that the future of Russia began to take shape.

The Kievan Period

After the death of Rurik in 879, his cousin Oleg—by all accounts an intelligent and efficient ruler—promptly disposed of Askold and Dir, moved to Kiev, and busied himself extending Russian rule. In 911, Oleg stormed Constantinople, where "the Russes inflicted many…woes upon the Greeks after the usual manner of soldiers." Whether or not Oleg actually put wheels on his ships, as the *Chronicle* reports, and contrived to have them blow into Constantinople (it seems unlikely), he did at least apparently conclude a favorable trade agreement with the Byzantine Empire.

Oleg's successor, Igor, ruled until 945, when he was killed by a rebellious Slavic tribe called the Derevlians. Rule passed to his wife Olga, as regent for their son Sviatoslav, and among the favorite tales of Russian history is the story of Olga's revenge against the Derevlians, whom she reportedly tricked by flattery into a gruesome end. Apparently a most independent and resourceful woman, Olga divided the increasingly unwieldy country into administrative districts and set up a tax-collection scheme. But she is perhaps most noteworthy for her conversion to Christianity, which probably took place when she visited Constantinople in 958.

Russia did not immediately become a Christian country, however. Olga's son Sviatoslav, along with most other Russians, refused to follow her in converting. As ruler, Sviatoslav spent most of his time expanding the Russian realm. Greek historian Leo Diaconus gave a concrete image of the early Slavs when he described the blue-eyed and snub-nosed Sviatoslav as "gloomy and savage," with a long, bushy mustache, his head shaven except for a single long lock on one side. "On one of his ears hung a golden earring adorned with two pearls with a ruby set between them. His white garments were not distinguishable from those of his men except for cleanness."

Upon Sviatoslav's death, the empire was divided among his three sons, beginning a conflict which was not resolved until 980 when Vladimir, the youngest son, became the sole ruler. He showed himself fully capable of following in his father's active footsteps, and soon had Russia in good order. Like many other tenth-century rulers, however, he decided that his country lacked a sufficiently organized religion, and sent out envoys to report on the various options available: Islam, Roman Catholicism, Greek Orthodoxy, Judaism. After considerable study, he apparently agreed with his grandmother Olga's choice, and decreed that Orthodox Christianity was to become the official religion of Russia.

Very likely, Vladimir was helped in this decision by the promise of an alliance with the Byzantine emperor, who sealed the bargain by marrying his sister off to the newly baptized Vladimir in 989. Seemingly in no time, whole cities full of reluctant Russians were being herded into the rivers for baptism, and the "heathen" practices of the old religion were thenceforth forbidden. With characteristic briskness, Vladimir had the old idols dumped into the rivers and commenced an ambitious church-building campaign.

However political the motives for Vladimir's choice may have been, he was seemingly sincere—or at least determined—in his personal conversion. Not only did he give up a reported eight hundred concubines (and seven wives), he also initiated a program of good works, giving money to the poor and sending food to the sick. In the thirteenth century, Vladimir was declared a saint by the Russian Orthodox Church.

Vladimir, later known as "the Good," apparently passed on his saintly inclinations to two of his sons, Boris and Gleb. After their father's death, the two brothers learned that their half-brother Svyatopolk had seized Kiev and intended to take over the whole kingdom. But as earnest Christians, they refused to take up arms against their brother, and rather than defend themselves, the two waited in prayer for the assassins sent by Svyatopolk to kill them. Boris and Gleb were widely regarded thereafter as embodying the greatest virtues of Russian Christianity, and the duo became a favorite subject of the icon painters.

"Svyatopolk the Accursed" ruled for only four years before being defeated by another of his brothers, Yaroslav, who was to rule over the greatest period of Kievan Rus. Under Yaroslav's direction, Kiev became a city of great beauty, highlighted by the Cathedral of

St. Sophia, and was reported by foreign visitors to "rival Constantinople." Schools and monasteries were opened, books were transcribed and collected, and the first Russian code of laws, *Russkaya Pravda,* was issued. The *Pravda* (a word meaning in Russian both "truth" and "law") established rules designed to limit—though not curtail—blood vengeance. It also created a system of fines for such offenses as cutting off someone's mustache (twelve *grivnas*) or riding his horse without permission (a bargain at only three *grivnas*). These many innovations in Russian culture earned Yaroslav the title of "the Wise."

Wise though he may have been, however, Yaroslav did not succeed in devising a scheme of inheritance which would secure the orderly transition of government. It was he who came up with a plan called the "rota," in which the eldest prince would receive Kiev, and the others be given, in order of age, lesser cities to rule. Theoretically, when an elder brother died, all the rest would move up. But the scheme was manifestly unworkable; in a short time, there would not be enough cities to go around. So after the death of Yaroslav, Kievan Rus began a swift descent into chaos.

During the next fifty years, the Russian empire crumbled into an assortment of petty principalities, with brothers in constant intrigue against one another, and nomadic enemies such as the Turkic Cumans taking advantage of the civil strife to harass the Russian trade routes. By 1113, the citizens of Kiev were desperate for leadership. Taking matters into their own hands, they turned away from the utterly unworkable rota system and offered the throne to Vladimir Monomakh, the good and honorable prince of Pereyaslavl. Over the objections of the other princes, the people's will prevailed, and their judgment was entirely vindicated when Vladimir Monomakh proved to be a wise, just, and effective leader. For a time, peace and order returned, and trade and learning flourished again.

Kievan Rus, however, was too far gone to be restored to greatness, even by one of Russia's most revered rulers. Its decline continued, and within a hundred years of Vladimir's death, Russia was little more than a loose federation of city-states, each ruled by one of the now-multitudinous offspring of the House of Rurik. These spoiled and selfish princelings, busy with their own quarrels, could offer little protection for Russia when the Mongol hordes appeared on the horizon.

The Mongol Period

The Mongol invasion and occupation created a two-hundred-year parenthesis in the political development of Russia, as well as changing forever the character of Russian culture. Although Russian unity had all but disappeared by the time the invaders arrived early in the thirteenth century, several of Russia's cities had already been groping their way toward a form of representative government. Improvements in both social and economic life were taking place throughout the country. But under Mongol rule, Russian life took a giant step backwards.

The Mongols are legendary for their overwhelming sweep across Asia. But originally, they were only one of many tribes inhabiting the vast desert of northern Asia, and they were never really numerous. Even at the height of the Mongol empire, the Mongols themselves numbered only about one million, with the vast majority of the famous Mongol "horde" actually made up of various Turkic peoples, referred to generically as "Tatars." The Mongols owed their ascendancy not to great numbers, but to one of history's greatest warriors: Temujin, the "Genghis Khan." Originally a minor chieftain, Temujin used his powerful vision of world domination to unite scattered clans and tribes into one vast fighting machine—a tightly organized military society, based on the principle of swift and impartial brutality. In 1206, he was proclaimed by the assembly of tribal leaders to be not just their *khan*, or supreme leader, but the *genghis khan*, the all-encompassing lord whose power was derived directly from the god of "the Eternal Blue Sky."

Although Genghis Khan was the great architect of Mongol success, it was actually his grandson, Batu Khan, who entered Russia in 1236 and brought that sprawling and disorganized land under the Mongol yoke. In some areas of Russia, the Mongols ruled directly; in others, they ruled through the local princes, but as a general practice, the Russians were allowed to carry on much as before so long as they paid taxes and provided conscripts for the Mongol army.

Church lands, however, were not taxed, and workers on church lands were not subject to conscription. Though the Mongols themselves converted to Islam in the fourteenth century, they encouraged Christianity in Russia, and by this means did much to solidify and expand the supremacy of the church in Russian life. Mongolian domination enforced upon Russia a cultural isolation which separated the country entirely from Europe's active intellectual ferment, and the Orthodox Church took advantage of this isolation to nourish the Russians' natural conservatism and to create an atmosphere of spiritual and cultural inwardness. During the Mongol rule there was virtually no intellectual debate in Russia, for new ideas were never even heard; as a consequence, there was no Russian Renaissance, no Reformation, no exploration, and little interest in science.

The long Mongol occupation left other legacies as well. Contrary to our popular impressions, medieval Russia was not a feudal state. Serfdom, which bound workers to the estates of their masters for life, was not introduced to Russia until much later, in the seventeenth century. Up until then, everyone but a few prisoners and indebted servants could legally (though perhaps not practically) own land in Russia. The majority of peasants had the right to work their own hereditary plots of land; craftsmen freely made and sold their wares; and movement about the country was unrestricted. The Mongols did not interfere with this system, but they did introduce to Russia an atmosphere of harsh penalties and repressive laws which changed the nature of class relationships.

The casual and extreme brutality of the Mongols was new to the Russians, but over two long centuries of occupation, the attitude took root in Russian society. The Mongols also brought with them certain Oriental customs which were absorbed into Russian culture, such as the seclusion of women. The Russian practice of confining upper-class women in separate households called *terems* was a product of exposure to the Mongols which outlasted the invaders by several hundred years. All in all, the Mongol period in Russian history resulted in the coarsening of Russian society, along with an almost complete stagnation of thought which was to set Russian progress back by centuries.

Only one part of Russia escaped the worst effects of the Mongol yoke. The city of Novgorod, by a combination of luck and cleverness, managed to avoid direct Mongol rule and to continue expanding business and trade, while developing a semi-democratic government. Novgorod was the only Russian city to elect its leader, and they had particularly good fortune with Prince Alexander, whose brilliant defeat of Swedish invaders beside the River Neva earned him the name Alexander Nevsky, and a place in history among the greatest Russian heroes. Seeing the fruitlessness of opposition to the Mongols, Alexander instead used scrupulous obedience to gain a relative measure of freedom from Mongol oversight. His strategy worked to the benefit of Novgorod, but even more important, it laid the foundation for the next great period of Russian history: the rise of Moscow.

The Muscovite Period

Because Moscow looms so large in our modern knowledge of Russia, it is surprising to realize that the city was not even founded until the twelfth century. In spite of its excellent geographic position near the center of the Russian waterways, Moscow remained a minor outpost until late in the thirteenth century, when Daniel, a son of Alexander Nevsky, acquired the fledgling principality and began the Muscovite line. Daniel and his successors followed the policy of cooperation with the Mongols, with the result that they acquired considerable wealth while simultaneously expanding the scope of Muscovite rule. Moscow, by virtue of its relative safety as well as its thriving trade, attracted *boyars* (noble landowners and merchants) from all over Russia, and its economic growth was nothing short of amazing.

Daniel's son, Ivan I, who swiftly earned the nickname of *Kalita* or "Moneybag," used his wealth to influence the metropolitan of the Russian church (the equivalent of an archbishop, then the highest church official in Russia) to move his official seat to Moscow, a triumph which sealed the destiny of Moscow. Ivan then announced himself grand prince of Russia, and was able to secure the Mongol Khan's assent to this title. He fortified the city's *kremlin*, or fortress, built the beautiful Cathedral of the Assumption, and generally set Moscow on the fast path to dominance. In 1380, his grandson Dmitry became the first Russian prince to launch a successful attack against the Mongol overlords. Although Moscow paid a fearful price for the victory (a reported twenty thousand killed in later reprisals against the city), this move proved to be the beginning of the end for Mongol dominion. Internal dissension had already begun to weaken the horde, and its hold on Russia was slipping away. Though it took most of another century, Russia was gradually to become free of the Mongol yoke.

Meanwhile, other events of critical importance to the future of Moscow were happening far away. The Byzantine Empire (which had amassed great power through its claim to be the "second Rome," true center of Christianity) was in its twilight. In 1453, its capital Constantinople fell to the Ottoman Turks, and the last emperor of Byzantium, Constantine XI, died defending her walls. His niece, Zoe Paleologus, ended up in the care of Pope Paul II, who shrewdly seized upon an opportunity to further the aims of Rome in Russia by proposing that Ivan III, now ruler of Muscovy, should marry his ward. This suggestion fit in perfectly with Ivan's own plans. Known as "the Great," Ivan III was a tireless strategist, bent on bringing the power of Moscow to a level which had not even been conceived by his great-grandfather Dmitry. Ivan had already made great strides toward his aim of Russian unification, but he knew the Byzantine connection would add enormously to his prestige in devout Russia.

Upon her marriage to Ivan in 1472, Zoe became known as Sofia, and proceeded to have at least some (though historians disagree about how much) impact on the fate of Russia. If nothing else, she probably encouraged Ivan's rebuilding of the Moscow *kremlin*. Master builders were brought from Italy, great churches were built, and even a palace of stone instead of the ubiquitous wood. By the end of the fifteenth century, Moscow was becoming a grand city, fit for a grand prince. But Ivan did not stop with aesthetic improvements. Having succeeded in curtailing the power of most of the other Russian princes and their cities, Ivan began to style himself not merely *tsar* (a Slavic version of the word *Caesar*), but *tsar* of all Russia. When that title was not challenged, he elevated himself still further: "Ivan, by the grace of God, sovereign of all Russia." By this means, Ivan gave notice that he was not merely a grand prince, first among equals, but in fact a ruler appointed by God.

His claim was actually only the final step in a process which had begun shortly after the fall of Constantinople, when the Russian Orthodox Church declared that Moscow was the "third Rome," new leader of Christendom. Ivan took pains to support and enlarge the idea by surrounding himself with imperial trappings, including a fur-trimmed crown reputed to have been worn by Vladimir Monomakh (a grandson of the first Emperor Constantine) and the Byzantine insignia of the double-headed eagle (which he had been granted the right to use as part of his marriage contract with Zoe). In the icon-loving Russian culture, these symbols were of great importance. From Ivan onward, Russian rulers placed great importance on their symbolic regalia *and* on their claim to direct inheritance of the mantle of Byzantium.

Ivan's death in 1505 brought Sofia's eldest son Vasily to the throne, and the twenty-five years of his reign brought relative stability to Moscow. All that ended, however, when he died suddenly, with a three-year-old son his only heir. The other princes and the boyars saw their opportunity to regain power, and although Vasily's young wife Elena proved a capable regent for the boy, she died mysteriously within five years. Her son was left at the mercy of powerful boyar families who effectively took over the rule of Moscow, and the boy lived in fear of his life until, at the age of thirteen, he suddenly ordered the arrest and execution of his chief tormentor. This swift and effective blow against the boyars was the first official act of Ivan IV, later known as *Ivan Grozny*—"Ivan the Terrible."

The appellation *grozny* applied to Ivan IV actually means in Russian "awe-inspiring," so the English translation "terrible" is somewhat misleading. It is certainly true, however, that this Ivan was unstable and unpredictable. Anthony Jenkinson, an Englishman who visited Ivan's Moscow several times, wrote of the tsar, "I think no prince in Christendom is more feared of his own than he is, nor better loved." For the first thirteen years of his rule, Ivan's piety was as intense as his temper. He was devoted to his wife Anastasia, daughter of a minor court official whose Prussian ancestors had arrived in Russia only in the fourteenth century. And he was guided by the zealous and mystical priest Sylvester, who encouraged him in a series of reforms which, while they did little to expand freedom in Russia, did codify the relationship of church and state, update the legal system, and strengthen the army. Ivan also created the *Zemsky Sobor,* an assembly of people appointed from throughout the land who gathered periodically for advice and the presentation of grievances. On balance, Ivan's early rule was successful.

But in 1560, Ivan seems to have been overtaken by his darker side. In that year, he banished Sylvester, of whom he had become increasingly mistrustful. Perhaps more important, Anastasia died, leaving behind only two surviving sons, one healthy (Ivan) and the other sickly and weak-minded (Fedor). Ivan immediately remarried and turned from a life of piety to one of debauchery. For years, apparently, he had brooded on the fear he had endured at the hands of the boyars as a child, and he had cherished a growing paranoid hatred of his "enemies." The rest of his rule was devoted to the merciless suppression of the threats he saw on every side, for which task he created a special security force, the *oprichniky*, to wage campaigns of terror across the countryside.

The scope and severity of Ivan's misdeeds were unmatched in Russian history. As one of his contemporaries wrote of the change in Ivan, "it was as if a terrible storm come from afar broke the repose of his good heart and he became a rebel in his own land." But the people of Russia had come to believe in the divine authority of the tsar and they feared the loss of his protection and strong leadership. Nothing was done—and perhaps nothing could be done—to curb the growth of Ivan's tyrannical authority. In the end, however, he received almost poetic justice. Although he had seven wives and produced several sons, it was the eldest of these, the beloved namesake born to Anastasia, who was designated by Ivan his successor. The *tsarevich* (or "young tsar," heir to the throne) was his father's closest companion, and was expected by everyone to become a strong and able leader. Then one day, as Ivan waited for news from a military campaign that was going badly, he was suddenly seized with a fit of anger over some remark made by his son. He struck out with his iron-tipped staff, and dealt the tsarevitch a mortal blow.

Torn by remorse, Ivan the Terrible was condemned to live out his final years in the knowledge that he had not only killed his best-loved son, but effectively ended the line of Rurik. The rule of Moscow would pass to Fedor, who was so physically and mentally infirm that no one believed he could rule successfully. Though Fedor had been married off, he produced no children, and upon Ivan's death, his wife's brother, Boris Godunov, became effective ruler of Russia. Godunov was in many respects a good ruler, but he was mistrusted by the boyars, and plagued by constant rumors that he had killed Fedor's half-brother Dmitri.

When Fedor died after fourteen years, Godunov was formally elected tsar, beginning what Russians called the "Time of Troubles." A curious story began to circulate that the young Dmitri had not really been killed, but was alive and living in Poland. Many Russians were eager to believe that a legitimate claimant to the throne might still be found, and soon the man who came to be known as "False Dmitri" had gathered a band of followers. His campaign took advantage of unrest among the peasants, which had begun when the de facto serfdom they had known under Ivan was made into law under Boris. The Cossacks, free men who had long lived as adventurers along the Russian rivers, also took up Dmitri's cause, along with dissatisfied boyars and even churchmen.

When Boris died suddenly in that same year, he was succeeded by his son Fedor Godunov, but only for a few weeks. The boy and his mother were murdered by the boyars, and False Dmitry was proclaimed tsar. This choice, however, almost immediately proved wildly unpopular. The very Russians who had acclaimed his entry into Moscow swiftly turned against Dmitry, whose Roman Catholicism and Polish manners offended them extremely. He in his turn was murdered (his ashes were shot out of a canon in the direction of Poland), and Prince Vasily Shuisky was installed as tsar. He too was soon killed off by the boyars, however, and when Poland launched an open attack against Moscow, Moscow was leaderless and defenseless.

The story of how the country was saved gives great insight into the unique national character of the Russian people. With all the people of power in disarray, the fate of Russia fell into the hands of—a butcher. Kuzma Minin, mayor of a provincial town, roused an army from the countryside and found a minor prince to lead it. They rode to the aid of Cossack forces holding the Poles at bay, and the combined forces, persuaded to cooperate by the intervention of the church, succeeded in saving Moscow. Even after this event, however, it does not seem to have occurred to the Russians to rethink their approach to government. Their first order of business, after the Polish threat had been put down, was to find a new tsar with the right credentials.

The mantle of divine authority now fell on the family of Ivan IV's first wife, Anastasia. Mikhail Romanov was the grandson of Tsar Fedor's uncle—a tenuous connection to the Rurik line, but enough to satisfy the now-desperate Russians. Mikhail was only sixteen and, not unreasonably, most unwilling to accept the office of tsar. In 1613, however, he gave in to great pressure and was crowned. The people were jubilant, and after a time, the troubles subsided. With his more practical father as co-ruler, the extremely pious Mikhail managed a respectable and lengthy rule before passing the throne on to his son Alexei.

Alexei, who shared his father's piety, earned the title of the "gentlest tsar." He believed it was his mission to provide kindly but firm leadership, protecting Moscow as the stronghold of Orthodox Christianity. In his personal capacity, Alexei was forthright, loyal, and genuinely concerned with doing right. Yet his public policy was unfortunate. Popular rebellions were continuing, as the burden of taxation grew and the power of the ruling classes became more onerous, but instead of moving toward a better social policy, Alexei became intent upon making the country administratively and economically stronger, while at the same time modernizing defense. Though the stringent measures he chose may have been necessary to restore and maintain order in the vast, unwieldy nation, they nevertheless created the conditions of inevitable revolution. Worst among Alexei's legacies was the Code of 1649, which indirectly institutionalized serfdom, tying the peasants not only to the land they worked, but to the landowners, who soon began to use them like chattels—trading, selling, and even gambling with them.

Alexei did see the need to bring new ideas into the country, however, and to forge a kinship with Western Europe. His introduction of modern ideas reached even into the ultraconservative Russian Church. During the long period of Russia's isolation, the Russian Orthodox Church had gradually grown away from the strict observance of Byzantine forms, developing a theological and liturgical style which, though by no means heretical, was distinctively Russian. When Alexei and his more progressive supporters began to turn Russia once again toward the West, they realized that Russian religious practice was now quite separated from that of Europe. In 1652, a militant, visionary priest named Nikon became patriarch (highest leader) of the church and set out to reform the Russian liturgy and ritual, bringing it more into line with the Greek Orthodox Church. The changes he initiated were small by our standards, seemingly mere details, but they aroused a furious passion in the Russian people. Many refused to follow the new precepts, and a schism was created in the church which lasted for centuries and significantly affected Russia's political climate.

In 1666, Alexei's first wife died, leaving him plenty of daughters, but only two sons—one sickly, the other mentally retarded. Accordingly, Alexei was in haste to remarry, but his choice of a new bride proved surprising. She was seventeen years old, the child of an impoverished Tatar family and the ward of Alexei's chief minister, a Russian who had married a Scottish woman and who lived an unabashedly European lifestyle. The young Natalia swiftly gave birth to a very healthy—indeed, an *amazingly* healthy—son. He was christened Peter.

IMPERIAL RUSSIA

Peter the Great

Peter the Great was so-called not only because of his achievements, but also because he was six feet seven inches tall! Even as a small child, he impressed all around him with an exceptional energy and curiosity. By the time Peter was five, his father Alexei was dead, and Peter's older half-brother, the frail Fedor, had been named tsar. Fedor ruled for only six years, but he did so with effort and good will, actually enacting some measures designed to curb the brutality of Russian custom and behavior. He failed, however, to produce an heir, and upon Fedor's death, a new crisis of leadership developed.

Since Fedor's brother Ivan was ill-equipped to govern, his half-brother, ten-year-old Peter, was proclaimed tsar, with his mother, the youthful Natalia, designated regent. All seemed to have been resolved peacefully, until Peter's half-sister Sofia—one of the many intelligent and ambitious women who influenced Russian history—attempted a coup. Determined not to be shut up in the terem, the ruthless Sofia gained the support of the *Streltsy* (a semi-autonomous military force originally created by Ivan IV) and engineered a violent uprising, in which many of those she considered enemies were killed. She was unable to rally enough support to have herself crowned, however, so Sofia next plotted the assassination of Peter and his mother.

The seventeen-year-old tsar proved too clever for her, though. Concealing himself in a monastery, Peter was able to organize a counter-coup; and in the end, Sofia was confined to a nunnery for the rest of her life. Thus, by 1689, young Peter had successfully weathered the first great crisis of his dramatic career, and a new chapter in Russian history was ready to be opened.

Peter I was larger than life in every respect. A physically powerful man with huge ideas, Peter resolved to sweep the cobwebs out of Russian culture and join the European Enlightenment. His father Alexei had recognized the need for modernization in Russia, but the "gentlest tsar" had proceeded carefully, fearful that too much change too soon would be ruinous to the country. Peter entertained no such caution. As holder of the most powerful office in a country of vast proportions and resources, Peter had the means to create his vision, and he did not hesitate to use them. His actions were often brutal, but Peter was not a cruel man, merely a determined one. The techniques he used were those common to his time, an era when authoritarianism was considered the God-given form of government and "human rights" was virtually an unknown concept.

Though some of Peter's actions were harsh, he did much that was intended ultimately to make life better in Russia. The range of his activities was truly amazing. He simplified the Russian alphabet and number system, promoted the creation of hospitals, orphanages, and fire-fighting services, introduced urban planning and landscape design, established the Academy of Sciences, and began the development of a secular literature. Although he frequently went too far in trying to mandate a wholesale overthrow of Russian traditions—even personally shaving off the boyars' beards and cutting the traditional trailing sleeves off their robes— his conviction that Russia could not endure without change was undoubtedly correct. As Russia fell further and further behind the times, the country became increasingly vulnerable to the more advanced military powers that coveted her rich resources. So Peter's obsession with modernization was also an obsession with Russia's security.

In 1697, Peter became the first Russian ruler to travel outside the country, other than on limited military excursions. Seemingly unable to do anything in an ordinary way, Peter began his grand tour disguised as a common citizen, supposedly accompanying a diplomatic delegation. He was anxious to avoid tedious state ceremonies and to concentrate on exploring, but inevitably, his unusual stature gave him away; in an age when the average height of men was considerably less than it is today, Peter towered over everyone. Thus Peter's passage through Holland, England, and Austria was not anonymous after all. The main objective of the journey was fulfilled nevertheless, for Peter managed to spend most of his time visiting shipyards, observatories, laboratories, universities, and all sorts of institutions far ahead of those in Russia.

After his first-hand experience of Europe, the anti-Western atmosphere of Moscow seemed more stifling than ever to Peter, and he spent as little time there as possible. When he was in Moscow, he was more apt to be found in the intellectually active Foreign Quarter—a large area of the city where all sorts of non-Russians had built a thriving, European-style community—than in the stodgy halls of the palaces. Among his closest companions were a learned and brave Scot, General Patrick Gordon, who had distinguished himself in the service of Tsar Alexei, and a sophisticated Swiss libertine, Francois Lefort. There were frequent large parties (bordering, reportedly, on orgies), as well as spirited debates, and Peter demonstrated amply that his personal appetites were as large as his political goals.

The Russian churchmen were, predictably, appalled by the new tsar's unroyal behavior. Many of the people were none too happy either. They had grown accustomed to the pomp and magnificence that surrounded their tsars, believing it to be a manifestation of Russia's primacy in God's plan. But conservative forces could not stand either against the tide of history or the forcefulness of Peter's new vision. Peter reorganized the Russian army and navy, decreed the development of industry, and perhaps most important of all, encouraged education and the practice of science. At the same time he undertook enormous campaigns of territorial expansion, finally wresting control of the Baltic from the Swedes.

This enforced expansion and modernization of Russia imposed harsh burdens on the people, for Peter's many civil and military projects were costly not only in money but in lives. The first nine years of his Northern War resulted in the conscription of more than 300,000 men; the fortification of Azov and the building of a naval base at Tganrog required 30,000 men a year, the construction of the Volga-Don canal another 30,000—and so on. Taxes were crushing, and peasants could escape forced service only by fleeing into the open land beyond the Urals or joining the Cossacks, who still zealously guarded their traditional freedom. Uprisings by the peasants and rebellions by the Cossacks and Streltsy were a constant threat during Peter's regime, and he frequently had to turn attention from his battles and building projects to the quelling of troubles at home.

Despite his advanced views in many areas, Peter seems to have had little interest in lessening the burdens and restrictions placed on so many of his people. On the other hand, Peter did introduce to Russia the possibility of social mobility. He abolished the old system of hereditary privilege, decreeing that everyone, no matter what his social status, had to begin in the lowest of fourteen ranks and work his way up. Whoever attained through service a specific rank enjoyed the titles and rights of that rank, and so it became possible for anyone of talent to reach positions once reserved for the nobility. "Rank" soon became the most important of all Russian social structures. It was this basic idea which created Russia's vast bureaucracies, and even shaped the Communist party organization.

Characteristically, Peter's reform of the social system was entirely directed toward giving power to the strong and able. A veritable dynamo himself, Peter had no patience with weakness of any kind, even in his own son. Tsarevich Alexei, born in 1690 to Peter's first wife, had been left largely in the care of his mother and her family—conservative Muscovites who thoroughly disapproved of Peter's unconventional ideas, to say nothing of his freewheeling life. When Peter took over Alexei's education, he made huge demands on the boy, expecting from his son the same drive and dedication he expected of himself. Alexei, however, fell far short of his father's measure, and soon developed an obsessive dislike not only of Peter but of all his policies.

Unable to stand up to the overwhelming tsar, Alexei turned to drink, attempted flight, offered to renounce the succession, and finally proposed to become a monk. Peter, however, was suspicious of his son's renunciation of power. He believed—and apparently, he was correct—that Alexei meant to seize the throne upon his death and not merely abandon reform, but actually destroy the many innovations Peter had brought about.

The conflict between Peter and Alexei was at heart the conflict between Moscow and St. Petersburg. Early in his reign, Peter had solved the problem of his hatred for Moscow by building a new capital city. St. Petersburg was constructed literally from nothing, in a swampy site on the estuary of the River Neva, and such was Peter's haste to produce his own European-style city that tens of thousands of workers perished during the building frenzy from disease and overwork. Peter himself decreed every detail of the city, including the types of houses to be built by the various classes of citizens. Dutch, French, German, and Italian architects were brought to design the many glittering palaces and ornamented buildings of the city, and nowhere in St. Petersburg was there a single onion dome (for centuries, the characteristic motif of Russian church architecture). In his beautiful new capital, Peter instituted a Western-style social life, complete with parties, fashions, and salons.

Peter's pride in his namesake city was virtually boundless, so it was perhaps the final straw when he discovered that his son Alexei planned, if he attained the throne, not only to leave Peter's cherished navy to rot, and drive all foreign influences out of Russia, but worst of all, to return the government to *Moscow*. Peter gave his son over to an independent court and instructed them to examine impartially and without fear the charges of treason against Alexei. Despite Peter's injunction to err on the side of leniency, the court sentenced the tsarevich to death, but the point was moot, since Alexei soon died of injuries received during his "interrogation."

Although Peter doubtless considered himself well rid of the feckless Alexei, he was left in a dilemma, for his own health was failing, and now he had no heir. Alexei had left behind a son, but the child was firmly in the hands of Muscovite conservatives, and Peter was determined that the crown should not pass into that circle of influence. But as the tsar continued to search for an acceptable solution to the problem of succession, time ran out. Peter died in 1725, leaving behind a vacuum which proved impossible to fill.

After Peter

During the next thirty-seven years, the Russian throne changed hands seven times, mostly among women. The first of these was Peter's second wife Catherine, whom he had married while his first wife still lived. A peasant girl who had been Peter's faithful companion through many travails, Catherine was by all accounts a generous, energetic, and sensible woman, but she did not have the training or the temperament to rule, so the real power lay in the hands of Peter's former lieutenants. In any event, Catherine did not long outlive her husband, and in 1727, Alexei's son Peter became tsar after all.

The headstrong Peter II was prevented by his regents from causing too much trouble during the mere three years he outlived Catherine, but he did manage to move back to Moscow with his court, which elated the conservatives. Their victory, however, was short-lived, because the next ruler moved right back to St. Petersburg.

The new winner in this royal roulette provided Russian government with one of its strangest interludes. Casting about for the claimant likely to be the least trouble, the powermakers at court settled on Anna, the daughter of Peter the Great's half-brother and co-tsar, Ivan V. Anna, who had been languishing for years in the small German duchy of Courland, was quick to accept the offer, agreeing to conditions which would have rendered her little more than a figurehead. But after hastening to Russia with her consort Biron, Anna promptly surprised her supporters by tearing up the agreement she had signed and proceeding to rule with considerable arrogance.

Anna established a dissipated court, composed mostly of Germans who brought with them the worst excesses of the Europeans. Loaded guns were kept at the palace windows so that Anna could shoot at passing birds, and for her more formal entertainments, she maintained a large troupe of dwarfs and freaks who performed at court and assisted in her grotesque revenges against those members of the old nobility who offended her.

Anna herself, of course, managed to offend just about everyone in Russia, and she could maintain her own security only through a reign of terror directed by Biron. Reportedly, he was responsible for the murders of 20,000 Russians suspected of criticizing the Empress. So when the childless Anna, near death, appointed Biron regent for her designated successor (a two-month-old nephew), the Russian people simply could take no more. They turned to Peter the Great's youngest daughter, Elizabeth, who within a year deposed the remnants of Anna's government and was crowned Empress.

As opposite to Anna as light to darkness, Elizabeth was soon beloved for her "tender, indeed bewitching, kindness." Though quite clever in matters of state, and capable of being severe, Elizabeth was exceptional in her generosity and general good nature. She forbade the execution of Anna's counselors, and early in her reign, abolished the death penalty. Her charm attracted the support of excellent men, who introduced a new standard of financial prudence and honorable service in the Russian court. Yet even so, Russian foreign policy during Elizabeth's rule involved the country in two costly wars.

Elizabeth herself, though a conscientious head of state, spent much of her energy in creating a lively court. She staged all sorts of social entertainments, including balls called "metamorphoses," in which the men wore petticoats and the women wore breeches. She also fostered the development of the arts in Russia. Plays were written, poetry flourished, opera and ballet were introduced. Under Elizabeth's patronage, Russia's first public theater opened in 1756.

Though she was known to have lovers, Elizabeth never married and produced no heir, so the seemingly eternal problem of succession persisted. Elizabeth settled on her nephew, the Grand Duke Peter, as the best of a bad lot of choices, and retrieving him from Germany, where he had been living, she undertook to educate him for leadership. When this proved hopeless, she determined to marry off the sickly and slow-witted youth in hopes he would produce a son with better qualities; and for his bride, she chose the insignificant princess of a small German state. This young lady, named Sophie by birth, but later rebaptized when she joined the Russian Church, was to become Catherine the Great.

The marriage was unsuccessful, from Elizabeth's point of view, for no son appeared. In fact, the young couple seems to have had little idea how to go about the required activities, and the immature Grand Duke took to drink and cultivated a scrupulous avoidance of his husbandly duties. After seven years of this, an exasperated Catherine took a lover and soon produced a son, Paul. Elizabeth, meanwhile, worked feverishly to secure her country's interests against the threat of young Peter's sympathies with Russia's great enemy, Prussia. She did not live quite long enough to achieve her aims, however, dying just after the Russian defeat of Prussia, but before the terms of surrender were concluded.

As Elizabeth had feared, the newly crowned Tsar Peter III immediately undid Russia's victory by allowing the Prussians to write their own terms. He then proceeded to insult virtually everyone in Russia, not least by decreeing that the Russian army should wear Prussian-style uniforms! He even attempted to force the Orthodox clergy to give up their glorious vestments and dress like Lutheran pastors. So although Peter also introduced some positive reforms—abolishing the secret police, granting freedom of worship to the schismatic Old Believers, and protecting the villages of the serfs—his general contempt for all things Russian alienated any potential supporters.

His wife Catherine behaved very differently. From the moment of her arrival, she had taken care to demonstrate her devotion to the Russian culture. She learned the language, carried out religious obligations to the letter, and made it clear to everyone that she did not share her husband's Prussian sympathies. Although she already had three children by three different lovers, Catherine was held in high regard by the Russian people, and only a few months after Peter was crowned, they enthusiastically supported a military coup which placed Catherine on the throne. Peter withdrew willingly, but was killed soon after in a brawl that just happened to include the brothers of Catherine's latest lover.

Ironically, Catherine, the German princess who had no conceivable blood tie to the throne of Russia, proved to be the spiritual heir of Peter the Great. She had his personal magnetism, his physical energy, and his largeness of vision. Her plans for Russian expansion were carried out with striking success, including the acquisition from the Turks of warm water ports on the Black Sea, the annexation of the Crimea, and the appropriation of a large territory from Poland. She also added greatly to the cultural life of Russia, encouraging theater and literature (she herself wrote several plays and published a literary journal), and inaugurating a golden age of architecture, which included the work of Russian as well as European architects. She even revitalized the stagnating Academy of Sciences, appointing as its director the remarkable Princess Catherine Dashkova. Dashkova launched the first dictionary of the Russian language, and even prevailed upon Benjamin Franklin to become an associate member of the Academy.

In matters of fundamental social reform, however, Catherine II was far less fortunate in her undertakings. She came to the throne at a time when humanitarian reform was desperately needed. Where once the Russian peasantry had endured many hardships but retained basic dignity, they had by now become no more than slaves. Serfs were routinely bought and sold, along with their families, and many were worked to death under inhuman conditions in factories and mines. The enormous tax burden of the country rested almost entirely on the peasantry, who paid taxes on anything they owned, everything they made, and even on their own lives, while the landed gentry applied themselves chiefly to expensive pretensions and political intrigues. Only centuries of religious indoctrination prevented full-scale rebellion, for the Russian Church had long taught that suffering and humility were great virtues and that the tsar was God's agent on earth.

Catherine recognized the urgent need for reform, and early in her rule, she composed the *Nakaz* ("Instruction"), a document intended to set out guidelines for a commission which would rewrite the laws of Russia. A tireless worker, arising at five every morning for reading and meditation before beginning a strenuous agenda, Catherine spent three hours each day for two years working on the *Nakaz*. In it, she applied some of the ideas of the French Enlightenment philosophers, including Montesquieu and Voltaire, whom she had studied while biding her time in the court of Elizabeth. When complete, the *Nakaz* was given with great fanfare to the assembly, and they were bidden to divide into committees and achieve the aims set forth in the document. Virtually none of the delegates to the assembly, however, had the slightest idea what the point of the document was, or how to go about their task. After a year of confusion, the project faded into obscurity.

The *Nakaz* won for Catherine a great deal of notoriety and admiration among the intellectuals of Europe, where it was circulated in several versions and received high praise. But unfortunately, she ended up doing much more in Russia to suppress freedom than to encourage it. It was Catherine who granted landowners the right to sentence their serfs to forced labor in Siberia, and who deprived serfs of the right to bring complaints against their masters. (This right of petition had been firmly upheld by Peter the Great.) At each of these steps, Catherine may have felt she was taking temporary action to protect social order, and she may have intended to introduce more advanced policies when her rule was more secure. A vicious cycle was already in effect, however. The more the serfs were oppressed, the greater the threat of uprisings. The greater the threat of uprisings, the more the landowners tightened their grip.

Catherine's own ambition ultimately prevented her from breaking this cycle. Her claim on the throne of Russia was virtually nonexistent, and in order to safeguard her own power, she had to satisfy the landowners. But even so, Catherine did not fail to see the consequences of this appeasement. After one particularly bloody uprising, she wrote to her minister of justice, "If we do not consent to diminish cruelty and moderate a situation which is intolerable to the human race, then sooner or later they will take this step themselves."

Catherine's appetite for power and luxury must have warred with her finer feelings and advanced ideas, but the love of power invariably won out over the love of justice. And as so often happens, the more she fell in love with her own power, the more she lost sight of the injustices upon which it rested. Her spending—on constant building, patronage of the arts, lavish entertainments, fabulous gifts to her favorites, clothes, jewels—was truly exorbitant, and since she had no personal fortune, she spent the government's revenues. Her never-ending profusion of grand schemes required ever larger amounts of money, and when she had wrung every *ruble* out of her own people, she turned to borrowing abroad. By the end of Catherine's reign, Russia was, for the first time in its history, in serious financial trouble.

Throughout her reign, Catherine guarded jealously against any competitor for power; thus, she never remarried, creating instead a very systematic process for selecting, installing, and dismissing a series of lovers (reportedly at least twenty-one in number). Many of these were chosen by Catherine's greatest love and lifelong friend, the dashing, brilliant, and wealthy eccentric, Grigory Potemkin. Master of romance, Potemkin was famed for his lavish gestures; at one dinner party, he passed crystal cups full of diamonds, from which the ladies were bidden to take their choice. But he was also an astute and courageous man (Catherine called him "bold mind, bold spirit, bold heart"), whose passionate interest in the arts brought great richness to the Russian court.

Unwilling to share her power with Potemkin or any other man, Catherine refused all close ties. In her later years, dismayed by the revolution taking place in France, Catherine repudiated all of her earlier ideas and systematically suppressed the very works she had formerly espoused, such as those of Voltaire (with whom she had carried on a lively correspondence) and Diderot. Her views grew increasingly reactionary, but she continued a life overflowing with activity well into her sixties. In 1796, apparently undisturbed that the country she bequeathed to her heir was a virtual powder keg, Catherine the Great died after thirty-four years as Empress of Russia.

THE WANING OF EMPIRE

The Last Autocrats

Catherine's determination to protect her personal power had not only alienated the peasantry, but embittered her own son. The iron-willed Empress kept the tsarevitch Paul far away from St. Petersburg and denied him any role in political life. Naturally, this course only deepened Paul's resentment toward a mother who had—from his point of view—usurped his throne. So it was not surprising that, when the forty-two-year-old became Tsar Paul, he was determined to assert himself quickly and powerfully.

A complete absolutist, Paul believed the ruler alone should have power and everyone else, including the gentry, should obey his dictates to the letter. In this spirit, he set about limiting the privileges of the landowners, even requiring them once again to pay taxes and serve in the army. Paul also enacted some relief for the serfs (though probably not so much to benefit them as to punish the landowners). But the new tsar's temperament proved so volatile, and his actions—such as dispatching troops to invade India—so unpredictable and even irrational that he ended up undoing as much as he did. Furthermore, he created numerous enemies without acquiring any friends. After seven years of Paul's whimsical foreign policy and internal offensiveness, a group of army officers paid a midnight visit to the tsar, in which the tsar (officially) suffered a fit of "apoplexy," doubtless brought on when he was hit over the head with a gold snuff box and strangled with a scarf.

Paul's son Alexander was expected by all to be an exemplary tsar, and though he took the throne reluctantly, Alexander began his reign with many promising reforms. He revoked the harsh measures enacted by his father, abolished the secret police (which had been reinstated under Catherine's rule), granted serfs the right to buy their freedom (an opportunity which very few of them could afford, of course), and established many new schools, some of which were (theoretically) open to all classes.

But over the twenty-four years of his reign, Alexander's idealism took many curious turns, becoming in the end a kind of mystical zeal. His early interest in internal reforms was soon eclipsed by a growing involvement in the high drama of world affairs. With America now independent and the French Republic in the hands of Napoleon, the old European order was swiftly changing, and Alexander was determined that Russia and Christianity should play pivotal roles in the reorganization of European power.

The first fifteen years of Alexander's reign were taken up with the problem of Napoleon, whose insatiable appetite for land and power threatened the stability of all Europe. The young tsar Alexander had begun almost immediately taking steps to insure peace in Russia, through treaties and agreements with Britain, France, and Prussia. But within a few years, having come to believe that war with Napoleon was inevitable, he proposed a grand alliance between Russia and Britain, to be supported by Sweden and Austria. (Russia's old nemesis Prussia was determined to remain neutral.) Alexander's purpose in pursuing this alliance was to create a "new Europe," free of French domination.

Tsar Alexander had already begun to form an image of himself as the leader of the Christian world—an image which was to become ever stronger throughout his reign. When Napoleon attacked Austria, Alexander (against the advice of his commander-in-chief) sent Russian troops to the defense of Vienna, where they suffered a rout. There followed other savage defeats for Russia, as Alexander tried to affect the course of the European war. Soon, even though Russia herself had never been attacked by France, Alexander was under pressure from his advisors to sue for peace.

But when Alexander and Napoleon met on a lavishly decorated raft in the midst of the Neman River, the encounter produced a peculiar and surprising result. For three hours, the two leaders met alone, and when Alexander emerged, he completely reversed the decades-long policy of Russia. Apparently convinced by Napoleon that Britain was the real enemy of both their countries, Alexander now embarked on a foreign policy organized entirely around the *support* of France. He joined enthusiastically with Napoleon's plans, first invading Sweden, then annexing Finland, finally even joining Napoleon's blockade against Britain.

The loss of trade with Britain, however, had a devastating effect on the Russian economy, and the Russian people were increasingly hostile toward Alexander's French alliance. Napoleon, meanwhile, committed a grave offense against Russian sensibilities by first pursuing and then rejecting a marriage with Alexander's fifteen-year-old sister, a debacle which reinforced the growing certainty that war between Russia and France must soon take place.

Never one to shrink from a fight, Napoleon invaded Russia in 1812, no doubt expecting a quick success against the considerably inferior Russian army. But events were not to turn out so predictably. True, the Russian troops numbered less than half of Napoleon's and could do little to stop his march toward Moscow. Yet by the end of the Russian campaign, Napoleon's invading force of over half a million troops was reduced to a mere 30,000 ragged survivors.

The Russians proved indefatigable and utterly fierce in the defense of their homeland. Though only one major engagement occurred between the Russian and French armies, Napoleon considered it the most savage he had ever fought; over 70,000 casualties were taken, including forty-seven of Napoleon's generals. Then, as the Russian troops strategically retreated, the Russians burned their own land and towns rather than let the French invaders live off their conquest. When Napoleon's army reached Moscow, they found the city smoldering, undefended.

For more than a month, Napoleon waited vainly in Moscow for the Russian surrender, and by the time he gave up and withdrew, winter was beginning. With few supplies, beset by bitter cold and the incessant attacks of Russian fighters, the French suffered staggering losses as they tried to make their way out of Russia. Alexander, now convinced of his divinely appointed role in history, pursued Napoleon all the way back to France, and in March of 1814, the victorious tsar led allied troops into Paris.

Alexander's glory was brief, however, for he followed his success with so many blunders that a frustrated Britain finally ousted the unpredictable Russian leader from the stage of world affairs. When he turned his attention back to internal matters in Russia, the tsar discovered an ironic twist. The Russian soldiers who had spent years fighting Alexander's wars in Europe were coming home with dangerous new ideas. Having been exposed to the lively intellectual and political climate of the West, Russia's young officers now found their own country horribly backward, unjust, and corrupt. They began to talk about change, and Alexander, fearful of open rebellion, commenced a campaign of suppression. Officers suspected of liberal thinking were imprisoned or exiled, but this policy only forced the new ideas into hiding, where they bubbled and seethed as if in a pressure cooker. Secret political societies, some influenced by Freemasonry, began to flourish, and the Russian "underground" was born.

Perhaps it was the increasing impossibility of combating new ideas which led Alexander in his last years to speak often of abdication. Indeed, his desire to leave behind politics and live a spiritual life was so well known that when he was reported to have died—quite suddenly and far from Moscow—in 1825, many believed that he had slipped away to the Holy Land. Some of those who saw the body declared the tsar so changed as to be unrecognizable, and years later, when a mysterious holy man closely resembling Alexander appeared in Siberia, speculation was renewed that the tsar had returned to his beloved Russia in the guise of Father Fedor Kuzmich.

Whatever may have become of Alexander, his departure from the throne sparked yet another crisis of succession in Russia. From the time of their father's death, Alexander's next-younger brother Constantine (who was notably forward-thinking) had firmly declared that he would never accept the crown. In this determination he did not waiver, and so the youngest brother, Nicholas, had been recognized by Alexander as his heir. Nicholas, however, was staunchly conservative, and the people were suspicious of him. They wanted Constantine to assume the throne.

In hopes of forcing Constantine to reconsider, liberal officers, with about 3,000 soldiers and other rebels, filled the palace grounds and attempted to prevent the installation of Nicholas as tsar. Government troops, led by Nicholas himself, at first attempted to outwait the poorly organized revolt. But as sympathetic protests spread through the city, an angry and fearful Nicholas finally ordered his gunners to fire into the hostile crowd which surrounded the palace. Dozens were killed, and the spontaneous uprising was quelled.

The "Decembrist Revolt" (so-called for the frigid month in which it happened) seemed a failure at the time; but in reality, it was the opening volley of the eventual Russian Revolution. In the aftermath of the revolt, over a hundred of its leaders were tried, and many Russians were shocked when five were sentenced to death—the first use of the death penalty since capital punishment had been abolished by Elizabeth. Now the two sides were firmly polarized: the budding liberal movement on one side, the change-resistant aristocracy on the other.

Nicholas, as expected, proved a harsh and inflexible ruler. His motto, "Orthodoxy, Autocracy, and Nationality," became the watchword for an aggressive anti-intellectual, anti-educational movement in the Russian government and the Orthodox Church. Public policy became as narrow as Nicholas himself, who was described by a youthful Queen Victoria as "severe and gloomy, imbued with principles nothing on earth could change." "I don't think he is very intelligent," she went on. "His mind is without refinement." Nicholas banished history and philosophy from university curricula and severely limited the number of students who could receive higher education, while enormously expanding the army.

The increasingly irrational nature of Russian policy was perfectly summarized by Nicholas in an address to the State Council in 1842: "There is no doubt that serfdom, in its present form, is a flagrant evil that everyone recognizes, yet to attempt to remedy it now would be, of course, an evil even more disastrous." Having seen the example of the French Revolution, in which aristocrats were enthusiastically slaughtered by the ill-treated French masses, the Russian nobility and gentry feared the same fate. It seems never to have occurred to them that fair measures, taken in time, might change the outcome of their own situation from inevitable bloody revolution to a peaceful reconstruction of Russian society.

The very idea of reconstructing society was, in fact, horrifying to entrenched Russian conservatism. The conservative view, as expressed by Nicholas's minister of education, was that "a Russian, devoted to his fatherland, will agree as little to the loss of a single dogma…as to the theft of a single pearl from the tsar's crown." Churchmen feared the loss of their absolute spiritual power as much as the privileged classes feared the loss of wealth and luxury, and in their determined alliance, the two groups stood squarely in the path of any kind of progress. The status quo was doggedly proclaimed the "true Russia," with any deviation denounced as traitorous and anti-national.

Such were the circumstances in which, ironically, began the greatest period of Russian intellectual life. The army—perhaps because it was so public—had proven a poor vehicle for the spread of revolutionary ideas, which now resurfaced amongst a growing new class called the *intelligentsia*. Writers and artists, philosophers and students met in small, secret groups to discuss the new ideas. These groups, which included such literary luminaries as Alexander Pushkin, Mikhail Lermontov, Nikolai Gogol, and Fyodor Dostoevsky, were closely watched by the secret police, who staged frequent raids and arrests in their relentless search for free-thinking "traitors."

The ideas which circulated among the intelligentsia included such "radical" notions as natural rights, equality, and democracy. Soon, the intellectual deliberation on these topics progressed from mere discussion of theory to a consideration of how ideals might become reality, and there emerged two very different factions. One group, the "Slavophiles," believed that any transformation of Russian society had to be rooted in the special nature of its own values and traditions; the "Westernizers," on the other hand, condemned all aspects of Russian culture and called for the adoption of modern, European ideas. These two attitudes were hotly debated, and were expressed by their proponents in works of art and literature; the great novelists Tolstoy and Dostoevsky were ardent Slavophiles, while Turgenev was among the most outspoken of Westernizers.

Although in many respects anti-intellectual, the rigid Tsar Nicholas nevertheless took an interest in the arts. He insisted on personally reviewing the poetry of the great Pushkin, with whom he developed a strange intimacy—even taking it upon himself to support Pushkin's family after the poet was killed in a duel. Nicholas also created the first public art museum in Russia, free and open to all. But in general, his effect on the condition of the arts in Russia was very restrictive. Under the tsar's rigid direction, the Academy of Fine Arts was converted into a bureaucratic machine, turning out a stream of mediocre painters skilled in the favored style of Neoclassicism. The more talented artists, meanwhile, turned in frustration to the rebellious ranks of the intelligentsia.

In foreign affairs, the reign of Tsar Nicholas was so fraught with excursions, alliances, reversals, and revolts that it would be very difficult to summarize. The entire Western world was by this time in a ferment. Territories changed hands like pieces in a board game, and nations made deals with one another for momentary gains, then moved on to new arrangements with different players. The two major concepts which dominated world politics were "expansion" and "balance of power." Each of the major nations sought to gain as much space and as many resources as possible, while also trying to ensure that none of the *other* nations formed associations which would be more powerful. So, for example, when Turkey threatened to become too powerful, Britain, France, and Russia all cooperated in the support of the Greeks against the Turks. But then Russia waged a victorious war against Turkey and gained control of the Caucasus, whereupon the balance of power shifted.

Now Russia's strength in the Near East became more threatening to her allies Britain and France than the possibility of Turkish expansion, and when Nicholas started another war with Turkey in 1853, Russian troops faced British and French as well as Turkish armies in the Crimea. In this grim war, both sides had great losses (the terrible British defeat at Balaklava was immortalized by

Tennyson in "The Charge of the Light Brigade"). In the end, it was amply demonstrated that the Russian army, in spite of its best efforts, was no match for the combined forces of Europe. Nicholas, who had devoted most of his life to building up the Russian army, was shattered by the realization that its organization and technology remained hopelessly behind that of the European nations.

In 1855, Nicholas died an embittered man, telling his confessor at the last rites, "I believe I have never done evil knowingly." Perhaps true, but the evil he had done unknowingly, through his refusal to confront reform, would haunt Russia for another century.

The Struggle for Reform

When Nicholas's son Alexander took the throne—finally, there was no question about succession—the day seemed to have come at last when Russia would have an enlightened ruler. At his coronation, Tsar Alexander II went far beyond the usual custom of bestowing gifts upon the people. He granted amnesty to all political prisoners, gave out tax concessions, halted military recruiting for three years, restored the privilege of foreign travel, and relaxed censorship. Soon it was rumored everywhere that Alexander would free the serfs, and the tsar informed the landowners that while he would not take this step immediately, it was not far off. The Crimean defeat had been widely interpreted, at home and abroad, as an indictment not merely of the Russian army, but of the entire Russian social system, and it was believed by most intelligent people that Russia could not progress without resolving the problem of the serfs.

Alexander asked the landowners to suggest how emancipation could best be accomplished, but the gentry refused even to consider this matter, and the disappointed tsar then named a committee to study the problem. When the committee would make no recommendations, he gave the chairmanship to his highly respected uncle Constantine, long a supporter of emancipation—but still nothing happened. It was increasingly plain that the vital restructuring of Russian society would not take place smoothly.

The problem of the serfs in Russia was far greater than the similar dilemma of slavery in the United States, for there were an estimated *fifty million* Russian serfs. The entire economy of Russia was dependent upon their labors, and there were no mechanisms of any kind in place to manage the productivity of the nation without the institution of serfdom. Therefore, the emancipation of the serfs required not only great courage, but great faith. Alexander showed both. He never wavered in his determination to bring freedom to the masses, and though his methods may be criticized, his sincerity cannot be questioned. After four years of negotiations with the landowners, Alexander set in motion the process of emancipation; in 1861, more than a year before Lincoln freed the slaves in America, the tsar's emancipation proclamation was read from the pulpit of every church in Russia.

The proclamation was a stirring document, but it did not even begin to solve Russia's problems. The serfs were now allowed to own limited portions of the land they had worked for generations, but only after many years of payments. The landed gentry still had great authority, and the serfs were as politically powerless as ever, so it rapidly became evident that reforms in local government, education, and military service would be needed in order to advance social progress further. The newly freed serfs were impatient, and there were scattered rebellions, but Alexander stood his course.

In the twenty-six years of his reign, Alexander made significant inroads into the social problems of Russia. He revitalized education; instituted a new form of local government, in which the peasantry was represented; and not only reformed, but civilized the backward Russian judicial system. Recognizing that many of Russia's problems could be alleviated by better transportation and communication, he increased the Russian railway (condemned by conservatives for encouraging "frequent purposeless travel") from 660 miles in length to 14,000 miles. As a result, trade improved, and the balance of economic power in Russia began to shift away from the landowners toward the merchants and industrial classes. Slowly but surely, all the elements were being put in place for a comparatively free capitalist nation.

Unfortunately, many Russians were more aware of the "slowly" than of the "surely." There was continued agitation among the intelligentsia for a representative national government. Alexander, however, was firmly against this idea. Although he supported popular government in other nations, he believed that the system would not work in sprawling Russia. "I can give you my imperial word," he told one liberal proponent, "that this very minute, at this very table, I would sign any constitution you like, if I felt that this would be for the good of Russia. But I know that, were I to do so today, tomorrow Russia would fall to pieces."

It will never be known whether or not representative government might have worked in nineteenth-century Russia. The most radical members of the intelligentsia, however, would settle for nothing less. As censorship and restrictions on political speech were relaxed, the radicals became more and more vocal in their advocacy of revolutionary aims and socialist theories. During the 1870's, the political activists not only increased their demonstrations but began terrorist operations such as arson, sabotage, and even assassination. Several attempts were made on the life of the tsar (the first deliberately planned to take place one year to the day after Abraham Lincoln's assassination), and each time, it was only by chance that Alexander escaped. But as the violence escalated, the radical movement began to lose the sympathies of more moderate factions. In 1880, Alexander commenced a new round of attempts at reform; the results of the initiative, however, still fell short of pleasing the radicals, who increased their terrorist activities.

Sadly, Alexander's long fight for the improvement of Russian society was finally halted by assassins on March 1, 1881, as he returned from attending the Sunday Parade. He had gone to the event against the pleas of his young second wife, Catherine, whom he had married only the previous year (though she had already borne him four sons). The tsar's assassination mobilized conservative forces, inaugurating a period of renewed repression which was to lead, inevitably, to the revolution of 1917.

THE REVOLUTION AND AFTER

Prelude

As Russia grew ever larger and the demands for progress increasingly strained its social system, pressure from beneath for greater social justice conflicted with pressure from above for tighter social order, and Russia rushed headlong toward calamity. It was precisely because of this conflict that Marxism gained the interest of the Russian revolutionaries. And in order to understand what happened next in Russia, it is important to understand the passionate appeal of Marxist ideas.

Today, we often use the terms "Marxism," "socialism," and "communism" more or less interchangeably, but they are not, in fact, all the same thing. "Communism," when spelled with a small "c," is an idea which can be traced all the way back to Plato, and it means simply a system in which groups of people share their resources communally. "Socialism," when spelled with a small "s," is a specific type of communism, developed from the viewpoint of an industrial (rather than an agricultural) society. The term "socialism" became popular among revolutionary theorists in nineteenth-century France, and there was born the famous slogan which sums up the socialist ideal: "From each according to his means, to each according to his needs."

When spelled with a capital letter, both "Socialism" and "Communism" describe political movements. The Socialists believed in an evolutionary approach, reforming political systems from within and working gradually toward the achievement of their political aims, while the Communists believed in the necessity of revolution. In both philosophies, however, the goal was a worldwide classless society, in which there would be no private property and no profit.

Karl Marx employed a kind of scientific approach to develop his own brand of socialist philosophy. According to Marx, all of human history had been determined by economic factors, and all conflicts were essentially conflicts between oppressors and the oppressed. Marx's interpretation of history, called "dialectical materialism," was based on the idea that each ruling class was always eventually supplanted by another ruling class. The noble class, for example, had once had the greatest power because they owned the means of production: the land. As economic conditions changed, a new class of profit-takers (such as merchants, manufacturers, and bankers) had achieved greater power because *they* now controlled the means of acquiring wealth. This class Marx called the *bourgeoisie*. Like all ruling classes, the bourgeoisie derived their profit from the exploitation of the laboring masses, whom Marx christened the *proletariat*.

Based on this theory, Marx predicted that eventually the proletariat would take over the means of production and the whole structure of class division would fall. Marx viewed this revolution as inevitable, since he believed (incorrectly, as it turned out) that workers and the capitalists they worked for could never reach any common ground. In the Marxian scenario, once the proletariat discovered its own power, revolution would spread through all nations, bringing an end to poverty and war—for with all things held in common, everyone would have enough. Religion, which Marx considered a tool used by oppressors to distract the oppressed from their suffering, would no longer be necessary. And after a time, even government itself would "wither away," unnecessary in the classless society.

Although Marx's theories seemed very logical, they failed to take into consideration many aspects of human nature, and things did not work out in practice as Marx predicted. England, America, and Western Europe developed labor union movements which actually resulted (though not without struggle) in important reforms. In these countries, wages increased, working conditions improved, and governments became more representative, so the pressure toward revolution subsided. In Russia, however, many factors conspired to prevent peaceful change. Among these factors were the sheer size of the country, the foolishness of the last tsar, the influence of the Orthodox Church, the tragedy of World War I, and perhaps above all, the iron will of a man called Lenin.

The events of the Russian Revolution actually unfolded over

more than a decade. In fact, there were really three revolutions, not just one. But the die was already cast in 1881, on the day Tsar Alexander was assassinated. His successor, Alexander III, was of quite a different outlook than his father, and he immediately instituted drastic measures to curb the growth of civil unrest. Censorship was increased and the power of district assemblies was sharply curtailed. Perhaps even worse, a new assault was made on Russia's ethnic and religious minorities. For some time, conservative forces had been blaming "foreign influences" and "Jewish conspiracies" for the widespread disaffection in Russia, and now, persecution of these groups was intensified.

The more repressive the government became, however, the more active and successful the revolutionary underground seemed to be. By this time, the huge numbers of factory workers who crowded Russian cities were just as oppressed and ill-treated as the rural peasants, and radical factions tirelessly distributed propaganda to the workers, organized labor unions, and encouraged strikes.

In 1894, the last tsar of Russia was crowned. Perhaps no one could have steered a successful course through the turmoil that afflicted Russia, but certainly this man was entirely unequal to the task before him. Easily swayed by others, especially his German wife Alexandra, Nicholas II made one mistake after another, never seeming to grasp the true nature of the Russian crisis. From the very beginning, when the public celebration of his coronation turned into a stampede that killed over a thousand people, his reign seemed doomed.

Almost as soon as he was crowned, Nicholas announced that all ideas of democratic reform were "senseless dreams," and as he continued and even intensified his father's policy of repression, terrorism and protest increased proportionally. In 1905, a huge but peaceful crowd of workers, led by the Orthodox priest Father Gapon, attempted to gather in the palace square to protest labor conditions. Unnerved by the size of the crowd, the palace guard fired on the demonstrators, leaving more than one hundred dead and many more wounded. Although the demonstration was never intended to be a rebellion, it provided the spark for a revolutionary "dress rehearsal," as strikes and riots quickly spread throughout the industrial cities of Russia. The massacre of Father Gapon's marchers became known as "Bloody Sunday," and public outrage over the event was enormous.

Fearful of a complete revolt, Nicholas finally followed the advice of his more sensible counselors and issued a decree promising the establishment of a Duma, or representative assembly. This was not enough to stem the tide of revolutionary energy, however. In a drama that was to become a symbol of the revolution, the crew of the warship Potemkin mutinied, seizing the vessel in the name of the people. Workers in St. Petersburg formed the first *Soviet*, or "council," which led a general strike in the city. The Soviet was soon arrested, however, and army troops were sent in to pacify the city, effectively ending the First Russian Revolution.

The Duma was held as scheduled, but even before the first meeting, Nicholas announced that its legislative powers would be severely limited. When the elected delegates demanded reforms, the Duma was dissolved. A second Duma was elected, and also dissolved. Revolutionary feeling was once again mounting in the country, and by the time the third Duma met, both sides were ready to compromise, at least to some extent. Various progressive measures began to be passed by the Duma, and tensions eased.

The revolutionary radicals had not given up, however. They mistrusted the Duma and continued to prepare for an overthrow of the government, but their plans were interrupted by the outbreak of World War I in 1914. The war, which Russia entered to defend its ally Serbia against an Austrian invasion, was at first popular with the people, and it was supported by the fourth Duma, then in session. But the war dragged on, with staggering losses (far greater than those sustained by any other country) among the ill-equipped and poorly supplied Russian troops. The Russian economy deteriorated drastically, and disillusioned soldiers deserted in droves, swelling the ranks of the revolutionaries. Nevertheless, the powerful in Russia were determined to continue the war, both for profit and for the promise of territorial gains.

Meanwhile, Nicholas continued a course of action which

further outraged the Russian people. The tsar's only son had been born with hemophilia, and both Nicholas and Alexandra were obsessed with keeping the child alive. They turned for help to a mysterious Russian peasant, Grigory Rasputin, who claimed to have healing powers. (There is still wide disagreement as to whether Rasputin's spiritual claims were genuine, fraudulent, or both.) The unconventional Rasputin was notorious for his drinking, womanizing, and poor sanitary habits, but the imperial couple remained irrationally devoted to him; before long, the sly Rasputin was exerting a powerful influence on government policy, even making military decisions. Desperate aristocrats made several attempts to assassinate the seemingly indestructible Rasputin, and in 1916, they finally succeeded by stabbing him repeatedly and dumping him into the icy river. But still Nicholas refused to change his course, instead surrounding himself with Rasputin's followers, and the more realistic factions in the court began to talk of a palace coup. They hoped that removing Nicholas from power would avert the impending revolution.

Before a plan could be agreed upon, however, new riots began in St. Petersburg, and now the soldiers brought in to quell the disturbances refused to fire on their compatriots. In one day, the entire garrison of the capital—more than 150,000 men—joined the uprising, and soon the city was in the hands of the revolutionaries. The Second Russian Revolution had begun, and within five days, with only about 1,500 casualties, it was over.

From Chaos to Totalitarianism

The revolutionaries had no clear leadership (most of their leaders were in exile or in prison) and no specific plan for implementing a new government, but years of discipline had prepared them for swift action. Almost immediately, a Soviet was established, made up of workers and soldiers who took over the practical activities of government. Pressure mounted for the removal of the tsar, and on March 15, Nicholas abdicated in favor of his brother Michael. The very next day, Michael too abdicated and a Provisional Government was formed. For the first time in many centuries, Russia was without a tsar.

The revolution was not over, however. During the next several months, a power struggle unfolded which was to determine the future course of Russia. The Provisional Government, made up mostly of liberals and moderates, wanted to institute a Western-style democracy. The members of the Soviet were dedicated to the ideal of a true Communist state, but they were divided into several factions. The most important of these were the Mensheviks (meaning "majority") who advocated gradual reform, and the Bolsheviks ("minority") who favored using every means to destroy capitalism and establish a proletarian state. While the Mensheviks supported Russia's involvement in World War I, the Bolsheviks insisted that the war was actually nothing more than a capitalist adventure, wasting the lives of the poor in order to enrich the oppressors.

In spite of their disagreements, the Mensheviks, the Bolsheviks, and the official Provisional Government maintained an uneasy cooperation until the exiled revolutionary leader Nikolai Lenin—a man of fierce purpose and ruthless determination—returned to Russia in April of 1917. Within a month of his return, the politically skillful Lenin took control of the Bolshevik agenda and focused it on bringing about an end to both the war and the Provisional Government. With slogans like "Peace, Land, Bread" and "All Power to the Soviets," the Bolshevik's massive propaganda campaign attracted more and more war-weary people. Demonstrations of as many as half a million people pressed the largely Menshevik Congress of Soviets to take over control of the country from the Provisional Government, and when the Mensheviks were unable to do so, the demonstrators turned their support to the Bolsheviks.

Fearful of the people's growing enthusiasm for Bolshevism, the Provisional Government responded with a wave of repression. They denounced Lenin, Trotsky, and the other Bolshevik leaders as counter-revolutionaries and agents of German imperialism, driving them into hiding. Bolshevik publications were suppressed and many of the government's own reforms were repealed. The land committees, which had been working toward redistribution of agricultural lands, were abolished, the death penalty was restored, workers in St. Petersburg were disarmed, and the establishment of an elected assembly was postponed. Within the government, reactionary forces were plotting to establish a military dictatorship.

Though the conservative coup was averted, Russia was now awash in a tide of political rivalries and recriminations. Lenin was poised to take advantage of the increasing chaos. He pressured the Bolsheviks into overthrowing the government by force, and this they did, almost bloodlessly, in the Third Russian Revolution (also called the "October" or "Bolshevik" Revolution). In the end, the most radical elements of the Russian revolutionary movement gained absolute power and became the dictators of Russia's future.

Under the direction of Lenin and the Bolsheviks, a Congress of Soviets convened to determine the new structure of Russia under an extreme version of Marxist ideology. Private property was abolished; all land was confiscated and placed under the control of agricultural communes; banks, railways, utilities, and factories were all nationalized (though in some cases, gradually). The new Russian government immediately withdrew from the war and called upon all nations to do the same. Government was placed effectively in the hands of a Council of People's Commissars, whose number included Joseph Stalin and Leon Trotsky. Lenin, of course, was elected head of the Council.

It is difficult to tell how much sincerity there was among the Communist leaders in those early days. Certainly, many of their actions were understandable, and some, even admirable. The new regime immediately granted the right of self-determination to nationalities—such as the Poles and Finns—which had been forcibly included in the tsarist empire, and declared an end to the persecution of ethnic and religious minorities. But although humane intentions and idealistic goals provided much of the enormous energy which fueled the revolution, within only a few years, the spirit of liberation was transformed into rigid ideology. The communist doctrine which Lenin impressed on Russia was not the utopian dream of Plato and Rousseau, but the "scientific socialism" of Marx and Engels. It proved to be neither a solution to Russia's practical problems nor a fitting milieu for the Russian soul.

Lenin's unexpected death in 1924 provoked a fierce power struggle within the party. Joseph Stalin emerged victorious, and soon began the most infamous period of Soviet history. An efficient and implacable organizer, Stalin pulled the newly autonomous national groups of the former empire together in a "Union of Soviet Socialist Republics" (U.S.S.R.) and began to steer the new federation rapidly toward an entirely socialist economic structure. The centerpiece of this approach was the "planned economy," in which Moscow set and enforced goals called "Five-Year Plans" for every farm, factory, and worker in all of the vast Soviet Union. Stalin's aim was to force massive industrialization of the backward, agrarian society, and in this he initially showed signs of being successful.

However, most of us today know the outcome of the Communist strategy. For one thing, centralized control of the huge Soviet economy proved absurdly inefficient. For another, it turned out that when people were deprived of the motives of competition, profit, and personal achievement, many of them simply did not put forth much effort. Meanwhile, a huge, cumbersome bureaucratic apparatus grew up to control every aspect of economic life, stifling all originality and preventing farms and factories from adapting to changing circumstances. With no market pressure to drive innovation and improvement, industry went on making things of poor quality that people didn't want, while a black market grew up, selling non-Russian items that people *did* want, at fabulous prices. And since members of the Communist party (which by Leninist doctrine did not include everyone, but rather a minority who were willing to make an intensive political commitment) were the only ones allowed to hold government or managerial positions, the "party elite" became a new privileged class.

Though these problems became more and more severe over decades, they began to be evident fairly soon after Stalin came to power. Alarmed by what they saw, factions both inside and outside the Communist party began to dissent from the party line, and by the mid-1930's, the Communists were ironically faced with the same problem which had plagued the tsars: in order to maintain power, they had to suppress freedom.

Stalin proved much more ruthless than his imperial predecessors. In a series of purges, often featuring elaborate sham trials, he executed or exiled virtually everyone in the Communist party who disagreed with his policies. Although the purges began at the top with some of the most important members of Stalin's government, it spread to every level of society. Professionals and intellectuals were targeted in the cities, while in the countryside, planned famines and huge resettlement projects killed or scattered every group that Stalin feared as a potential threat. During the period from 1934 to 1938, it is estimated that at least ten million and perhaps as many as thirty million citizens of the Soviet Union were killed in the Great Purges.

War and Peace

Communist doctrine condemned war as a tool of the capitalist conspiracy which, they believed, sought to dominate the world and oppress the workers. But at the same time, the Communist party actively sought to overthrow non-Communist governments. So understandably, other nations were wary of Russian power. Even though America and most of Europe finally, reluctantly, recognized the existence of the Soviet Union, Russia's place among Western nations remained so insecure that when Hitler gained power in Germany and began to cast a hungry eye on Russian territory, the U.S.S.R. feared capitalist governments would seize the opportunity to form an anti-Communist alliance. Taking the offense, Stalin concluded a 1939 alliance with Germany, and by this means, the U.S.S.R. was able to buy time not only to rebuild its army, but also to annex a large chunk of Poland.

In less than two years, however, Germany turned its war machine against the Soviet Union, and the Communists were forced to ally themselves with England and America. The Russians fought heroically during World War II to save their country from the

German invasion and defeat Hitler. In a "scorched earth" policy reminiscent of the tactics used to defeat Napoleon, they frustrated the German advance by destroying their own factories, dams, and bridges, flooding their mines, and burning their crops. The city of Leningrad (formerly St. Petersburg) endured a siege of nearly two years, taking casualties of more than one million (nearly half the city's population), before the Germans were finally turned back in 1942.

Not long afterwards, Soviet forces captured most of Germany's Sixth Army in the epic battle of Stalingrad, and Hitler's Russian offensive was broken. Nevertheless, it was not until 1944 that the German invaders had been driven completely out of the Soviet Union, and by this time the once-backward Russia had developed into a huge military and political power. The Russian army did not stop at its own borders, but drove all the way to Berlin, where Stalin used his new power to dominate post-war negotiations and gain control over virtually all of Eastern Europe.

With its huge territorial gains from World War II, and its rapidly developing military technology, the Soviet Union assumed a forceful role in world affairs. Over the next forty years, the Soviet government was able to incite and support Communist insurgencies in third-world countries like Cuba, while crushing any dissent in its European "client-states" such as Hungary. And by converting their nation's education and industry almost entirely into the service of building military might, the Soviets succeeded in becoming the first nation to place a satellite in orbit, as well as in building a huge arsenal of both nuclear and conventional weapons. Lenin and Stalin became mythic figures, commemorated everywhere with monumental statues and murals.

The Soviet Union, like all totalitarian states, closely controlled information and used it to manipulate the people. Much government energy was poured into propaganda extolling the virtues of the state, and into the censorship of any voices which might raise questions or reveal unpleasant truths. Not only was political reality, such as the extent of Stalin's purges, unknown to most Russians, the government concealed and even denied news of natural disasters like earthquakes.

An elaborate network of informants and secret police constantly harassed Soviet citizens, who had as little freedom under Communism as their parents had had under the tsars.

Though the quality of material life at first improved for those who had been at the bottom of pre-Revolutionary Russian society, living conditions in the Soviet Union never really became more than marginal for most. So much of the country's resources went into military production that there was little left over for other social needs. And in spite of many shifts in policy, the Soviet leadership was never able to make Marxist economic theory work in practice— which was inevitable, since Marx had completely misunderstood human nature.

Nikita Kruschev, who proved the winner in an intense power struggle after Stalin's death, attempted to modernize Soviet economic and political structures, but his attack on Stalin's cult of personality, and an inclination to brinksmanship (for example, in the Cuban Missile Crisis) resulted in his ouster. Leonid Brezhnev, his successor, proved to be a stolid conservative who doggedly held the Communist line in the U.S.S.R., in spite of mounting evidence that progressive capitalism is far more likely to improve people's lives than militant socialism. The legacy of Brezhnev's policies brought the Soviet Union near economic collapse and necessitated what is now sometimes called "the Fourth Russian Revolution."

By the close of the 1980s, it was plain that the Soviet Union could not survive. Although Mikhail Gorbachev attempted to preserve a liberalized version of socialism and at the same time institute democratic reforms, he brought too little change too late. The people of Russia, who had been waiting nearly a century for the freedom and prosperity promised by the revolution of 1917, turned to Boris Yeltsin. Led as before by a strange coalition of disappointed workers and disaffected intellectuals, the people demanded a transformation to real democracy and a free-market economy.

Today they are getting some of what they have wished for, but the suffering continues. Economic dislocation has produced food shortages, hyper-inflation, organized crime, unemployment, and a host of other hardships. Conservative forces continue to impede progress. Ethnic rivalries, long held in check by tight Soviet control, are flaring up in many parts of the former Soviet Union. The social security once provided by the Communist state has collapsed, leaving the elderly and the infirm in nearly hopeless straits. And the Russians are realizing that their country, once filled with beauty and rich with natural resources, has been reduced to a depleted and polluted wasteland.

Yet in the midst of all this, the Russian spirit is reasserting itself. People are recovering their religions, rediscovering their arts, and reclaiming their heritage. For many who grew up with an idealistic belief in the future of Communism, the shock of its loss may be too great to overcome; and even for those who can adapt to new ways, peace and plenty will be a long time in coming. But with luck, those growing up now will have the chance to build a new future, in which beauty will return to Russia, and the soul of this remarkable people will at long last be set free.

Chapter 2

The Russian World

*A*n old Russian proverb says, "Russia is not a country, but rather a world." Geographically vast, and isolated for centuries from foreign influences and ideas, traditional Russia became its own universe. Drawing on the power of the Russian landscape and the diversity of Russia's ethnic heritage, the Russian people developed a unique approach to the realm of art and imagination. Although much can be understood about Russia through its history, to get a broad sense of the land and its people we also have to look at what they believe in and what they create.

MYSTERIOUS RUSSIA

The imaginative and spiritual traditions of Russia are quite different from those of our own culture, and even from those of most cultures in which Westerners have taken an interest. For many years, students of philosophy and metaphysics have been fascinated by Eastern ideas, and more recently, by such traditional cultures as those of the American Indians, Australian aborigines, and various African tribes. But we have known little of what has animated Russian spiritual life.

Today, of course, Russian spirituality is as much in change and disarray as Russian economics or politics. But the history of spiritual experience in Russia is still of great interest. Like Russian art, Russian spirituality combined many different influences and then added some unique Russian twists. The result was a rich and diverse experience of the spiritual realm which saturated the lives of Russians for a thousand years. Christianity was the dominant force during most of that time, but the roots of Russian spiritual experience go much further back.

Myth and Folklore

We know relatively little about the mythology of pre-Christian Russia. Nomadic cultures like the Sarmatians and the Scythians passed along their stories and beliefs orally, so we have only some ancient artifacts to offer vague suggestions about their religious life, which doesn't seem to have been highly developed. The early Slavs were more settled, and probably had a fairly rich mythology, but most traces of it were wiped out with the coming of Christianity. From what we do know (mostly by way of linguistic comparisons and references in later Russian documents), the Slavic religion had much in common with the Persian religion of the time. Both were very nature-oriented. Slavic gods were associated with the wind, the sun, the frost, and the earth. The most powerful god in their pantheon appears to have been Perun, a solar deity whose emblems were thunder and lightning, the oak tree, and the horse.

The pagan Slavs apparently built temples, such as the one described by a tenth-century German bishop as "decorated with magnificent carvings of gods and goddesses." But little of their sacred architecture remains, in part because the temples (and probably most of the artifacts) were made of perishable wood; and in part because historically, wherever Christianity was adopted, the Church was effortful in obliterating the old "pagan" religions that had preceded it. Sacred sites and objects were destroyed, rituals were prohibited, and stories of the old ways were suppressed. In Russia, as soon as Christianity was declared the official religion in 989, carved wooden statues of the old gods were unceremoniously pulled from their places of honor and dragged into the river. Then a vigorous building campaign erected Orthodox churches on the very grounds where the old gods had once been worshiped. In many places, mass baptisms were enforced, often upon people who had no idea what their new religion was actually all about.

In Russia, as almost everywhere else, however, people refused to give up the old ways entirely. Country people were likely to keep aspects of their old beliefs and graft these onto their new religion, and even the more sophisticated city-dwellers echoed pagan beliefs in their superstitions and social rituals. This practice was referred to in Russia as *dvoeverie*, or "double-faith," and it persisted almost throughout Russian history. In 1845, the St. Petersburg Academy of Sciences compiled an immense two-volume encyclopedia of folkways called *Beliefs, Habits, Superstitions, Songs, Riddles and Games of the Russian People*, in which were recorded the many beautiful and sometimes strange customs that still flourished in the countryside. There, the year still had its mysteries, and every day was marked by special properties. September, for example, was called "Women's Summer," and on the first day of the month, old mattresses were burned and replaced with new ones to placate evil spirits.

The Russian people read the stars and watched nature for signs and portents. For example, wolves seen near a village on October 30 presaged war or famine, while Venus was said to help a person see the truth. The bear, an important symbol of the old Slavic god Perun, was a continuing character in Russian festivals and sports (performing bears and bear-wrestling contests were for a time prohibited by the Church), and was even seen in icons, church frescoes, and coats of arms. Many superstitions revolved around the bear, whose name pronounced at sea was thought to bring storms, and whose fur, burned at the proper time, would smoke out evil spirits.

Indeed, superstition was always a hallmark of the Russian people. One English visitor wrote in the late 19th century that among the Russians there was "the greatest faith in love philters and charms, talismans and crosses." There were lucky and unlucky days, dates, and numbers, as well as a whole array of practices designed to propitiate the many spirits who were thought to inhabit homes, fields, forests, and streams. Among the most potent of these spirits was the *domovoy*, or house spirit, thought to live behind the stove or under the threshold. Mischievous and easily aggrieved, the domovoy had to be given regular gifts of bread and salt, or pancakes.

Other spirits included the *Poludnica*, who guarded the fields and field-workers, making them sleepy at mid-day; water spirits such as the ogre-like Vodanoy who caused floods; their wives the *Rusalki*, who lured men to death by drowning; and the *Vili,* forest fairies who ruled the animals and befriended hunters. But the most important spirit revered by the old Russians was that of the earth, variously known as *Mokosh* (meaning literally, "moist") or *Mati* (short for *Mati Syra Zemljz,* "Moist Mother Earth"). Mokosh is known to have been worshiped in pre-Christian Kiev, and for hundreds of years after Orthodoxy took over Russia, the Church complained that women would still "go to Mokosh," that is, worship the earth goddess. Like her numerous counterparts in other cultures, Mokosh/Mati was associated with fertility and child-bearing.

Each of the seasons was also represented in many parts of Russia by a goddess, who was honored each year at the appropriate time. The goddess of Winter, *Marena,* was thrown out in effigy each Spring after being carried through the village. The Spring-goddess *Kostrubonko* was impersonated by a young girl who would lie as if dead while the villagers mourned her, then arise as a symbol of rebirth. In the Summer, the goddess *Kupalo* was represented by a straw figure who was ceremonially burned or allowed to float away, taking away the evil of the village.

The "old woman" of Autumn was closely associated with a character known to Eastern European Slavs as *Baba,* who inhabited the last sheaf of harvested grain. In Russia, this harvest spirit became Baba Yaga, a witch-like woman who rowed through the air in a mortar, with a pestle for an oar. The awful *Baba Yaga* lived in the depths of the forest and devoured passers-by, after scaring them to death.

Baba Yaga was the prototype of the fairy-tale witch, and in fact, there is nowhere on earth where fairy tales were more fantastic and full of life than in Russia. As Suzanne Massie explains in *Land of the Firebird,* these Russian tales "stressed the values of the humble over the rich and powerful, the strength of the true and clean heart, a closeness and respect for nature." Besides Baba Yaga, there was the evil sorcerer Kaschei the Immortal; the beautiful Snow Maiden; the clever simpleton, Ivan Durachok; the good and pure Ivan Tsarevich; and Volkh, the wizard-hero who could change into a wild ox with golden horns, or a gray wolf, or a flashing falcon. These colorful characters, along with adventurous and often funny stories, and beautiful, song-like rhythms, have made Russian fairy tales among the most cherished in the world.

In the nineteenth century, these fairy and folk tales, along with the more elaborate heroic epics called *bylini,* were recognized by Russian poets and artists as a rich reflection of the Russian soul. These stories became part of an artistic renaissance that focused on the old ways and values of the peasantry, inspiring Pushkin, Gogol, Tolstoy, and other literary greats. Scenes from fairy tales were beautifully illustrated, and in the twentieth century, when icon-painting was no longer permitted under the Soviet regime, icon-painting villages such as Palekh and Mstera turned their talents to the creation of a fairy-tale world on lacquerware items such as boxes, trays, and other artifacts.

The world of folk and fairy lore persisted for so long in part because Christianity failed to meet many of the people's deeper needs. Christianity offered an "either/or" picture of reality (heaven or hell, good or evil, God or man), while folklore described an "in-between" world, where strange things could always happen. Christianity stressed suffering, tolerance, and acceptance of one's fate, while folklore offered "magical" procedures for bringing about change. And Christianity offered an abstract and distant theology, while folklore attached meaning to particular places and objects. Among the Russians, whose lives and hearts were so much connected to the land, the sacredness of plants and stones, trees and streams remained immensely important, and so they supplemented the rather abstract and austere Christian world with nature spirits, witches and wizards, and "superstitious" rituals.

Yet even so, the Russian Orthodox religion remained the center and soul of Russian culture almost from its arrival until the Russian Revolution. Understanding the Russian church is vital to understanding the Russian world.

The Orthodox Church

St. Andrew is the patron saint not only of Scotland, but of Russia as well. Andrew, who was Simon Peter's brother, was born near the Sea of Galilee, and pious Russians believed that he made an early mission to the north coast of the Black Sea and east to the Volga. He was said to have preached to Scythians, Sarmatians and Slavs on the hills of Kiev before going on to Britain.

Whether or not St. Andrew ever set foot in Russia (and there's no evidence that he did), this story is a good example of how the Russians appropriated and elaborated Christianity. Within a few centuries they went from cheerful paganism to a way of life so deeply rooted in the Christian church that they firmly believed Russia to be the last bastion of true orthodoxy, the "Third Rome" and truest defender of the faith. Although the Russians initially borrowed their religion whole-cloth from the Byzantine Greeks, they stamped it with the deepest imprint of Russian values and made it into their own.

The special emphasis of Russian religion on aesthetic experience actually began with the choice of Christianity and the Byzantine model. The story is told that when Vladimir sent emissaries to all of the great religions in order to decide which of them would be best for Russia, he rejected Islam because of its prohibition against alcohol ("To drink is the joy of the Russes," he explained), and rejected Judaism because the Jews were condemned to wander the world ("Would you have us share this fate?"). The envoys then reported that when they attended mass at the great Greek cathedral Hagia Sophia, they could hardly tell whether they were "in heaven or on earth," and Vladimir was immediately sold. From that time on, the direction of the Russian church was ever more toward creating a religious experience saturated in the experience of heavenly beauty. To that end, they filled their churches to overflowing with icons and frescoes, gold and precious gems, incense and embroidery, all carrying in one way or another the message of Christ's redemptive power.

Few Russians could read, even up until this century, and their education as Christians was accomplished not through words but through images. In fact, not only reading but even listening was unimportant in Russian religious services. The congregation was separated from the altar by a very large and ornate screen; behind this screen, mostly out of sight or hearing, the mystery of the mass took place. The screen, or *iconostasis*, was a unique Russian invention. The iconostasis, formed of tier upon tier of icons (arranged with the patriarchs and prophets of the Old Testament at the top, the events in the life of Christ in the center, and popular Russian saints at the bottom) symbolized the boundary between earth and heaven. While the sacred mysteries unfolded behind the screen, the worshippers could look at its images and contemplate the presence of God on earth.

This elaborate concealment of the sacrament developed as a distinctive feature of Russian Christianity. The Russian congregation didn't usually share in the ritual of the mass, as Roman Catholic worshippers always have. But neither did they stand silently watching as the Eucharistic drama unfolded out of sight. In Russian churches, worshippers came and went—sometimes several times, as the services were very, very long; they talked amongst themselves, and moved about the church freely. This freedom contrasted, or perhaps complemented, the extreme formality of the Russian liturgy and the many religious obligations which structured the lives of ordinary Russians. In Old Russia, nearly every day was a day of some religious observance, feast, fast, or festival, and communal life revolved to a great extent around the Church.

Because of its emphasis on aesthetic experience rather than on conscious understanding, the Russian Orthodox Church grew increasingly different from Roman Catholicism or even from Greek Orthodoxy. It became more mystical and more dramatic than these other forms of Christianity. Extreme piety was widespread. During the height of Russia's religious life, monasteries grew so large that they became small cities, and devout ascetics called *starets* wandered the countryside to inspire and chastise the people. Everyone, from the tsar himself to the ordinary peasant, observed long and frequent fasts, and princes vied with one another in an endless contest of church-building.

There was very little of abstract theological debate in the Russian church, and no equivalent of the Protestant Reformation, but there was a "Great Schism" in the seventeenth century brought about by the reforms of Patriarch Nikon. The reforms in question were not at all about ideas or questions, but rather about forms—whether to make the sign of the cross with two fingers or three, for example, and how to spell the name of Jesus. Yet so passionate were many Russians about their religion that groups of them called "Old Believers," or *raskolniki,* committed mass suicides by burning themselves alive in their wooden churches, rather than give in to changes in their historical and distinctively Russian way of worship.

Among many Russians, this religious fervor lasted well into the eighteenth century, long after rationalism and secular interests had overtaken Europe. But with the increasing Westernization that followed the rule of Peter the Great, the Russian Church gradually lost its all-consuming hold on Russian culture. In the cities, especially among students, artists, and scientists, a more questioning and even anti-religious attitude arose. Because Russian Christianity had always emphasized the virtues of patience and humility (the most beloved of Russian saints, Boris and Gleb, had martyred themselves rather than cause trouble), many came to see the Church as little more than a tool of government greed, duping the peasantry into a life of poverty-stricken toil by glorifying suffering and promising that a better life would come in heaven.

The Marxist interpretation of religion as the "opiate of the people" was eagerly embraced by Russian intellectuals, and accordingly, among the results of the Russian Revolution were the destruction of many religious sites and artifacts, the dismantling of the Church and its hierarchy, and the repression of religious activity or symbolism. In effect, Communism did to Christianity what Christianity had done to the old pagan religions, assimilating its rituals into a new doctrine. Marxist theory replaced theology. Great military parades imitated the solemn processions of the mass. Even the iconographic tradition was absorbed into the new Communist

Russia, with giant icon-like paintings of Lenin, Stalin, and other Communist leaders adorning every public space. And in many homes, the old "beautiful corner" was still kept, only now it was filled with political pictures and memorabilia instead of religious paintings and relics.

Throughout the Communist domination, underground worship continued in spite of intermittent attempts at suppression, and in recent years, with official anti-religious pressure removed, Russians have flooded back to the Church. The Russian Orthodox religion is no longer unchallenged in Russia, however. Western-style evangelical Protestantism has attracted many followers in Russia and throughout Eastern Europe. Perhaps this is not surprising, since the whole history of Russia attests to the longing of the people for absolute values and for intensity of experience. These qualities may be provided even more strongly by fundamentalist religions than by the pomp and ritual of Orthodoxy.

Evangelical fundamentalism is not the only new influence entering into the world of Russian belief today. Eastern philosophies, New Age ideas, and magical schools are all making appearances in a new Russia eager for new answers. But Orthodox Christianity was for so long the only spiritual outlet in Russian society that there is very little in their own tradition for the Russians to draw on in seeking metaphysical alternatives.

Esoteric Traditions in Russia

There has always been a strong mystical strain in Russian life, both in folk tradition and in the Orthodox Church. Slavic culture was infused with what we might call today "nature mysticism"; Mother Earth was considered a living being, and trees, water, hills, and fields were all believed to be inhabited and animated by spirits whose energy could affect human life. Slavic healers are thought to have treated the sick not only with herbs and other natural medicines, but with "places of power" and the energies of trees (energy-giving oaks, for example, to treat fatigue; energy-sucking aspens to drain fevers or inflammations).

Many of these healing practices are reputed to have continued in the Russian countryside even up to the present. (It's rumored that Communist Party leaders might secretly seek out a village "sorcerer" when conventional medicine failed to alleviate their ills.) But for the most part, the rich, mystical Slavic heritage was driven to the margins of Russian life after the tenth century, when Russia was converted to Christianity.

The Russian church took its beginnings from Greek Orthodoxy, which, unlike the Roman Catholic Church, was very much influenced by Neoplatonist and Gnostic ideas. These ideas form the basis of most esoteric teachings, and they emphasize the importance of developing "inner life" and acquiring "mystical knowledge." A special type of mysticism, called *kenosis* or "emptying," was practiced by extremely devout Russians. Saints Boris and Gleb were Kenotics, and so was St. Theodosius (creator of the Jesus Prayer, known to readers of J.D. Salinger as the prayer that preoccupied Franny Glass in *Franny and Zooey*). Another peculiarly Russian type of mysticism was practiced by the *yurodivy,* or "holy fools," who abandoned conventional reality-testing altogether and offered topsy-turvy insights sometimes called "crazy wisdom."

But even though mystical practices and magical beliefs were deeply a part of Russian culture for centuries, it was not until just over a hundred years ago that occult activities took on any real significance in Russia. There was almost no tradition there of ceremonial magic, alchemy, or any of the activities which shaped occult history in the West. Perhaps because the Orthodox Church was so powerful and so pervasive, other forms of spiritual experience did not readily take hold.

Probably the best-known occult figure to emerge from Russia was Helena Petrovna Blavatsky, founder of the widely influential Theosophical Society. Madame Blavatsky (or HPB, as she was often called) mixed spiritualism, Eastern philosophy, and all sorts of esoteric lore into the doctrines of Theosophy. With her charismatic personality, she attracted many spiritual seekers in Europe, England, and America; in her native Russia, however, she was known not as a mystic but as "Radda Bai," a writer whose romantic stories of exotic

India appeared in Russian literary journals. A few esoteric articles by and about HPB appeared in a Russian occult journal called *Rebus*, so a small circle of Russian intellectuals and aristocrats were familiar with her work. But when HPB died in 1891, there was still no official group of the Theosophical Society meeting in Russia.

Between 1890 and 1925, Russian interest in occult matters increased dramatically. Theosophy began to attract popular interest, and occult ideas influenced many well-known Russians, including prima ballerina Anna Pavlova, noted philosopher Nikolai Berdyaev, and impresario extraordinaire Sergei Diaghilev. In Russia, as in Europe, interest in the occult was widely intermingled with experiments in poetry and art (such as Symbolism and Abstraction), attracting the creative edge of society.

Occult influence was felt in another quarter as well. The infatuation of Tsar Nicholas and his wife Alexandra with the controversial holy man, Rasputin, is well known. But less widely known is the fact that the French physician and occultist Papus, author of the classic work *Tarot of the Bohemians*, was a member of the imperial inner circle. Between 1901 and his death in 1916, Papus visited Russia four times, offering occult counsel to Nicholas and Alexandra—reportedly even performing a ceremony to summon the spirit of Nicholas's father. Papus's Christianized approach to occult matters was especially appealing to the Russian spirit; and the tsar himself, along with a number of his relatives, was a member of the Martinist Order (a secret society established by two eighteenth-century Christian adepts) led by Papus.

Only a year after Papus's death—which Alexandra reportedly saw as a sign of doom for the Romanov monarchy—the Russian Revolution took place, bringing an apparent end to occult activities for the next seventy years. Life under the new Communist regime became so inhospitable to esoteric ideas that another of Russia's best-known mystics, G.I. Gurdjieff, departed with a small group of his followers. Born near Russia's border with Persia, Gurdjieff had left home at an early age and, for twenty years, traveled the world in search of ideas about the meaning of life. In 1912, he appeared in Moscow, and began to teach a "method" for achieving enlightenment. His method, which he called the "Fourth Way" (that is, the way of normal life as opposed to the way of the monk, yogi, or fakir) incorporated both traditional mysticism and modern Western science. The combination of these ideas began to attract followers from among the intelligentsia. Gurdjieff taught his students a process of "self-remembering" which would help them "awaken" from their mechanical lives and create a higher state of being.

Among the Gurdjieff enthusiasts who left Communist Russia with the master was the journalist and Theosophist P. D. Ouspensky. Gurdjieff established his new center of operations in Paris, while Ouspensky (who had begun to distrust his teacher's emphasis on "slyness" as a path of enlightenment) went on to begin his own work in England and America. Whereas the colorful Gurdjieff followed in the tradition of Russia's "holy fools"— provoking and playing tricks on his students, and generally behaving unpredictably—Ouspensky was much more serious-minded and conventional. But Ouspensky did much to popularize Gurdjieff's often difficult ideas. Ouspensky also stimulated interest in the Tarot images, which he incorporated into his books *A New Model of the Universe* and *Symbolism of the Tarot*.

Though not a great deal is known about it, there is said to have been a Gurdjieff-influenced circle in St. Petersburg which pursued work with the Tarot. The author of *Meditations on the Tarot*, Christian mystic Valentin Tomberg, was exposed to the ideas of this group. Tomberg, who later converted to Roman Catholicism and lived in England, stipulated that *Meditations on the Tarot* (which uses the Tarot images as a vehicle for profound reflections on Christian hermeticism) would be published anonymously and only after his death. Since its publication, the book has attracted great admiration for its sincerity and depth.

The Western world knows mainly those Russian esotericists, such as Blavatsky and Gurdjieff, who left Russia. But throughout the Communist regime, there thrived in Russia a religious underground which included not only Orthodox believers but many different esoteric and occult groups. These various groups included some which derived from the work of earlier teachers (students of Gurdjieff and followers of Theosophy continued to work in the spiritual underground), and others which were started by ordinary citizens who experienced spontaneous spiritual awakenings. In this second category was the group which followed Porphyry Ivanov, a peasant whose amazing physical health enabled him to wear nothing more than shorts even in the depths of the Russian winter. After a mystical vision in the 1930's, he began to teach his nature-oriented philosophy to others, who tuned themselves to Mother Earth by such practices as yoga-like breathing exercises and ice-water bathing.

Another group which focused on natural experience encouraged "conscious conception" and taught parents to communicate with their unborn children. Among this group, many mothers gave birth in the Black Sea, where it is said that dolphins often came to support the mothers in labor. But leaders and members of these groups were systematically persecuted by the Soviets, who imprisoned Ivanov for a time and denied birth certificates to the Black Sea babies. One favorite Soviet tactic was to place spiritual seekers in mental hospitals and treat them with anti-psychotic drugs.

Nevertheless, these groups and others continued to practice their work, and today are experiencing a renewal. There is great interest in reviving Slavic paganism and other intrinsically Russian types of experience, but there are also eclectic influences from all the world's great spiritual traditions: yoga, tai chi, Taoism, Tibetan Buddhism, Sufism, shamanism, and many more. The Theosophical Society was officially reestablished in Russia in 1991, and followers of the exiled Russian mystic and artist Nicholas Roerich are once again publicly pursuing their search for Belovodye (the Russian equivalent of Shangri-La) in summer outings among the Altai mountains. Meanwhile, groups working with "energy technology" continue the study of paranormal phenomena—ironically, this was an area of intense interest for the Soviets, who believed "psi" skills could be developed and used for military purposes.

There is no way of predicting the future of Russian spiritual life. At present, there are hundreds of associations dealing with esoteric and occult matters, ranging from the bizarre (one group practices "astral karate") to the sublime. The Russians, long starved for metaphysical nourishment, may be easy prey for charlatans and fanatics. But whatever happens will be of great interest and significance. As Gnostic scholar Stephan Hoeller writes, "purged in the fire of terror and martyrdom, held back for many decades from satisfying its deepest needs, but nourished by inner springs of mystic fervor and insight, the Russian soul has much to give to the spiritual traditions of the world."

CREATIVE RUSSIA

No country is more legitimately famed for the diversity and richness of its artistic traditions than Russia. From earliest times, the Russians lavished imagination on the decoration of their homes and tools. During their long Middle Ages, they incorporated and elaborated traditional motifs into the creation of some of the world's most gorgeous churches and liturgical accouterments. Their creative skills reached new heights of beauty and delicacy during the imperial period, when great palaces were built and the lives of the nobility were furnished with the most beautifully wrought luxuries. In the nineteenth century, through the rediscovery of their folk heritage (ignored, and even disdained by the Europeanized upper classes for almost two hundred years) and the reexamination of their cultural values, Russian writers produced an almost unparalleled body of literary works. Then finally, before the descent into Communism, Russia provided the world with an outburst of innovation that greatly influenced the development of modernism in all the arts.

To understand the importance of the creative arts in Russian life, we can look briefly at the history and the special character of several different areas of artistic achievement.

The Visual Arts

Painting and sculpture, the two great expressive traditions of the visual arts, developed very unevenly in Russia. Because of the

Orthodox prohibition against the creation of "statues" (which were feared to encourage idolatry), there was virtually no tradition of fine sculpture in Russia until the eighteenth century. Until that time, almost the only three-dimensional art was found in the low-relief friezes which were used in some churches, and in the beautifully carved wooden implements and decorations which adorned peasant life. When fine sculpture was finally introduced to Russia, it became mainly a derivative art form, dedicated for the most part to reproducing the style and content of classical European sculpture.

Painting, on the other hand, was literally a religion in Russia. Not only the paintings themselves, but everything associated with them was considered sacred. The lives of the icon-painters were expected to reflect a deep religious commitment. Strict rules laid down by the Church for icon painters decreed that they were to live like priests, and to observe very specific conventions in their painting. (Certain scenes, for example, were always to have the same composition, and particular colors were associated with particular figures or objects.) Icon painters were not to sign their works, for the artists were thought to be the instruments, not the creators, of these holy images.

Iconopis, or religious painting, originally borrowed its form and content from the Byzantine Greeks; but very early, the Russians developed their own style. Russian icon painters introduced new forms to the tradition, such as narrative icons, figures in motion, and backgrounds embellished with scenery. Also, while Byzantine iconography employed a contemplative mood and favored dark colors, Russian artists created more vigorous interpretations with bright, luminous colors and simplified outlines. Certain images were especially favored by the Russians, primarily those that portrayed qualities of warmth and loving kindness.

Icons were customarily painted on wood, and the selection and preparation of wood for the panels was the important first step in the process of producing the icon. Many of the areas which became centers of icon production were located near sources of especially excellent wood. (Cypress from the Russian south was at one time preferred for icons, but later, northern pine became more popular.)

Tempera, a mixture of powdered mineral earths dissolved in a preparation of fresh egg yolk, water, and *kvass* (rye beer), was used to paint the icons. The mixing of the tempera was in itself an art, and painters developed their own formulations to achieve the rich colors they sought.

Icon painting became increasingly complex as the demand grew for ever more beautiful icons. By the sixteenth century, no fewer than six different "specialists" were required for the process of creating an icon. The first selected and prepared the wood; the second composed the outline of the picture, following traditional form; a third was in charge of gilding. Clothing and buildings were painted by a fourth expert, natural forms by a fifth, and faces—considered the highest of all the forms—were given their other-worldly expressions by a sixth artist.

The characteristic appearance of icons derives in large part from their "flatness"; everything in the picture is on one plane, with no foreground or background. Although perspective, a method of imparting a more naturalistic depth to painted scenes, was widely employed in European painting from the fifteenth century on, Russian artists continued to use the traditionally flat style. Though the Russians knew about perspective, they rejected it, as they did so much of Western European culture. The tradition of icon painting was, after all, much more than just an artistic activity. It was a divinely inspired process. So not until non-religious painting began in Russia did perspective begin to be seen in Russian art.

Zhivopis, or naturalistic painting, began to gain favor in Russia at the end of the seventeenth century. Like their Western European counterparts, the Russian secular painters typically used oil paints and painted from live scenes of nature or people, rather than from prescribed subject matter. But even though the secular artists of eighteenth and nineteenth century Russia had greater creative freedom, they never produced any art which compared in intensity and originality to the anonymous works of the icon-painters. In fact, it was not until the early twentieth century, when artists like Vasily Kandinsky and Kasimir Malevich rediscovered the icon-painting tradition and used it as a springboard for their bold leaps into abstraction, that Russia produced any painters who had real stature and influence in the art world.

From the seventeenth century on, icon-painting gradually declined in importance, and naturalistic painting became more widely practiced. Many Russian artists were employed in creating works for the numerous palaces and official buildings of the Empire. But the Russian nobility did not fail to notice the relative inferiority of Russia's own visual arts. In an attempt to make Russian art competitive with European art, they brought many painters, architects, and artisans into Russia from Western Europe, and sent a number of Russian artists abroad to learn to imitate European technique. What's more, the tsars and tsarinas amassed large collections of Western art, with the result that some of Europe's finest works have long resided in Russian museums.

During this time, Russia's own native art, still made and loved by the peasants, came to be regarded by the gentry and the academics as primitive and embarrassing. But in the second half of the nineteenth century, a new generation of artists recognized the unique vitality of the old folk art, as well as the formal achievements of Russian iconography. Their movement began with a rebellion against the increasingly stuffy Academy of Fine Arts. This institution, which bestowed valuable government rank on its graduates, confined the activities of art students to precise reproduction of neoclassical themes and discouraged any attempt to paint from real life or personal feeling. In 1863, a group of students refused to paint the official subject ("Odin's Entrance into Valhalla") of the annual competition, and, resigning from the Academy, formed an artists' cooperative called Artel.

This group became the nucleus for a movement which included noted naturalistic painters Ilya Repin, Vasily Maksimov, and Vasily Surikov, as well as hundreds of others. Calling themselves "The Wanderers," these artists not only traveled the countryside sketching and painting from real-life scenes, they abandoned the museums and patrons of the art "establishment," and began their own traveling exhibitions. So successful were they in captivating the interest of Russian society that The Wanderers were soon recognized as a national school, and eventually the leading artists of the group—now prosperous and well-respected—took over the very Academy against which they had originally rebelled. But of course, it was not long until these former revolutionaries were themselves under attack from a new generation of artists. The younger artists invented new styles, to which they gave such dramatic-sounding names as Primitivism, Rayonism, and Cubo-Futurism.

The artistic flowering in Russia that began the twentieth century was expressed in the founding of the magazine *The World of Art* (*Mir Iskusstva*) in 1898, and in the first exhibition organized by the group of that same name the following year. *The World of Art* proclaimed the doctrine of "art for art's sake," and undertook to introduce French ideas to Russia, such as Impressionism and Symbolism. Centered in St. Petersburg, the movement gave a focus to the artistic ferment going on in Russia: a creative explosion in which the thousand years of Russian artistry and craftsmanship was sparked into newness by the end of tsarist repression.

Drawing on the stylized and attenuated forms created by the master icon painters, as well as on the popular arts of the Russian peasantry, modernist painters soon set out to create an entirely new kind of art, purely Russian and free of European ties. Husband and wife Natalia Goncharova and Mikhail Larionov introduced Primitivism, a style which sought to return to "pure" forms, undistorted by history or idea. Their early work incorporated imagery from medieval icons and the wood block prints (*lubki*) which had been a mainstay of peasant art. But the two painters became more and more involved in abstraction, and in 1912, they staged an exhibition which brought together their own art with that of Cubist Kasimir Malevich and the mystical painter Marc Chagall. Meanwhile another Russian, Vasily Kandinsky, was working in Germany on his own revolutionary approach to art.

Malevich and Kandinsky were developing a style in which all recognizable objects were eliminated, and only color and texture, composition, and contrast remained. This approach to art, called "abstraction," was intriguing painters throughout Europe, but it was pursued most radically in Russia, where the whole intellectual climate was intensely revolutionary. The artistic movements which developed in Russia before and just after the Revolution stripped away every "realistic" aspect of phenomena in an attempt to depict a higher, or spiritual, reality in painting and sculpture. Malevich carried this rationale to the extreme with his famous 1918 painting *White on White,* a white square on a white ground.

Malevich's movement in painting, called Suprematism, was paralleled by Vladimir Tatlin's Constructivism, which brought abstraction into sculpture and focused attention on synthetic materials and the formal precision of a machine-made world. Like most of the avant-garde artists in Russia, Malevich and Tatlin believed in an absolutist vision of the future, shaped in large part by the emerging wonders of technology and the eventual triumph of the proletariat. Their art was considered by Trotsky and many Bolsheviks to be an appropriate expression of the Revolution, so after the Revolution, Malevich was appointed a professor in the Leningrad Academy, and many expatriate artists, including Kandinsky, returned to Russia in the belief that the worker's paradise would also be a fertile new ground for the arts. Lenin, however, always disliked modern art, and as he gained the ascendancy over Trotsky in the infighting that followed the Bolshevik Revolution, he cut off first support and then freedom of expression for the avant-garde artists. By 1922, almost all of them had fled, many of them to join the thriving art scene in Berlin.

Ironically, the two greatest achievements of Russian visual art—the icon tradition and the abstract movement—were both renounced by the Communist regime. In Soviet Russia, all art was required to be not only representational, but educational. The sole end of art was deemed to be the glorification of social progress, and art became almost indistinguishable from propaganda. Soviet culture derided and destroyed the beauty of its own past, while it approved and applauded works of "socialist realism" such as the monumental (and unforgettably titled) sculpture *Machine Tractor Driver and Collective Farm Girl.*

Music, Theater, and Dance

In terms of a serious art form, Russian music was as late-blooming as Russian sculpture, for although music was always integral to Russian life (visitors to Old Russia frequently commented on the Russians' enthusiasm for singing at all occasions), Russia showed little inclination to develop its own instruments or its own musical idioms. Liturgical music was limited to vocal polyphony rather more like chanting than singing, and folk music revolved around the singing of stories to the accompaniment of such fairly simple instruments as the balalaika and the pipes. In the eighteenth century, Italian composers brought to Russia by Peter the Great and by Catherine II greatly influenced Russian court music by emphasizing European forms and themes.

Early in the nineteenth century, however, Russian music began to blossom. The turning point was the performance of Mikhail Glinka's opera, *A Life for the Tsar,* in 1836. Another of Glinka's operas, *Ruslan and Ludmila,* inaugurated the use of folk stories and musical themes in Russian music. Then in mid-century, a group of composers emerged whose number was small but whose talent and influence was great. Dubbed the "Mighty Handful," these men, who included Mussorgsky, Rimsky-Korsakov, and Borodin, established a style of programmatic music based on themes from Russian history and folk life. Borodin made wonderful use of Russian orientalisms in works such as *In the Steppes of Central Asia* and his opera *Prince Igor*, while Rimsky-Korsakov exploited the unusual qualities of Russian folk music in his many works—such as *The Snow Maiden* and *The Golden Cockerel*—based on Russia's rich treasury of fairy tales.

After the Mighty Handful came the lush romantic composers Tchaikowsky and Rachmaninoff, the stunning visionary Scriabin, and finally, modernists Stravinsky, Prokofiev, Shastakovich, and Khatchaturian. Taken all together, these Russians created a surprisingly large portion of the musical repertoire played today throughout the West. Their music, which continues to enjoy broad popularity because of its drama and accessibility, established Russia as a distinctive voice in the world of classical music.

The dramatic quality of Russian music was perfectly suited to the confluence of music, dance, and theater which was to take place in Russia at the beginning of the twentieth century. Dance, of course, had been passionately adored by Russian society since the introduction of ballet in the seventeenth century. Ballet is a delicate, disciplined, and highly European art form which might at first have seemed the antithesis of Russia's own lively and down-to-earth folk dance tradition. (The best-known of those Russian dances today is the lusty Cossack dance, which involves a difficult trick of squatting and kicking at the same time.) But in its highly stylized and utterly unreal character, classical ballet was not unlike iconography in motion, and it struck a resounding chord among the Russian people. Just as they had borrowed icon-painting from the Greeks and taken it to new heights, the Russians took French ballet to its greatest extremes of formal beauty. Although the classical ballet declined in the rest of Europe, it was preserved and perfected in Russia.

Then, early in the twentieth century, Russia was introduced to the flamboyant Isadora Duncan and her modern interpretation of ballet, which abandoned the stylized formality of classical ballet in favor of a more natural, flowing movement. This innovative approach to dance was quickly adopted and elaborated by the great Russian choreographers Mikhail Fokine and Leonide Massine, and two of the world's most legendary dancers: Anna Pavlova, famed for her perfect fluidity in *The Dying Swan,* and Vaslav Nijinsky, whose effortless elevations gave rise to speculation that he could levitate! Under the leadership of one of the century's most influential artistic figures, Sergei Diaghilev, these artists (together with painters Leon Bakst and Natalia Goncharova, and the avant-garde composer Stravinsky) formed the Ballet Russes in 1909. Over the next few years, they produced a body of work among the most important in all of modern art.

The great impresario Sergei Diaghilev was truly multi-faceted in both his love of art and his entrepreneurial skills. Born in Russia's mountainous Ural region, Diaghilev went to Moscow as a law student in 1890, but soon abandoned his studies to pursue his fascination with art. He was a founding member of the World of Art group, and an enthusiastic influence among the avant-garde artists. Diaghilev developed a strong interest in gaining public exposure for the arts of Russia. Under imperial patronage, he mounted an enormous exhibition of Russian portraiture in St. Petersburg in 1905. The next year he took a sumptuous exhibition of Russian art to the Petit Palais in Paris, and soon after returned to Paris to present five concerts of Russian music—with such great success that the following year he mounted the Western premiere of Mussorgsky's *Boris Godunov.*

On May 19, 1909, when his newly-formed Ballet Russes made its debut in Paris, Diaghilev achieved instant acclaim. Pursuing Diaghilev's desire to evolve a new art form, in which dancing, painting and music would be "inseparably combined," the Ballet Russes created such world-famous works of dance theater as *Afternoon of a Faun, Daphnis and Chloe, The Firebird,* and *The Rite of Spring.* In these works, unfamiliar harmonies and bold rhythms, exotic colors and fantastic scenery, and an uninhibited, often primitive style of dancing combined to produce a festival of sensuous performance that proved both shocking and thrilling to the audiences of pre-1914 Europe. Conceived as a touring company which would reveal the greatness of Russian artistry to the world, the Ballet Russes exerted a huge influence on the fashionable worlds of Paris, London, and New York, imprinting its unique style on clothing, interior design, books, and the popular imagination.

The Ballet Russes, however, never played in Russia. Although the expertise and inspiration which created this marvelous achievement were wholly Russian, fate seemed to carry it away from its origins. In 1912, a St. Petersburg season was scheduled, but the theater burned down before performances began, and thereafter, the demand for the company abroad was so great that a Russian performance never materialized. After the revolution, Diaghilev and the other great artists of the Ballet Russes became effective expatriates.

Meanwhile, the other most famous and influential Russian

theatrical endeavor never *left* Russia. The Moscow Art Theater, begun in 1898 by Konstantin Stanislavsky, was as revolutionary in its own way as the Ballet Russes or Malevich's Suprematism, for it brought both realism and poetry into the theater after a long period of stagnation.

Like the classical ballet and academic painting, the dramatic theater had become mannered and dry, not only in Russia, but throughout Europe. Stanislavsky almost single-handedly overturned the old theatrical tradition and introduced radical new ideas about performance and staging. He asked his actors to act from the "inside out," drawing on their own feelings and emotions to give reality and dimension to their characters. (This technique became famous in the West as "method acting.") He transformed theatrical settings from stilted scenes, framed by the proscenium like picture postcards, to artful evocations in which the audience seemed to be peering into another world. For example, Stanislavsky added ceilings to interior sets and even placed some of the furniture with backs to the audience.

Perhaps most important of all, Stanislavsky's Moscow Art Theater brought the poetic realism of plays by Chekov and Gorky to the stage. In 1898, the company's production of Chekov's contemporary work *The Seagull* was such a great success that the seagull became and remained the emblem of the Moscow Art Theater. The play's evocative portrayal of Russian life touched its audiences, even though its seemingly aimless dialog and lack of a traditionally structured plot were at first shocking to many.

Continuing to reflect literary innovations of the times, the theater staged Gorky's *The Lower Depths* in 1902, and in 1908, Belgian playwright Maurice Maeterlinck's symbolist fairy-tale drama, *The Blue Bird.* The company toured abroad and gained international prestige. This reputation, along with its emphasis on Russian culture, enabled the Moscow Art Theater to survive the Communist regime better than most of the Russian art groups. But by the 1940's, it had become mired in its own tradition, and not until the 1970's, when Soviet control of the arts began to relax, did the theater start to regain something of its innovative edge.

For the most part, music, theater, and drama, like the visual arts, were required under the Soviet regime to serve the propaganda purposes of the state. Yet paradoxically, the intense training and classical perfectionism which had made Russian ballet unparalleled was continued by the Soviets, not only in the ballet but in the training of musicians and athletes as well. Perhaps this was because Communist materialism emphasizes the physical aspects of life, and values those skills which can be enhanced by training and measured by precise standards. Certainly it also reflected the Soviet regime's great desire to convince the world of Communist superiority. In any event, some of the greatest pianists, dancers, gymnasts, skaters, and other performers in the world were produced by the Communist state, employing the same techniques used under the tsars to create the incomparable Imperial Ballet.

Literature

For many centuries, Russian literature was comprised almost entirely of heroic poems called *bylini* and folk tales called *skazki,* which were passed on from generation to generation by singers and story-tellers. The only written works were a few historical and moral treatises recorded by churchmen. In the seventeenth century, some poems and plays were written. Then, in the eighteenth century, satires, epics, fables, and other types of secular literature became more widely produced; but for the most part, these works copied their form from European literature.

The nineteenth century, however, saw an astounding leap in the development of Russian literature. This new epoch began at the very dawn of the century, with the work of Alexander Pushkin, who is still recognized as Russia's greatest poet. Born in 1799, Pushkin grew up in a time when Russian literature was little more than a slavish imitation of European styles. The young Pushkin was raised by a devoted *nyanya* who passed on to him her deep love of Russian fairy stories and folk lore. (These early teachings inspired his beloved poetic tale *Ruslan and Ludmila,* which Glinka later turned into an opera.) He learned little of self-discipline, however, and even though his talent was evident from an early age, Pushkin spent much of his time in sensual self-indulgence—gambling, drinking, and carrying on a prodigious number of love affairs. Chronic misbehavior soon led to his exile in Bessarabia, where he seems to have lived for a time with the Gypsies.

This experience became the subject of a long poem, *The Gypsies*, which he wrote while banished to the countryside. With little else to do (and only the company of his old nanny), Pushkin began to produce great quantities of writing, including a play, *Boris Godunov*, and his most famous work, *Eugene Onegin*. These works, like all of Pushkin's writing, were extremely innovative; they drew on Russian themes, history, and daily life, creating the basic model of Russian literature which was to be perfected during the nineteenth century.

Ironically, the brilliant Pushkin finally lost his heart at the age of thirty to a vain and shallow teenager. Marriage to the young beauty proved his undoing, for she kept up a social whirl that left the poet impoverished, exhausted, and wildly jealous. When Pushkin was killed in a duel with his wife's purported lover, the whole of Russia mourned. (In a single day, 32,000 people filed past his casket.) But he had left a great legacy, not only in his literary works, but through his influence on other writers. Pushkin had befriended the talented but difficult Nikolai Gogol, and by way of encouragement to the young writer, is said to have given Gogol the ideas for his two most famous works, the novel *Dead Souls* (in which a cunning character contrives to exploit the greed of landowners by selling them the ownership of serfs who are actually dead) and the play *The Inspector General* (a mocking look at the stuffy Russian bureaucracy).

These biting satires reflected a dark view of Russian life, for Gogol's personal vision was a tormented one. In reality, Gogol never intended to be a social critic (he privately defended serfdom and autocracy), and was dismayed that his work was seen by most not as an exploration of human nature but as a commentary on political ills. Though his work was popular, Gogol never achieved either the literary or social acceptance he craved, and he roamed discontentedly about Europe for most of his life, finally succumbing to a strange religious fanaticism in which he rejected his own writing and starved himself to death.

No two men could have been more different in their vision than Gogol and Pushkin, for in spite of his extremes and melo-dramas, Pushkin was passionately in love with life, and with Russia. Henri Troyat wrote in a biography of Pushkin that Russians found in the poet's work "the eternal image of their land, the simple line of the horizon, the long roads leading to the end of earth, the flight of sleighs over moon-soaked snow, the trembling of the leaves through the lindens in provincial parks, the scent of tea and lilacs and the laughter of girls." But the romantic vision of Russia which Pushkin created was changed indelibly by the work of his most famous successors, Tolstoy and Dostoevsky, creators of that great body of work known today as the Russian novel.

Both Tolstoy and Dostoevsky inherited from Pushkin a lively interest in Russian history, folklore, and folk life. They continued his development of a true Russian literary style, independent of European fashion. But they created their own fictional worlds in which the beauty and heroism that Pushkin extolled were inextricably intertwined with horror, suffering, and ambiguity.

Tolstoy, like Pushkin, was a larger-than-life figure, though in rather a different style. Born in 1828 on the spacious estate *Yasnaya Polyana* ("Clear Glade"), Tolstoy was the son of a count and a princess. After many adventures, which included extensive gambling losses, several successful years as a soldier, and a number of amorous liaisons, Tolstoy turned seriously to writing. This he did, in part, to support his ambitious plans for bringing about social change through education. Like so many Russians, Tolstoy was something of a mystic, but unlike most of his class, he admired the peasantry and enjoyed their way of life. He started a school for the peasants at Yasnaya Polyana and began to develop a unique philosophy that advocated a return to the "natural" peasant life of hard work and deep religious faith.

Thanks in part to his young wife, who painstakingly copied and recopied his manuscripts (she wrote out the immense novel *War and*

Peace seven times in all!), Tolstoy's writing career was a great success almost from the beginning. Sofia, who married Tolstoy when he was thirty-four and she just eighteen, also bore her husband thirteen children and managed every detail of estate, household, and finance. Yasnaya Polyana became a thriving enterprise, and as Tolstoy's fame increased, it became something of a literary shrine.

Tolstoy's two most beloved works were *War and Peace* (1869), an intricate, enormous tale that traces the fates of a host of characters during the time of the Napoleonic Wars, and *Anna Karenina* (1877), a complex tragedy in which a woman is destroyed by her passions. These works made the writer both rich and famous, but he ultimately cared little for the two melodramas, or for most of his other novels, stories and plays. In the last three decades of his long life, Tolstoy became increasingly obsessed with developing a kind of anarchistic religious philosophy. He detested social life, preferring to plow the fields or aid famine victims, but he continued to take an interest in world affairs and emerging generations. His writings about a new world order based on the principles of Christian love inspired a huge following, and he was regarded by many as a prophet.

Both Tolstoy and Dostoevsky believed that the Russian people had unique spiritual qualities which were of great value to the world. Their approaches to life and writing were very different, however. Tolstoy's works combined precise observations of human nature with the detailed evocation of a vanishing way of life, while Dostoevsky's explored the darker recesses of the human soul, extolling the importance of redemption through suffering. In his best-known works, *Crime and Punishment* (1866) and *The Brothers Karamazov* (1880), Dostoevsky reflected not only on some of the most important social and moral themes of Russian life, but also on the driving forces of his own tumultuous life. An addiction to gambling kept the great novelist in constant financial straits, and epilepsy impaired his health. But by far the most influential factor in the shaping of Dostoevsky's work was his youthful arrest for involvement in a political conspiracy. He was sentenced to death, and only as he was actually standing before a firing squad was he reprieved and instead exiled to Siberia for four years.

The impact of this event never left Dostoevsky. The protagonists of his novels are men forced to confront their own demons, as he himself had been. They sin, and their punishment is not given out by law but discovered in the depths of inner experience, or imposed upon them by an implacable fate which grows out of their own natures. In *Crime and Punishment*, the protagonist Raskolnikov kills a greedy pawnbroker, and must contend with his own guilt until he comes to understand the nature of suffering and the power of love; in *The Brothers Karamazov*, three very different brothers—a mystic, a man of passion, and an intellectual—are forced to face their own natures when one of them is accused of murdering their drunken father. In all his works, Dostoevsky illuminates the ambiguous relationships of good and evil, love and violence, power and weakness.

Tolstoy and Dostoevsky never met, although they greatly admired one another's work. Dostoevsky called *Anna Karenina* "a perfect work of art," while Tolstoy wrote of Dostoevsky's prison memoir, *House of the Dead*, "I do not know of a better book in all modern literature." But circumstances never brought them together, and in 1881, Dostoevsky died suddenly at the age of sixty, worn out by his own intensity. Tolstoy lived until 1910, when he at last determined to abandon secular life once and for all. The eighty-two-year-old Tolstoy set out, dressed as a pilgrim, to join a band of "Tolstoyan" ascetics in the Caucasus, but he caught pneumonia and died in a railroad station along the way.

Tolstoy and Dostoevsky shared a personal and literary bond through their mutual interest in spiritual life. But this preoccupation was scorned as a waste of time by the disaffected writer Turgenev, whose best-known work, the 1862 novel *Fathers and Sons*, introduced the term "nihilism" to describe the alienation of the Russian intelligentsia. Turgenev and Tolstoy, once great friends, quarreled after Tolstoy fell asleep reading *Fathers and Sons*, a spare but moving tale portraying the conflict between a new generation of scientific rationalists and the values upheld by their fathers: honor, patriotism, love, and beauty. Turgenev retaliated by severely criticizing *War and Peace* ("Who are these young ladies?" he wrote, "Some kind of affected Cinderellas?"), and the two did not speak for seventeen years.

Though Turgenev later said grudgingly of *War and Peace* that "probably nothing so good has ever been written," his interests so far diverged from Tolstoy's that even after the two reconciled, the relationship was never again warm. Turgenev was a Westernizer, Tolstoy (like Dostoevsky) an ardent Slavophile. Not surprisingly, Turgenev became the first Russian writer well-known outside Russia, and indeed, he lived for much of his later life in Germany and France. But in his own way, he had perhaps as great an influence on Russian affairs as Tolstoy, for his works incorporated thinly veiled attacks on serfdom which embarrassed the Russian government and encouraged reform.

Much the youngest of the great Russian writers, Chekov was not born until 1860. He began writing at nineteen, and before his untimely death from tuberculosis in 1904, he wrote not only the four dramatic masterpieces for which he is best-known— *The Seagull* (1896), *Uncle Vanya* (1899), *The Three Sisters* (1901), and *The Cherry Orchard* (1904)—but also nearly six hundred short stories. Tolstoy greatly admired Chekov's fiction, but deplored his plays, which the hearty Tolstoy described as "endless conversations of neurasthenic intellectuals." Though the two were close friends, Chekov's vision was quite different from Tolstoy's, for Chekov believed that the artist should be "not the judge of his characters and their conversations, but the unbiased witness." Where Tolstoy was an impassioned partisan, Chekov was a neutral observer, carefully and luminously revealing human nature without commentary.

In this, he had much in common with his contemporary and fellow playwright, Maxim Gorky. These two founded the school of Russian "realism," but where Chekov was delicate, Gorky was extreme; where Chekov chronicled the collapse of Russia's elite, Gorky narrated the rise of the working class. Gorky, whose name (meaning "the bitter one") was adopted as an expression of his writing style, ran away from a youthful life of poverty to live as a vagabond, and among the lowest economic strata of late nineteenth-century Russia he found the characters who populated his plays and stories. Committed to the Communist cause, Gorky was arrested and exiled for his revolutionary activities, but after the Bolsheviks took power, he became chief of propaganda, and later, the first president of the Soviet Writers' Union. Though he is best-known outside Russia for his grim play *The Lower Depths*, Gorky became most famous in his own country for his role in shaping the official Communist literary method, known as "socialist realism."

According to official Soviet doctrine, socialist realism was "a truthful, historically concrete depiction of reality in its revolutionary development." In practice, however, this enforced style mainly produced simplistic writing, devoid of experimentation or imagination. Only a few Russian writers managed to produce works of lasting merit during the Stalinist era; the best-known is Nobel laureate Mikhail Sholokhov's long novel of Cossack life, *And Quiet Flows the Don*. The most famous Russian writer of the period, Vladimir Nabokov, left the Soviet Union, and after 1940 wrote mostly in English.

Following Stalin's death in 1953, restrictions on literature were somewhat relaxed. Aleksandr Solzhenitsyn's novel *One Day In The Life Of Ivan Denisovich,* about the Soviet labor camps under Stalin, was published in the U.S.S.R during this thaw, but his slightly later novels, such as *Cancer Ward* and *The Gulag Archipelago* had to be published abroad. Boris Pasternak's huge and much-loved novel, *Doctor Zhivago*, was banned in the Soviet Union, and when Pasternak was offered the 1958 Nobel Prize for his works, the Russian government forced him to refuse the award. Solzhenitsyn, however, was awarded the 1970 Nobel Prize for literature.

Perhaps because poetic imagery is difficult to pin down (and maybe because poems are shorter and easier to hide than novels), poetry proved more resistant to Soviet censorship than fiction. Poets like Osip Mandelstam, Anna Akhmatova, and Boris Pasternak were able to circulate their poetry even during Stalin's regime, and in the 1960's, a group of young poets including Yevgeny Yevtushenko used their work to criticize the Soviet regime.

In the Russia of today, newly free, many long-suppressed works are being published. Not only the works of Russian writers, but poetry, plays, and novels from all over the world are eagerly read. But the future of writing in Russia remains an unknown. Like every aspect of Russian life, the literary world is a flurry of new ideas, with few sure directions.

Architecture and the Decorative Arts

"Suddenly I saw spring up thousands of painted towers and sparkling domes," exclaimed the Marquis de Custine, French traveler and journalist, in recording his approach to Moscow on an August evening in 1839. "This first view of the capital of the Empire of the Slavs, which rises brilliantly in the cold solitudes of the Christian East, produces an impression one cannot forget. You have before you a sad landscape, but vast like the ocean, and to animate the emptiness, a poetic city whose architecture has no name."

That nameless architecture was distinguished above all by the spires and domes of Russia's churches. The earliest church-builders adopted the classic Byzantine domes, low and rounded, but gradually these were replaced with the characteristic "onion" shape that distinguishes the Russian domes. The bulbous shape is said to have been invented in Novgorod, and recent research suggests that it evolved during the building of wooden cupolas, when it was discovered that the stress placed on the timbers was best absorbed by an onion-shaped construction. But however practical their real origins might be, the onion domes (*lukovitsa*) have their own romance and lore; faithful Russians believed the bulbs captured their prayers and directed them to heaven.

Most buildings in early Russia were made of wood, churches and houses alike. Since wood was spectacularly plentiful, the Russians became very adept at utilizing it, and wooden buildings (even very complex ones) were frequently built without the use of iron in nails or frameworks. One of the few surviving examples of Russia's great wooden architecture is the Church of the

Transfiguration on the small island of Kizhi. There is not a single metal part in the pyramid-shaped church, which stands 120 feet high and has twenty-two cupolas. Like most of Russia's early houses (and indeed, almost everything else in the tree-covered land), the Church of the Transfiguration was made almost entirely with that ubiquitous Russian tool, the ax.

Perhaps to contrast with the plentiful snow and the dark evergreens, Russian structures were usually heavily decorated and brightly colored. Homes were adorned with elaborately carved and painted weathervanes, gates, shutters, birdhouses, window boxes, and other wooden ornaments. The patterns and images used so lavishly in Russian folk art took their symbolism from the natural phenomena that shaped the course of the peasant's life—the seasons, plants and animals, wind, water, sun, and earth. Used indoors and out, these ancient motifs were worked into stone and wood, stitched into linens and homespun, and painted on ceramics and lacquerware.

Even though the Orthodox Church attempted to suppress pagan imagery, the old symbols kept their place in secular crafts; the ancient sun god, for example, was depicted as a circle or as a flaming horse (sometimes with three heads) and was worked into diverse designs, such as mirror frames and distaffs. Folk art influences can even be seen in many Russian churches. For example, rich floral and animal carvings cover the white stone facade of the Cathedral of St. Dmitri (1193-97), and colorful echoes of Russia's exuberant countryside make the fantastical multi-towered and polychromed Cathedral of St. Basil (1555-1559) Moscow's most famous landmark.

In the seventeenth century, the color and vitality of Russia's characteristic architecture and decoration began to be eclipsed by the more formal Western European styles. Peter the Great and his imperial successors brought artists and artisans from Italy and France to build and decorate their elaborate palaces, design their Western-style clothing, and create the awesome array of fine objects with which they surrounded themselves.

In Imperial Russia, architecture was undertaken on such a

grand scale that palaces, churches, and state buildings continued to evolve over centuries, changing styles as the Russian rulers' tastes and foreign alliances shifted. The Winter Palace, principal residence of Russia's royal families, provides a wonderful example of this process. Built first in the severe, square Dutch style by Peter the Great, the Winter Palace was later replaced with a simple two-story building designed by a German architect, and next enlarged by a Swiss architect. Then it was remodeled during the reign of Elizabeth (1741-1762) in the flourishing Russian Baroque style, which featured immense scale, Italianate features, and brilliant color (the refurbished Winter Palace was painted turquoise with white trim). Catherine the Great, however, preferred the more austere and antique neoclassical style; finding the high-spirited and huge (it housed as many as six thousand people!) Winter Palace little to her liking, she built the quietly elegant Hermitage next door to it for her own use.

Work on the Winter Palace continued into the nineteenth century, and there have been many restorations since the building was "finished." But it is only one of the spectacular imperial building complexes for which Russia is famous. Perhaps the most fascinating is *Tsarskoe Selo*, the "Tsar's Village." Richly embellished under both Elizabeth and Catherine, Tsarskoe Selo evolved into an array of gardens, pavilions, and palaces, even featuring a whole "Chinese" town. The Agate Pavilion—a mere trifle in the overall scheme of Tsarskoe Selo—contained libraries, reception rooms (including one in which the walls were made of solid jasper, interspersed with red agate) and even a "Philosopher's Gallery" filled with busts of Catherine's favorite thinkers. Underneath the pavilion were elaborate Roman-style baths, with a swimming pool, spacious "relaxing rooms," and the marble equivalent of today's hot tub.

The opulence of imperial life in Russia was unparalleled, for the most fabulous materials—precious stones, furs, gold and silver—were abundant in the vast Russian realm. Highly skilled, almost-free labor was also plentiful. These resources enabled Russia to become a showplace for the power of wealth. Not only were the structures and interiors of Imperial Russia grand almost beyond imagining, everywhere in the fantasy palaces (and even in "middle class" homes) were *objets*—picture frames, jeweled flowers, teapots, chess sets, writing pens, umbrella handles, enameled miniatures, ad infinitum—of such superb workmanship that Russian goods were coveted all over the world.

Beginning in the time of Peter the Great, enormous workshops were constructed for the creation of tapestries, porcelains, silver, jewelry, furniture, and even fine papers. (In one paper factory, a visitor reported finding eight hundred workers dressed all in snowy white, and each wearing a novel paper hat of his own design.) The most famous of the great Russian craft workshops was the renowned House of Fabergé, best known for the bejeweled imperial Easter eggs which opened to reveal intricate miniature scenes. But Fabergé came to prominence near the end of Russia's long history of craftsmanship.

One of the crafts which was introduced to Russia in the eighteenth century was lacquerwork, a method of using high-gloss varnishes in many layers (usually on wood or papier-mache) to create decorative objects. Lacquerwork was invented and perfected in China, and at first, the Russians copied the Chinese masters, but after a time, they developed a distinctive style. The inventive Russians began to apply lacquerwork to metal, and Russia became famous for its lacquer trays. Factories scattered around Moscow and St. Petersburg turned out large quantities of wood and paper lacquerware; especially in demand were snuff boxes, for these small, popular items took full advantage of the Russian talent for miniature-painting.

The skill of painting in miniature was highly developed in Russia, where there existed a long tradition of creating exquisite paintings in enamel, porcelain and oil, diminutive enough to be worn as jewelry yet fine enough to be regarded as works of art. Miniature painters were adept at using the smallest brushes (some only the thickness of a single hair) to create the fine details of portraiture, landscape, and still life.

It was the combination of skilled miniature painting and the Russian flair for color that made Russian lacquerware distinctive and sought-after. The vivid colors loved by Russians were especially effective against the characteristic black background of lacquerwork. The icon-painting tradition, too, made a contribution, for although Russian lacquerware designs were mostly secular, they displayed the richness of subject matter and the graceful composition that had always marked Russian icons.

In fact, the icon-painting tradition and the lacquerware tradition finally converged after the Revolution of 1917, when Russian icon-painters could no longer work as they had always done. Whole villages of icon-painters were faced with finding new occupations, and several (Fedoskino, Mstera, Kholui, and Palekh) turned to lacquerwork. They combined their talents as icon-painters and miniaturists with themes from Russian history and folklore to produce a unique style of lacquerware, for which they have since become famous. The artists of Fedoskino continued to paint in the naturalistic manner of the old Russian masters, but the other villages developed an unusual approach that blended Persian influences (miniature-painting had reached perhaps its greatest heights in Persia) with scenes from the history and fairy tales of Russia. This unique hybrid is the very style that we see in the Russian Tarot of St. Petersburg.

The development of the lacquerware industry in Palekh and the other villages was fostered by the Communist government, which in its earliest days provided enthusiastic support for Russian folk art. An active movement to reanimate the traditional beauty and beliefs of Russian life had begun in the nineteenth century among artists, writers, and intellectuals, who strongly affected the foundation of the revolutionary movement. So although many of the imperial palaces, noble estates, and Orthodox churches and monasteries were looted by the revolutionaries, and more were soon turned into office buildings, warehouses, or collective farms, the cultural traditions and arts of the Russian peasant were at first encouraged by the new Soviet government.

But as the Stalinist state became more and more militaristic and totalitarian, the emphasis in architecture and decoration rapidly shifted from the pursuit of beauty to the achievement of modern, practical efficiency. The state buildings created by the Soviets were uniformly huge and stolidly ugly; Soviet "houses" were mostly featureless high-rise apartments, stacked by the thousands next to drab factories. The decorative arts, meanwhile, became nearly extinct in Soviet Russia, where utilitarian design was encouraged and the pursuit of beauty was derided as "bourgeois." Those who could afford nice things generally bought imported goods, often on the black market, and the old Russian crafts were practiced mainly in more isolated rural areas.

Today, much of Russia's venerable architecture has fallen into decay, and many of the artifacts which remained in the hands of churches and families are being sold by those trying to survive in the faltering Russian economy. Yet the work of salvaging and even renewing Russia's architectural and decorative heritage goes on, as Western museums and preservation groups offer support through new alliances with the Russian people. It will be interesting to see what new styles develop in the rapidly changing artistic climate of the new Russia.

Part II

The Russian Tarot of St. Petersburg

Chapter 3

The Art and Symbolism of the Russian Tarot of St. Petersburg

The Russian Tarot of St. Petersburg is filled with the beauty and lore of Russian culture. Drawing on Russia's fertile folk heritage for the deck's imagery, and employing the distinctive Palekh style for its execution, artist Yury Shakov has created a set of cards that not only illuminates the Tarot, but also offers a glimpse of Russia's great past.

The richness of the Russian Tarot of St. Petersburg can best be appreciated by exploring the many levels and themes which have been built into the deck. Now that we've learned more about Russian history and culture, it's time to consider in greater detail the imagery and symbolism that fills these beautiful cards.

Every card in a Tarot deck is, in a sense, complete in itself. Each of the trump cards has its unique archetypal image, and each of the minor arcana cards has its special combination of suit, and number or person. So it is possible to talk about each card individually, looking at it as an isolated group of images and meanings.

But seventy-eight unrelated cards would probably not have the power and fascination that the Tarot has! Every card in the Russian Tarot of St. Petersburg *also* takes part of its meaning from its resonance with all the other cards in the deck. From studying this whole, we come to understand each of the parts; and from studying the parts, we learn to see the whole. Through the interaction of these two points of view, the Tarot becomes rich and real.

So we approach the Tarot both by learning about individual cards and by exploring the many overlapping structures of the deck. In just the same manner, we gain the fullest appreciation of a particular deck, such as the Russian Tarot of St. Petersburg, by looking not only at the way the artist has executed each card, but also at the motifs and patterns used throughout the deck. The Tarot artist creates a miniature world, with its own colors and costumes, its own places and objects, its own visual style; to grasp the nature of that world, we have to see it as a whole.

Later in this part of the book, we will look at each card in turn and probe the elements in each that gives it its own nature. But first, it's important to see some of the artistic structures that make the Russian Tarot of St. Petersburg a special and distinctive world.

Style

"Style" is simply the *way* in which something is shown or done. Donald Duck and Daffy Duck are both ducks, but they are not much alike as characters. It's not just that one is white and one is black. Each is drawn and animated in a different style, so we think of them as different ducks. A duck drawn by Audubon is even more different from Donald and Daffy than the two are from each other. And if Picasso or Michelangelo had drawn ducks, the results would be unmistakable. Almost anyone could instantly tell a Picasso duck from a Michelangelo duck because those artists had such completely different styles.

But while Michelangelo's and Picasso's styles are familiar to us because they are part of our own visual tradition, the Russian icon style is foreign to most of us. To appreciate fully the visual character of the Russian Tarot of St. Petersburg, it's very helpful to understand more about icons—not only how they look, but *why* they look that way. Something about the icon-painting tradition has already been explained above, but it would be useful now to review the icon style and look at it in a bit more detail.

The hallmarks by which we can recognize the icon style include lack of perspective, the flattening of figures and objects, and the absence of a light source within the picture. All of these characteristics combine to make the images look two-dimensional, and so quite different from the more natural-looking rounded figures we are accustomed to seeing in drawings and paintings. The reason behind this general flatness of Russian icons was actually theological rather than aesthetic. The Orthodox Church forbade sculpture for religious purposes, believing that realistic figures might too easily become objects of idolatry.

Accordingly, icon-painting avoided any suggestion of three-dimensionality, and it was this restriction, in part, which forced icon-painters to develop their characteristic emphasis on color and composition. Also, since the actual content of religious pictures was carefully dictated by the Church—for example, an Annunciation scene had to be portrayed in a particular way, with certain elements always present—the icon-painters focused their concentration not on originality, but on the achievement of expressive shapes and a harmonious blend of colors.

Although there were as many as forty different schools of icon-painting, each with its own subtle variations of style, the basics remained the same throughout Russia for hundreds of years. It was not until the late sixteenth century, when Oriental and Western influences began to have an impact on Russian art, that a significantly new style was introduced to icon-painting. A school of painting named after the wealthy Stroganov family combined the brilliance of the Persian miniature with the familiar subjects and figures of the icon, producing a much more flowing and glowing type of art. This style was later to influence the lacquer painters of Palekh and Kholuy, and its characteristics are clearly seen in the Russian Tarot of St. Petersburg. The bright colors, ornamental borders, and delicate detail of the cards are all inherited from the Stroganov school.

If you look carefully at the images of the Russian Tarot of St. Petersburg, you will note that although the figures are somewhat rounded, most objects are shown as flat, and there is very little separation between foreground and background. You will also see that, although there are suns, moons, and windows in the pictures, there is no light coming from these sources. For this reason, figures and objects do not cast shadows and there is no impression of realistic space in the pictures. These factors contribute to the overall iconic quality of the images.

The figures and objects in the pictures are also given a "cut-out" appearance by being placed on a solid black background. This aspect of the deck's style derives directly from the lacquerware produced by the former icon-painting village of Palekh, as discussed earlier. The three suits created by the second artist (Swords, Coins, Clubs) are more similar in style to those lacquerware designs; they are dense and curvilinear, filling the entire elliptical space with swirling shapes. The suit of Cups and the major arcana cards created by Yury Shakov place more emphasis on the central figures and there is a much greater use of black space.

Yury Shakov set the basic style of the Russian Tarot of St. Petersburg, defining its overall look. In his career as a miniaturist, Shakov painted in many different Russian styles, sometimes in the Moscow icon-painting tradition, sometimes in the naturalistic "old master" style, and sometimes in the naive folk art style. But many of his most delightful works reflect his interest in the Palekh lacquerware tradition, and that is the style which can be clearly seen in the Russian Tarot of St. Petersburg.

Vladimir Guliayev could almost be describing the Russian Tarot of St. Petersburg when he explains, in his beautiful book *The Fine Art of Russian Lacquered Miniatures*, how the Palekh style differs from that of the other lacquerware villages:

> The Palekh compositions seem to blossom against the deep black glimmering background. The pattern is graphically expressive, constructed on precise lines and contours, and seems to be permeated with the finest gold and silver threads. The treatment of images is explicitly symbolic, figures and gestures are emphatically dynamic, and the coloration is clear and pure.

Guliayev goes on to discuss how the Palekh style creatively utilizes the black space of the background, just as Shakov does in the Russian Tarot of St. Petersburg trumps:

> The background performs quite a notable role in the Palekh miniature. The black colour not only brings out the nuances of the hues but really sets the rhythm of the entire composition. It may signify the sky, the ground or just an abstract space lacking references to time and place.

The influence of Shakov's Palekh training can be seen even more clearly when Shakov's paintings are compared with those of the second artist. While the three suits created by the second artist are lovely in their own way, they lack the precision and the elaboration of detail which marks Shakov's work. The best way to see the difference between the styles of the two artists is to take a close look at two cards that are otherwise similar. Put the Page of Cups and the Page of Swords next to each other, and let's compare them.

The first thing you'll notice is that Shakov's Page of Cups looks much brighter, more illuminated, than the second artist's Page of Swords. The brighter effect of Shakov's card is produced by putting in more contrast (for example, between the pattern and the background in the fabric of the Page's costume) and by the technique of "beading." Notice how little white dots edge the hem and collar of the Page's garments, and decorate his boots. The buildings in the distance also appear quite different; Shakov's church is a more intense white, the exterior more delicately detailed. And the ground beneath the Page of Cups appears rocky and chiseled, while the Page of Swords stands on a smoother, more flatly painted outcropping.

Painted from Shakov's original specifications, the second artist's work retains the basic conventions of the Palekh style—black background, strong colors, bold figures—but does not have the same level of careful detail and traditional technique. It has a rather illustrational, perhaps more contemporary quality. Yet when seen as a complement to Shakov's work, rather than as an imitation, it succeeds well in its own right. Many of the second artist's cards have great charm, distinguished by sweeping lines and interesting color combinations.

Taken altogether, the cards of the Russian Tarot of St. Petersburg are a vivid, exciting testament to Russian creativity. The Palekh style, with its echoes of the icon tradition, can be seen clearly as the organizing principle of the deck.

Colors

Among the most visually striking features of the Russian Tarot of St.
Petersburg is the use of color. The vibrant colors of the deck are very
much in keeping with the character of traditional Russian culture,
where almost everything was lavished with color, perhaps as a
psychological defense against the monotony of rolling steppe and
drifting snow. Suzanne Massie, in *Land of the Firebird,* describes
how the Russian penchant for color brought gaiety to houses so
often swathed in the unrelieved whiteness of winter:

> Houses and their decorations were brightly painted with
> diamonds and squares in blue, red and green. On a carved
> board over balcony windows, bright-green lions might lie
> against a turquoise background. The inside of the eaves
> was boarded and painted with large red and blue flowers
> and bunches of grapes; shutters with thin black branches,
> dark-red berries, roses and flowers.

These mixtures of color and pattern are a characteristic expression
of the vitality and variety which marked traditional Russian culture,
and they lend great energy and distinctiveness to the Russian Tarot
of St. Petersburg.

Russian icon-painting, while more restrained than decorative
art in its use of color, also took a wide-ranging and inventive
approach. As the wonderfully informative book *Art Treasures in
Russia* explains:

> The Old Russian masters were not restricted in their
> treatment of color: they were free to paint any object in
> whatever color they chose. We find blue horses, red
> mountains, multicolored buildings and costumes such as
> never existed, and grounds either golden or bright red.
> With such freedom, color harmony could always be
> achieved. In Russian icons the colors rarely have a conven-
> tional allegorical meaning—their meaning is defined by
> the overall impression, the coloring of the whole.

The same attitude can certainly be seen at work in the Russian Tarot
of St. Petersburg, where each card features a suite of colors which

work together to create an overall impression. Although most figures and objects are realistically colored, the color values are often unnaturally bright.

The whole deck employs a very distinctive "palette," or group of colors. In different segments of the deck, however, the palette is reorganized to create specific symbolic connections. So, while the major arcana cards mix many colors to create lifelike scenes with rich tones and textures, the minor arcana suits each emphasize one specific color which brings out the special associations of that suit. The major arcana cards are also noticeably warmer in tone, giving the impression that they are bathed in golden light.

In order to see the use of color at work in the deck, you may find it interesting to lay out the cards in groups. First, look at the major arcana cards all together, preferably against a black background and from a distance of three or four feet. By this means, it's possible to see the "glow" created by the use of colors gently toned with red or gold. You will also notice that in each image, some details are in colors which highlight or contrast the others, producing an impression of visual activity and density. For example, the Empress is seated on a bright pink cushion which has a very different quality from the other more toned-down colors in the image; the same color is repeated, however, in the hem of her dress.

You may also want to look at each of the minor arcana suits together as a group. Each suit has its own distinctive color scheme, with the diversely colored Cups taking their cue from the rainbow, the Swords using strong red accents against the dominant elements of luminous, lavender-tinged blue. The Coins, appropriately, feature rich purple set off by bright gold, and the Clubs use strong areas of intense green. These differences will become even more apparent if you look at groups composed across the four suits. For example, take all the threes or all the nines and observe how differently color is handled in each of the suits.

Ornamental Borders

The ornamental borders on the Russian Tarot of St. Petersburg designs recall the *rizas*, decorative coverings made of metal, which were used on many icons. Fine rizas were made of wrought silver or gold, to enhance the value of the icon, while less expensive rizas of stamped tin or some other alloy were used in mass-produced icons to reduce the amount of painting required. Rizas also served to heighten the symbolism of the icon as a "window" into heaven, by creating an effect of actually looking, as if through a peephole, into another world. The same effect was utilized in the famous Fabergé Easter eggs.

Each segment of the deck—the major arcana and each of the suits—has its own variation of the basic ornamental border. The card backs for the entire deck have another variation. The basic border is a rectangular frame around an elliptical center opening. The frame is filled with a branching (or "foliate") pattern based on a lily motif and punctuated with rosettes. In the center of each side of the rectangle is a stone in a rosette. The major arcana frames and the card backs have a lotus blossom at each corner of the frame. The minor arcana cards feature the suit tokens in the top corners.

The type of pattern used in the borders is called "arabesque" or "grotesque." (Both of these terms mean something quite different when they are used to describe decorative patterns than when they are used in other contexts!) "Arabesque," which means simply "Arabian," describes any type of intertwining pattern, usually based on floral elements, but also sometimes including human and animal figures. Arabesque patterns are not actually based on Arabian or Moorish decorative styles at all, but rather derive from the "grotesque," a term referring to the type of patterns found in the decorations of Roman grottoes. The grotesque usually includes fantastic elements and distortions of natural objects; while the arabesque is typically symmetrical, with its foliation branching out gracefully from a vertical axis.

The components of an arabesque or grotesque each have their own symbolic meanings. Lilies, which are found in the ornamental borders of the Russian Tarot of St. Petersburg, typically signify purity, and are linked with both the Virgin Mary and Easter, the most important of the Russian Orthodox holy days. The lily, which lends its form to the French *fleur de lis*, is also associated with royalty. Another form found in the border is the rosette, a stylized emblem of the rose, a flower symbolic of both love and perfection. The larger rosettes in the border have eight "petals," symbolizing regeneration.

The emblems and intertwining patterns of the arabesque and grotesque have been associated with Gnosticism, for Gnostic sects— long persecuted as heretical—are thought to have given symbolic representation to their doctrines and concealed these symbols in decorations and other seemingly meaningless forms, such as the watermarks set into paper. In fact, the suit markers of the Tarot (Cups, Coins, Swords, and Wands) seem to have been among the many Gnostic emblems, and some scholars believe this supports the idea of a direct connection between the Tarot and Gnosticism. But whether or not such a connection exists, it is certainly the case that arabesques and grotesques are made up of elements that have symbolic significance. And beyond the various elements, the intertwining and symmetrical nature of these patterns has its own significance, representing the world of phenomena and the coherent unfolding of existence.

Card Backs and Faces

The card backs feature the four suit signs in ensemble—Sword, Club, Cup, and Coin—"crowned" by a warrior's helmet. (The helmet appears to be one which was believed to be worn by the thirteenth-century hero Alexander Nevsky, and which was restored as a national treasure by the first Romanov tsar.) The ensemble is shown on a pebbled or hammered background, surrounded by an elliptical outline resembling silver beading. The ornamental border on the card backs is similar to that of the major arcana card faces, but with red lotus blossoms rather than blue. There is also an inner border to the frame, surrounding the ellipse; in this border, four green stones are set in rosettes, and double lotus blossoms punctuate the pattern at top and bottom.

The open ellipse on the card face is considerably larger than the one on the card back, so the front borders are smaller. A scrolled border at the bottom of each card holds the card title. The scrollwork borders are different on each of the suits. To compare the various borders on the major arcana, look at the four aces together. The differences add visual interest to the cards, but don't seem to have any particular symbolic values.

Figures and Costumes

Almost every card in the modern Tarot features a figure, either human or angelic. In the Russian Tarot of St. Petersburg, these figures are not just abstract symbols, but actually characters, each taking part in the miniature drama of the card image. In the major arcana images, most of the figures shown have a specific historical or allegorical significance, described in the commentaries on the cards. In the minor arcana cards, however, the figures are generic, representing various aspects of Russian society. So in order to interpret the various characters in the deck, it's helpful to know some of the conventions of costume which are used to distinguish the different social types portrayed in the card images.

In Old Russia, before the reign of Peter the Great, the same general kinds of everyday clothing were worn by most everyone, but of course differences in social station were marked by differences in the cut and fabric of clothing. These distinctions were even more obvious in the dress-up clothes worn for festive occasions, and they reflected ethnic and geographical differences as well as economic ones. But after Peter's introduction of Western fashion, the differences of style among the peasantry, the middle class, and the aristocracy became much more extreme. While the upper classes adopted the exaggerated fashions of Western Europe, the peasantry and the Old Believers stuck closely to their traditional costumes.

Robert Ker Porter, an English artist who visited Russia early in the nineteenth century, wrote that anyone who has studied the sculptures in Gothic cathedrals and cemeteries "will not doubt of the fact, but immediately perceive that the peasantry of Russia in the 19th Century, are contemporaries in fashion with those of England in the 14th." The basic costume was a garment that fell straight from the shoulders and flared somewhat at the hem; the male version of this A-line item was called a *kaftan*; the female version, a *sarafan*. These garments might go over or under other clothing, such as petticoats or leggings, vests and aprons, and they might be floor length or knee length. The sarafan was sometimes worn with a belt or girdle, and was frequently used as a jumper over a blouse, while the kaftan was most often seen as a coat.

The kaftan and the sarafan are worn by many of the figures in the Russian Tarot of St. Petersburg. Men are also shown wearing the typical costume of full trousers tucked into high boots, with a belted overblouse. This costume is known as "Cossack style" outside of Russia, but it was worn at one time or another by most Russian men, not merely the freewheeling Cossacks. A kaftan-style coat was often worn over this dashing outfit, with a tall fur hat to complete the ensemble. The kaftan and fur hat were the marks of Russia's merchant class, the boyars, many of whom refused to give up this traditional style even when Peter the Great declared the kaftan out of favor.

Although the sarafan is worn by most of the females in the deck, it was not the only garment worn extensively by Russian women. The *ponyova*, a fullish skirt usually worn with a blouse and a colorful apron, was the staple work costume of Russian women, and elaborately decorated versions were worn over petticoats for festive occasions. Festival outfits were heavily embroidered, often with pearls, gold coins, and other valuables. So rich were the costumes created for special occasions that they were handed down from one generation to the next, and in these ornate outfits, peasants could scarcely be told apart from royalty.

Whatever the occasion, whether dressy or everyday, a woman's costume was always complemented with a suitable headdress. This might be a simple kerchief or open hoop, or it might be a winged *kokoshnik,* a foot tall and encrusted with gold and semi-precious stones. *Kokoshniki* were basically hoops with shaped front pieces, but there were many variations—peaked, crescent-shaped, even horned—from region to region, town to town. Some kokoshniki had long veils of muslin or gauze attached to them, while others featured networks of gold, silver, and pearls which fell over the forehead. The kokoshniki and other popular types of headdresses emphasized the importance of the Russian woman's hair, which was truly thought to be her "crowning glory." By tradition, married women concealed their hair from strangers, while unmarried girls advertised the luxuriance of their hair by wearing it in a single long plait.

Men, too, placed great importance on their hair—that is to say, their facial hair. A man's beard was as precious and as carefully cultivated as a woman's plait. Virtually all men in Russia wore beards until the time of Peter the Great. Peter at first outlawed beards altogether, cutting off many of them personally, but then allowed men who chose to keep their beards to pay a "beard tax." Peter's rule against beards did not apply, however, to peasants or to the clergy, and for that reason the beard became a symbol for Russians of both the old ways and the true faith.

Because of the harsh Russian winters, Russians wore a great many clothes during most of the year. The rich lined their cloaks with fur and wore heavy felt or leather boots, while the poor swathed themselves in homespun and wrapped their feet with straw. But as one English lady wrote, the visitor who saw the Russian people "not wrapped up in their sheepskin coats but in their summer attire," found "something quite classic in Russian dress." "The closely setting folds of the women's sarafans," she continued, "are very like those in Greek paintings and on Etruscan vases; the loose shorts tied round the waist worn by men, their mustached and bearded faces, looked very like the friezes of the Athenian temples." In summer, heavy boots were replaced with latticed shoes, called "bast" shoes, tied about the ankles and quite reminiscent of Greek sandals, while women's headdresses gave way to crowns woven of flowers.

Many of these varied aspects of Russian costume are depicted in the Russian Tarot of St. Petersburg, and more specialized costumes are also accurately portrayed in the deck's images. The regalia of the Emperor and Empress, for example, are very like the royal outfits worn before Peter the Great, when the traditional kaftan and sarafan were made up in sumptuous fabric for the regal wardrobe. Folk styles, featuring bright colors and lively embroidery, are shown on such characters as the Hanged Man and the Lovers. The Hierophant's robe is a very good depiction of the garb worn by Russian Orthodox patriarchs; the Hermit's homespun robes and bast shoes are true to the costume of the *starets*, or wandering holy men; and the Fool's motley is a cheerful rendition of the outfits worn by the wandering jesters called *skomorokhi*.

But there is as much of fantasy in the Russian Tarot of St. Petersburg's costumes as there is of fact. The colors and patterns of the costumes borrow a great deal from the clothing seen in Persian miniatures, which provided inspiration for the fairy-tale style of Palekh lacquerware. The capes worn by so many of the men are features commonly found in icons, but they were not, apparently, ever widely worn by real Russian men. Overall, the costumes present an exotic and Orientalized vision of Russian dress more nearly than they portray the reality of clothing in Old Russia, but much can be told about the meaning of each card from the specific garments, headgear, footwear, and hairstyles given to each character.

Scenery

The scenic backgrounds found throughout the Russian Tarot of St. Petersburg deck include both wild nature (rough hills, dark streams, star-laden skies) and civilization (walled cities, church domes, craggy towers, homely cottages). Although we will look at the scenery of the cards in terms of these two categories, they aren't really separated in the design of the cards. Figures are shown in the context of a fully developed "world," in which nature and people coexist.

Most of the cards in the deck feature some element of nature in the picture. Of the trumps, only the first three (The Magician, The High Priestess and The Empress) are obviously set indoors. All the others, except the two adjacent cards Wheel of Fortune and

Justice, show something of the natural world. Of the fifty-six minor arcana cards, only ten scenes are entirely indoors, and all of these have windows through which the sky may be seen.

In its use of the outdoor world as a visual and symbolic element, the deck follows the Waite Tarot closely. Waite's pictorial emphasis on nature was something of a departure from Tarot tradition. In the earliest decks, the trump images in the first or "social" part of the deck (from The Magician through the thirteenth card, Death) depicted scenes and characters against patterned backgrounds, in a sort of abstract space; outdoor settings were used only in the second or "philosophical" part of the deck (Temperance through the World). Later, in the Marseilles-type decks, the patterned backgrounds were abandoned. A few blades of grass or sketchy hillocks are seen in the first part of the deck, indicating vaguely that the figures are not indoors, but there is still no real development of nature imagery.

Pamela Colman Smith's illustrations for the Waite deck are, by contrast, a riot of vegetation, replete with streams and pools, rocks and clouds, and all manner of natural elements. This development of a more romantic, organic look for the Tarot was in part related to the Art Nouveau style popular in decorative design during the early part of the twentieth century, featuring sinuous, curving lines suggestive of vining plants, along with floral motifs arranged in fluid, symmetrical patterns. Other reasons for the "flowering" of the Tarot under Waite and Smith were probably Smith's own interest in folk art, which frequently draws on nature for its designs, and Waite's preoccupation with symbolic imagery.

Although the Russian Tarot of St. Petersburg follows the Waite/Smith deck in its inclusion of natural settings and nature-related symbols, it does so with a decidedly Russian twist. Where the Waite deck is lush and verdant, the Russian Tarot is for the most part spare and almost harsh in its landscape, taking its design values from the Russian land itself. Outdoor locations are usually not fully depicted, but only suggested, frequently by using the symbolic shorthand of the icon-painters. Like the traditional icons, the Russian Tarot of St. Petersburg images are not meant to be realistic, but rather evocative, revealing the landscape of the natural world through stylized renditions which have been charged with meaning through long use.

Most explicit among the borrowed landscape conventions of the deck are the "hills" included so frequently in the trump images. These look more like oddly shaped rock outcroppings or even shingled roofs than like hills. Nevertheless, they are depicted here in just the same way they appear in early Russian icons. They are called *pyatochki,* or "little heels," and they represent in exaggerated form the shaley rocks that make up the few, low hills breaking the vast flatness of the Russian steppe. This stylistic convention was introduced by the Novgorod school of icon-painters, and later, in the seventeenth century, became so elaborate that the hills in their paintings looked almost like coral growths.

The treatment of water in the trump images is also drawn from the icon-painting tradition, which indicated the fluid nature of water by means of little whorls: spirals, S-curves, and commas. In the Russian Tarot of St. Petersburg, water is not colored blue or green, but left black, suggesting mysterious, other-worldly depths. Only the ruffled tracings which punctuate the surface let us see that the water is alive with movement.

It is in keeping with their greater formality that the trumps use this icon-like treatment of the landscape, while the minor arcana images show a much more decorative picture of the outdoors. In the pip card images, especially those of the three suits painted by the second artist, hillsides and promontories are graceful, almost sculptural, and the bright blue water is caught in waves that look like woodcarvings. These warmer, more lifelike settings resonate comfortably with the intimate, "everyday" character of the lesser cards.

Blending into the landscapes of both Major and minor arcana cards are the evidences of human habitation. In the major arcana, the characteristic walled cities (kremlins) of Old Russia are seen behind the Emperor and the Hierophant, signifying their dominion over worldly life. Several minor arcana scenes also include as an element or as a background the city walls, symbolizing in some cases (such as the Ten of Cups and the Six of Coins) the importance of communal life, and in other cases (such as the Seven of Swords and the Ten of Clubs) the militant fortifications that protect the people from their enemies.

The most striking features of the cities we see throughout the Russian Tarot of St. Petersburg are the onion domes and tent-style roofs of the many churches. Church architecture in Old Russia was, as we have already learned, not only architecturally, but also theologically unique. Although the distinctive Russian roof styles did serve the practical purpose of preventing snow accumulation, their symbolic usefulness was perhaps equally great. According to Suzanne Massie, one poetic interpretation is that "the cupolas assumed their characteristic shape to catch the prayers of the faithful and send them to heaven. Another is that they took the form of the helmets of Kievan soldiers because Russia was the last line of defense of the West against the East, and her churches stood like soldiers, protecting the West from annihilation."

Not only the shape of the domes but their number was accorded symbolic importance. A single dome represented God as the head of the church; three domes symbolized the Trinity; five, Christ and the Four Evangelists; seven, the Holy Sacraments; and nine, the celestial hierarchies. The grandest array of domes is thirteen, representing Christ and the Twelve Apostles.

Although the bulb-shaped cupola is the most visible symbolic element, the whole structure of the Russian church is a symbol in itself. The physical church represents the physical human being, standing on earth, reaching toward heaven. Accordingly, the word for the dome means "head" or "forehead." The dome stands on a drum called the "neck." Other parts of the church include a rounded gable called the "shoulder," and below the drum, a sectional vaulting known as the "bosom." The small arches often arranged in receding tiers on the gables are named *kokoshniki*, after the tiara-like headdresses worn by the women of Old Russia. Although there are no kokoshniki visible in the Russian Tarot of St. Petersburg churches, all the other customary features of Russian church architecture are faithfully depicted in the cards.

Individual homes, the centers of Russian family life, are absent from the grand images of the major arcana. They are seen, however, in the minor arcana, where the craftsman works before his modest wood hut in the Seven of Coins, and a happy couple in the Four of Clubs stands in front of their beautifully carved and painted country house. The grand palaces of the upper ranks, on the other hand, are seen only at a distance or from the interior.

Interiors

The major arcana cards of the Russian Tarot of St. Petersburg show virtually nothing in the way of interior views; only sketchy windows behind the Magician, the High Priestess, and the Empress. In this respect, they follow tradition, for as we have already seen, the trumps have always been given either abstract or outdoor settings. The minor arcana cards of the Waite deck continue the outdoor theme, and only a few of their illustrations (all in the suits of Coins and Swords) suggest interior spaces.

In the Russian Tarot of St. Petersburg, Yury Shakov's Cups images follow Waite, but the second artist has introduced a more intimate feeling into the other three suits, adding several interior scenes to those shown in Waite. These scenes are rich with color and texture, in keeping with the traditional decor of Old Russia. Featured throughout the Clubs, Swords, and Coins suits are rooms with intricately patterned tilework, carved stone ledges and balustrades, arched and leaded windows, beautifully woven carpets, and intricate woodwork. The interior backgrounds of the court cards, particularly the Queens, are especially sumptuous.

These glimpses into the decorative arts of Russia are of great interest. For most of her history, Russia's gift for creating beauty was concentrated in two areas: the glorification of God and the adornment of everyday life. The artistry and craftsmanship of the Russian people is legendary, and they applied their skills ceaselessly to the manufacture of beautiful places and objects. Whole families and entire villages were dedicated to the production of the most intricate metalwork, the most elaborate carving, or the most painstaking needlework. For centuries, the resulting treasures enriched not only the churches and palaces of Russia, but also the homes of the Russian people.

The interiors shown in the Russian Tarot of St. Petersburg depict a world where European elegance blends with the essential character of Russian artistry. From the churches of Greek Orthodoxy and the mosques of Islam, early Russia had borrowed a tradition of decorating walls, floors, and even ceilings with mosaics and friezes. This custom they wed to their own vivid color schemes and extraordinary woodworking skills, producing a highly textured style, warm and imposing all at once. When European decorative elements such as the brightly glazed tile, rich parquetry (inlaid patterns made with various colors of wood), and woven tapestries shown in the deck were introduced to Russian decor by Peter the Great, the geometric designs and brilliant colors used in these decorations recalled Russia's Byzantine heritage.

The brilliance of Russian woodcarving is amply shown in the only two kinds of furniture found in the Russian Tarot of St. Petersburg: tables and chairs. The chairs run the gamut from simply carved wooden stools, a typical kind of seating in Old Russia, to elaborate thrones. The profusion of thrones shown in the deck is true to life, for Russian nobles were connoisseurs of these lavish chairs, commissioning them to be specially designed, or receiving them as gifts from trade delegations and foreign emissaries.

Although wood was the most beloved and the most lavishly worked of all materials in Russia, stone too became an important part of Russian design, and was ornately carved, utilizing the same patterns traditional to woodworking. In the Russian Tarot of St. Petersburg, figures are frequently shown standing in front of archways, screens, columns, and balustrades, carved in both wood and stone. These scenes, like all the interiors shown in the cards, combine elements of traditional Russian craft and design with the fantasy settings of fairy tales and Oriental miniatures, in a style that recalls the Russo-Oriental "exoticism" of Diaghilev's Ballet Russe productions.

Chapter 4

The Deck in Detail

THE MAJOR ARCANA: GENERAL OBSERVATIONS

The twenty-two trump cards of the Tarot are generally referred to as the "major arcana" (meaning "greater secrets"). They are also sometimes called the "keys." Historically, the trumps appear to have developed separately from the four-suited deck, known in the esoteric interpretation of the Tarot as the "minor arcana" ("lesser secrets"). The origin of the trump images is unknown, but many students of the Tarot find them profoundly significant. They seem to offer a concise description of the archetypal states of being through which humans progress, from the innocence of The Fool to the completeness and harmony of The World.

The sequence of the trumps can be viewed as a diagram, representing the journey through life from birth to death, or the progression from the material to the spiritual. The various cards can also be seen as symbolizing the basic characters (mother, father, teacher, leader, magus, etc.), forces (love, strength, justice, evil, hope, fate, etc.), and events (change, conflict, salvation, etc.) that make up the drama of human life.

Because they offer such depth of meaning, and because they appear to have connections with esoteric systems such as alchemy and the Kabbalah, the trump images are frequently used for meditation and for magical purposes. When the Tarot is used in divination, the trumps are believed to have greater power and wider application than the minor arcana cards. They are usually thought to represent forces which come from beyond the individual and to signify the effects of synchronicity, or meaningful "co-incidence," in life.

So, for both historical and esoteric reasons, the trumps are the heart of the Tarot. Throughout the five hundred years that the Tarot has been known, there have been numerous versions of the trump images, but there has also been an essential continuity in most of the images. Only a few of the trumps—notably The Moon, The High Priestess (originally called The Papess), Strength, The Lovers, and Wheel of Fortune—have changed materially between the first known Tarot decks and the most recent ones.

It's very helpful in analyzing the Russian Tarot of St. Petersburg to understand something about the history of the Tarot trumps and their design. Yury Shakov created the trumps by examining several different Tarot decks and selecting from among the various versions of each image those elements which best suited his own conceptualization. These compositions from the history of the Tarot were then embellished with elements from Russian history, to produce the unique depth and distinctiveness of the deck. Therefore, in discussing each of the Russian Tarot of St. Petersburg trumps, we will need to consider the relationship of the card's image to the whole Tarot tradition.

Generally speaking, there are three distinct parts to the Tarot tradition. The first can be broadly described as the "Visconti-Sforza period," taking its name from the family which is thought to have sponsored the creation of the first hand-painted Tarot trumps. These images featured many references to the affairs of Italian noble families, and clearly reflected the styles and motifs of the late medieval and early Renaissance culture.

During the fifteenth century, the earliest period in the development of the Tarot, there were many variations in the card images. It was not until late in the century that a more-or-less standardized set of trump images emerged, now called the "Marseilles" style after an important French center of card manufacturing. The Marseilles-type of Tarot was the basis for almost all deck designs until the appearance in 1910 of a deck conceptualized by Arthur Edward Waite and executed by painter Pamela Colman Smith. The so-called Rider-Waite deck, which elaborated the original Tarot images with a great deal of added symbolism (as well as introducing story-type illustrations for the minor arcana cards), became the most popular and widely-used Tarot of the twentieth century.

The majority of Tarot decks being created today follow the basic pattern either of the Marseilles or the Rider-Waite decks, though each new deck has its own special character. The Russian Tarot of St. Petersburg incorporates aspects drawn from every period of Tarot history in its major arcana images. Although the overall form of the deck is taken from the Rider-Waite design, specific trumps are based directly on the Marseilles-type deck, and a few elements even refer back to pre-Marseilles designs.

In order to highlight the special nature of the Russian Tarot of St. Petersburg, the commentaries that follow will bring out the similarities and differences between the images created by Yury Shakov and the core images of the Tarot tradition. The distinctive meaning of each of the Russian Tarot trumps can be captured most fully by analyzing the traditional elements which have been left in the image, the traditional elements which have been left out, and the new elements which have been added.

Here's an example: The Star card has the central figure common to both the Marseilles and the Rider-Waite decks—a woman by a stream pouring liquid from one jug into the water, and from another jug onto the land. Above her are the conventional six small stars and one larger star. But in traditional images, the woman is kneeling, while in the Russian Tarot of St. Petersburg, she is standing. Traditional images also include a bird (often interpreted as a symbol of the soul) perched on a nearby bush, but the bird has been left out of the Russian Tarot of St. Petersburg image. Included instead are mountains and tents in the far distance. The woman, who is nude in other decks, is here clothed, and wears the traditional Russian hat called a *kokoshnik*, with a *fata*, or veil. On the edge of the stream there is an empty costume, an element which has no parallel in any other deck.

The choice to show a clothed woman standing, rather than a nude woman kneeling clearly seems significant, especially since other traditionally nude figures, such as the dancer on the World card, *are* depicted as nude in the Russian Tarot of St. Petersburg. What associations might this suggest for the woman? And what is the significance of the empty costume (a man's costume, by the way) on the bank? Why is the bird missing, and where did the tents come from?

These are the sorts of questions which repay speculation by suggesting a pattern of specifically Russian references woven into the major arcana. Many of these references are drawn from the intensely religious, symbol-centered culture of Old Russia, and although some of them are apparently political (those tents in the Star card, for example, are of the style used by Napoleon's armies on their disastrous progress through Russia), it's important to remember that political and spiritual matters were inseparable in Old Russia. There was no such thing as a "secular" part of the culture, and everything that happened—birth, death, famine, war, creation, discovery, and love—was bound up in the all-encompassing faith of the Russian Orthodox Church. In this sense, more than any other, the culture of traditional Russia was very, very far from our own.

But *not* far at all from the culture which produced the Tarot trumps. Whether the Tarot originated at the whim of an Italian nobleman or as a tool of some Gnostic sect, or in some circumstance we haven't even considered yet, it certainly emerged from an environment drenched in the power of symbolic imagery, an environment very like that of Old Russia—mystical, passionate, mysterious, powerful, and intimately connected with both the rhythms of nature and the sense of a living god. For this reason, the Russian Tarot of St. Petersburg is more than just a picturesque rendering of the Tarot images; it is a valuable evocation of a time and place in which the Tarot would have been in its own element.

With this in mind, we can understand how all the various allusions and motifs in the Russian Tarot of St. Petersburg images are interrelated, forming a significant whole in each card, and a significant pattern in the overall composition of the deck. The specifically Russian themes introduced into the images are not a separate "layer" of meaning, but a set of references that illuminate the essential intentions of the cards. For example, the Star card discussed earlier has some added elements (the woman's costume, the tents, the empty costume on the bank of the stream) and a missing element (the bird on the bush). The woman, remember, is wearing the traditional Russian headdress called a *kokoshka,* over the veil called a *fata,* a name from the same root as our own word "fate." The tents are emblematic of Napoleon's assault and the Russians' epic defense of their homeland. But how does all this fit together— and what about the empty costume?

A very careful look will reveal that, in the lower right-hand corner of the picture, there are not actually two flowers, although it may appear that way at first. (Keep in mind that these cards are miniatures, and the smallest detail may have meaning.) The yellow "blossom" is in fact a butterfly. And the butterfly, like the bird, is an ancient symbol of the soul. The bird, however, represents the "winged" or "free" soul, while the butterfly represents the *resurrected* soul. The costume on the bank, then, is an empty shell, the resurrected soul alight beside it. So we see in the picture both the soul *clothed,* a symbol of mortality, and the soul *unclothed,* a symbol of resurrection.

The distant tents remind us that the Russians burned their own cities rather than surrender them to Napoleon's armies, and that in the end, the "soul" of Russia was victorious over the army which had overrun all of Europe. Brigadier General Coxe, an Englishman in Russia on a diplomatic mission during the war, wrote: "This morning I waited with Count Rostopshchin, the Governor of Moscow, to see him fire his palace and all surrounding premises. It was a magnificent act, executed with feeling, dignity, and philosophy." Russian faith stood its greatest test during the invasion, and was rewarded. Czar Alexander said afterward, "The burning of Moscow brought light to my soul and judgment of God on the icy fields filled my heart with warmth and faith…I owe my redemption to God's redemption of Europe from destruction."

Thus, with a few subtle symbols, the Russian Tarot of St. Petersburg brings to the Star a greater and more complex resonance. The traditional meaning of the Star is hope, or aspiration, and it has also been identified with immortality. The Russian Tarot of St. Petersburg image gives specific historical and theological reference points for these meanings, through the medium of symbolic imagery. Moreover, the card brings into play a whole range of allusions to other Tarot decks: the woman in the Star card of the earliest Visconti-type decks is clothed, but is holding a star, not pouring from two urns; the figure pouring from two urns is a feature of the Marseilles-type deck, and is carried over in the Rider-Waite deck and most others, all of which have a bird; only the Oswald Wirth deck of 1889, one of the earliest esoteric deck designs, substitutes a butterfly for the bird.

The message of the Russian Tarot of St. Petersburg Star is one of hope for victory of the soul against all odds, and for resurrection of the soul against all fears. The added dimensions of this image are visible only through a knowledge of both Russian culture and Tarot history, and this is the perspective which I hope to offer for each of the cards in the following commentaries. Not all of the questions raised by the composition of the Russian Tarot of St. Petersburg yield a clear answer, of course, so a substantial residue of mystery remains in the cards. But there is much that can be understood through careful observation and a willing interest.

THE MAJOR ARCANA: CARD BY CARD

0 The Fool

The character of the Fool began as an idiot or wild man in some decks, a beggar in others, then progressed to a wandering, somewhat ragged court jester, and ended up in the Rider-Waite deck as an insouciant young man out for a stroll. Along the way, a dog was added to the picture, at first appearing to attack the Fool, and later seeming to be his companion. In later cards, the Fool is shown walking heedlessly toward a precipice.

The Russian Tarot of St. Petersburg Fool is of the jester type, and is clearly modeled on the wandering performers of Old Russia called *skomorokhi*. Clowns, minstrels, and puppeteers, the skomorokhi appeared first in Kievan Russia, and for centuries they traveled in groups through the cities and countryside, or served in the courts of the noblemen. Our Fool, as can be seen from his patched clothes and knapsack, is a wanderer, and he seems to be accompanied by a gray, wolfish-looking dog. His "motley" or many-colored costume is a traditional symbol of his calling, like the bells at his waist and on his shoes. He carries a be-ribboned rattle, and a puppet which looks exactly like himself.

The puppet is the most interesting addition to the Russian Tarot of St. Petersburg image. The puppet does not appear in any traditional Tarot decks, but puppets were the ubiquitous companions of the skomorokhi, so this is obviously a Russian reference. The meaning of the puppet is less clear, however. The most obvious point of departure for considering the puppet is that it's identical to the clown. The clown, in turn, seems to be focusing intently on the puppet. This suggests a self-absorption, even narcissism, which is commonly associated with the Fool in its negative aspects. It is this self-absorption which leads the Fool to folly, to thoughtless or impulsive action. This is also the source of the Fool's frequently noted irrationality and frivolousness.

The Fool

On the other hand, The Fool is traditionally considered to be a very powerful image, and as the only unnumbered card, it is thought to create a "circle" of trumps by being both the first and the last card in the sequence. From an archetypal perspective, the Fool can be viewed as the self starting off in narcissistic innocence, and—after much experience—ending up as the "wise fool" who depends on insight rather than reason. At the beginning of the cycle, the Fool is a fool because he takes himself too seriously; at the other end of the cycle, the Fool *appears* to be a fool because he does *not* take himself seriously (having discovered his place in the cosmos). Thus the *skomorokh* in our card may be gazing at his own image in fascination, or laughing at himself in affectionate wisdom, depending on the context in which the card is considered.

The holy fool is a figure of divine innocence much loved in the Russian culture. Dostoevsky, the great nineteenth-century Russian novelist, explored this character in *The Idiot*. The "idiot" of the title is Prince Myshkin, a naive soul whose goodness perplexes everyone with whom he comes into contact, and causes a great deal of inadvertent trouble. Throughout the many passionate and curious events which swirl around Myshkin, the reader is left to puzzle about whether he is a saint or a simpleton, a moral genius or a social incompetent. In the final analysis, many readers conclude that, like the Tarot Fool, he is both, just depending on how one is looking at it. But above all, Myshkin's great point is that "the essence of religious feeling doesn't depend on reasoning." The holy fool, who abandons reason for faith, has a very strange effect on the world of those who suppose that truth is rational.

The same is true of the Tarot Fool, who, whether selfish or selfless, can be dangerous to those overly dependent on reason, but quite illuminating to those who can trust their intuition.

The Magician

I The Magician

The Magician, like the Fool, started off as a character who would, in our society, be called "marginalized"—that is, outside the accepted social structures. The original character was a peddler, a tinker, or a mountebank (better known as a flim-flam man). In the Marseilles-type deck, he wore a hat of fashionable French design which resembled a figure-eight lying on its side, and this shape was later interpreted as a lemniscate, the mathematical symbol of infinity. In esoteric decks, therefore, the magician (originally the sort of magician who entertains with tricks) became the Magician (a practitioner of the hermetic arts), and the lemniscate was shown floating above his head. The objects on the table in front of him, which had at first been thimbles or other implements, became the suit tokens.

Of all the trumps in the Russian Tarot of St. Petersburg, The Magician differs least from the traditional Tarot image. The picture follows the symbolism of the Rider-Waite deck completely; even the roses which grow profusely in the Rider image are included, here tumbling out of the Cup onto the table and floor. Like all his Tarot predecessors, the Magician holds a club (rod, wand, baton) in his uplifted hand, and like his Rider-Waite forebear, he wears a flowing cape. The few Russian elements are circumstantial; the table and stool are the sort of design common to Russian furniture, and the stone wall and window are the same features used to denote interiors throughout the deck. This lack of Russian references in The Magician may be due in part to the fact that there is no tradition of hermetic magical practice in Russian culture.

In any event, the only unusual feature of the Russian Tarot of St. Petersburg image is the addition of wings on the lemniscate, a small detail which turns out to be more important than it might at first appear. For one thing, it may be a reference to Crowley's Thoth deck—the only such reference in the Russian Tarot of St. Petersburg, as far as I can discover. Crowley placed over the head of his Magician a winged Eye of Horus, an Egyptian symbol of prophecy, in order to explicitly link the Magician with Thoth/Hermes (the mythical Egyptian/Greek magus who was imagined by Court de Gébelin and other Tarot theorists to have been the creator of the Tarot trumps). It's also possible, however, that the wings in the Russian Tarot of St. Petersburg image are a direct reference to Hermes, who is frequently depicted in Greek and Renaissance art wearing a winged helmet. Either way, however, it seems likely that the addition of the wings does relate The Magician to the great Hermes, fountainhead of the hermetic arts, father of alchemy, and messenger of the Greek gods.

Another possibility is that the wings relate to the winged figures used to symbolize the four Evangelists (Matthew, Mark, Luke, and John). The Russian Tarot of St. Petersburg includes the symbolic representation of the Evangelists (depicted as an angel, a winged lion, a winged ox, and an eagle) in the same places they are found in the Rider-Waite deck—that is, on the Wheel of Fortune and World cards. But Yury Shakov also included the winged lion, Mark's emblem, on the Two of Cups, suggesting that he intended the Evangelists to play an even greater symbolic role in the overall composition of the deck. So it may be that the wings are part of a Christian theme, either instead of or in addition to a hermetic reference.

So what is the meaning of The Magician in the Russian Tarot of St. Petersburg? In Waite's interpretation, the Magician is one who possesses and communicates gifts of the spirit. In Crowley's view, the Magician is a figure of power, possessing skills and wisdom, knowledge of science, and the power of healing. Their Magicians both are shown in the traditional position, one hand pointing at the sky, the other at the earth, in accordance with the dictum "As above, so below," long attributed to Hermes and believed to mean that all aspects of creation are inextricably interlinked. Negative aspects of The Magician include deceit (Crowley) and disquiet (Waite).

From an archetypal standpoint, The Magician occupies the "beginning" place in the cycle of the Tarot trumps, and represents the child's first attempts to exercise power over his environment. It is the birth of the will.

As we've already seen, the Fool is an unnumbered card which floats at both the beginning and end of the deck. When placed at the beginning of the sequence, it constitutes a pair with the Magician. The Fool is "absolute" beginning, formlessness; The Magician is "human" beginning, the first form.

The next two cards, The High Priestess and The Empress, constitute the second pair, representing the feminine dimensions of the soul and of the environment.

II

The High Priestess

II The High Priestess

For most of Tarot history, this card was called The Papess, and featured a woman in a nun-like habit, wearing a bishop's miter. The Papess was based either on the probably-mythical character of Pope Joan (a woman elected Pope by credulous male cardinals) or on a relative of the Visconti family who really was invested as "Pope" of a heretical sect. In esoteric decks, beginning with Wirth's designs and carried further in Waite's, the Papess was radically transformed into a priestess of Isis, accompanied by symbols of the moon and flanked by pillars representing the mystic temple.

The Russian Tarot of St. Petersburg figure of the High Priestess is more similar to the old designs than to the new. It features a woman in noble dress, seated on a throne bearing the heraldic device of the lion rampant, and holding in her lap what appears to be a royal decree. Like the Papess, she is wearing a bishop's miter. Clearly she is not a nun, but certainly she is not a priestess of Isis! Even so, there are references in this image to the Waite deck's High Priestess; the pillars of the throne recall the pillars of the temple, and the red swath which wraps the throne suggests the veil of the temple from Waite's card.

Just as important as these connections with Tarot history, however, is the connection with *Russian* history. The Russian Tarot of St. Petersburg High Priestess wears a Russian cross (rather than the Roman cross worn by early Papesses or the solar cross worn by Waite's Priestess of Isis) and a bishop's miter in the Russian Orthodox style, ringed with small icons; her wooden throne is carved in the traditional Russian folk style. She is almost certainly Princess Olga of Kiev, the first Russian ruler converted to Christianity and the greatest early heroine of the Russian people. Olga's husband, Prince Igor, was slain in 945, and Olga became regent. Her much-admired deeds, recorded in the *Primary Chronicle* (the earliest written account of Russian history), included responding to a marriage proposal from her husband's murderer by having his emissaries buried alive. (When a second group was sent, she had them boiled in a bath.)

A few years later, Princess Olga became a Christian, under the sponsorship of the Byzantine Emperor Constantine. While it is unclear whether her conversion was motivated by political or spiritual considerations (for Olga was a very astute administrator, and trade with Constantinople was a mainstay of the Kievan economy), it is certain that this event had momentous consequences in the shaping of Russian culture. Although there would be two more generations before the wholesale Christianization of Russia, it was Olga who began the rejection of Russia's old polytheistic paganism and introduced the idea of a monotheistic state religion. She symbolizes feminine strength, spiritual awareness, and the union of sacred wisdom with common sense.

Traditionally, this card represents intuition, mystery, and the eternal feminine in its positive aspects; secrecy and manipulation in a negative context. In the archetypal cycle of the trumps, the High Priestess represents the development of the "anima" or feminine archetypal principle, also called the "soul." From the anima arise imagination and fantasy; it is the anima that connects consciousness with unconscious life and "animates" our perception of the world as a meaningful, symbolic environment.

One interesting note: the Russian Tarot of St. Petersburg High Priestess differs from all her sisters in holding aloft her right hand, as if giving a blessing. Notice the position of her fingers. She seems to be making the sign or *mudra* (sacred gesture) associated with the Hindu deity Kali, in her manifestation as the "Mother of the World." This symbolic gesture resembles horns, and was used in many European cultures both as a sign of the devil and as a defense against the "evil eye." Horns are also associated with Isis, and for that reason, Waite's High Priestess wears a horned headdress—one surprisingly similar to the *kichka,* a cap with padded horns worn for centuries by women in certain Russian provinces.

III The Empress

The Empress changed considerably between the original Tarot designs and the later esoteric interpretations. In the earliest decks, she was clearly a royal figure, throned and crowned and accompanied by a shield bearing the imperial eagle. By contrast, in the Waite card, she is a sort of earth-mother figure, seated on a divan in a field of abundance, near a stream; her imperial shield is replaced by a heart with the symbol of Venus.

Once again, the Russian Tarot of St. Petersburg follows the earlier pattern, but with some esoteric allusions and one very important change. The Empress's crown is in the style of a popular Russian headdress (often worn at weddings), and it is outlined in stars, referring to the crown of stars worn by Waite's Empress. She wears traditional Russian dress, but the profuse floral pattern of her gown reminds us of Waite's Empress, whose dress is patterned with pomegranates, symbolizing both fertility and chastity. The Russian Tarot Empress wears over her gown a short, full jacket called by the Russians a "soul-warmer," and its ermine trim denotes her imperial status. But the most significant element in the picture is her shield bearing the two-headed eagle which symbolized the Byzantine Empire, looking both east and west.

The presence of this shield suggests that the Empress is a very special character in Russian history: Zoe Paleologus, who became Grand Princess Sofia, second wife of Ivan III. As a niece of Emperor Constantine XI, Zoe came from one of Europe's most important families, but she was orphaned at a very young age, and grew up in Rome as a ward of Pope Paul II. The Pope, wishing to increase Roman influence in Russia, offered her hand to Ivan, and in 1472, they were married. As part of the marriage contract, Ivan gained the right to use the Byzantine double eagle, which remained the crest of the tsars until the revolution of 1917.

Zoe turned out to have a considerable influence over the tide of Russian history, not only politically but also aesthetically. Having grown up among the splendors of Constantinople and Rome, she inspired and encouraged the renovation of the Moscow Kremlin, which by the end of her thirty-one years as Grand Princess was well on its way to becoming an architectural showplace. Zoe, who was fluent in several languages, and very well-educated by the standards of the time, also passed on to her son Vasili sophisticated tastes in art. As Grand Prince, Vasili continued the ambitious remodeling of the Kremlin. But it was only by dint of considerable scheming on Zoe's part that Vasili became Ivan's heir, for his claim to the throne was rivaled by Ivan's grandson Dmitri, and much intrigue is thought to have gone into securing his succession.

All in all, Zoe seems to offer an excellent synopsis of the character of the Empress. Creative and nurturing, fruitful and sensual, the Empress may also be vain, superficial and controlling. In the archetypal cycle of the trumps, The Empress represents the effects of the mother, both good and bad, as well as the development of the feminine principle of action in making, doing, and giving birth. The Empress is traditionally associated with the mother goddesses Demeter and Ishtar, and with Aphrodite/Venus, goddess of love.

More horn lore: Look at the newels on the back of the Empress's throne. At first glance, they appear to be fleur-de-lis, but closer inspection will reveal that the center "petal" is not attached to the rest of the "flower"; block it out, and you will see that each newel is in fact the horned headdress of Isis, quite similar to that worn by Waite's High Priestess. (The third "petal" is actually a flame floating above the horns.) This is a most interesting association, because the Egyptian hieroglyphic for Isis was a throne, and the Pharaoh's throne was actually thought to be the lap of Isis, its arms surrounding and protecting the Pharaoh like the goddess's wings.

By connecting the symbol of Isis with the throne of the Empress, the Russian Tarot of St. Petersburg reminds us that the High Priestess and the Empress represent the two complimentary aspects of Isis, both the source of mystery and the mother of all. These two cards are also the two aspects of the anima—the inward principle of imagination and the outward principle of creativity.

The High Priestess and The Empress show us the dimensions of feminine consciousness. Similarly, The Emperor and The Hierophant reveal the dimensions of masculine consciousness. These four cards form two "couples"—the material parents and the spiritual parents.

In the Russian Tarot of St. Petersburg, these pairs of cards represent not only some of the archetypal characteristics attributed to the masculine and feminine, but also the historical roles of men and women in Russia. Both of the female figures in the cards are shown inside, *where high-born women in Old Russia were expected to remain, and both of the male figures are shown* outside, *seated before the cities they ruled.*

IV The Emperor

Little change has taken place in the image of the Emperor over the history of the Tarot. The only alterations, really, are in his posture. He was originally shown in profile, but Waite-type decks depict him facing forward; Marseilles-type decks show him with crossed legs (appearing to form the figure "4"), but other decks, both old and new, show both his feet on the ground. Either way, he is surrounded by Imperial trappings, usually crowned (but sometimes helmeted), and most often with an orb and scepter. Esoteric decks, such as Wirth's and Waite's, add ram's heads to the throne (emphasizing the Aries association) and top the scepter with an *ankh* (the Egyptian cross, symbolizing the creative energies of the male and female), rather than the traditional fleur-de-lis.

The Russian Tarot of St. Petersburg Emperor differs little from his predecessors in most respects. In a compromise, he faces mostly forward but looks slightly to his right; he is richly garbed, and holds the conventional orb and scepter. As with the Empress, the most interesting thing about the Emperor is his identity in Russian history, and fittingly enough, he is Ivan the Great, Zoe's husband. The fur-brimmed crown he wears is the *chapka Monomakha,* a crown which had been worn by the 12th-century prince Vladimir Monomakh, and which was reputed to have been the hat of his maternal grandfather, Emperor Constantine. Ivan the Great, first to claim the title "Tsar of all Russia," used the legendary *chapka,* along with Zoe's dowry of the double eagle, to bolster his political position by establishing the appearance of a direct link with the powerful heritage of the Byzantine empire.

This image of the Emperor actually resembles Ivan the Great, who wore a dark, fairly short beard like the one shown. (Unfortunately, there is no way of knowing whether the Empress looks like Zoe, because no images of her have remained.) Ivan truly was a great figure in Russian history, for he consolidated power as much by diplomatic cunning as by might, and though he was far from being benign, he did not exhibit the capricious cruelty which marked many Russian rulers—including, most notably, his

IV

The Emperor

grandson Ivan the Terrible. Ivan the Great brought order to a disorganized country, and turned Moscow into an Imperial city. He also created a new concept of rulership. Traditionally, the Russian title *tsar* (a Slavic form of the Latin *caesar*) meant merely that a ruler owed allegiance to no one else. But under Ivan's manipulation, the term came to be understood as implying a God-given right to rule.

Ivan the Great exhibited all the characteristics long associated with the Tarot Emperor: strength, confidence, leadership, originality, virility, and a sense of order. He also embodied several of the negative qualities of that character, sometimes putting ambition ahead of all else, occasionally acting from malice or spite, and usually being autocratic. Generally speaking, Ivan offers a good example of the archetype of the father or authority figure, the place occupied by The Emperor in the archetypal cycle of Tarot trumps. The Emperor represents the *animus,* the masculine counterpoint of the *anima.* Within the psyche, the animus constructs and enforces rules, creates a will to order, and is a source of both energy and aggression.

The Russian Tarot of St. Petersburg offers one other interesting Russian connection for the Emperor. The carved facade of the Emperor's throne depicts a favorite subject of Russian art, St. George slaying the dragon. St. George was widely revered among the Russians as a symbol of bravery, and of the triumph of good over evil. The conventional story of St. George is that he was a second-century Christian soldier who slew a dragon in order to save a maiden from sacrifice, and whose heroism converted the pagans to his faith. In fact, however, the story of St. George is really an allegory, in which the dragon represents paganism and the maiden represents the city. Most importantly, however, St. George illuminates the figure of the Emperor by reminding us that, ideally, strength and goodness are joined in the hero.

V The Hierophant

Unlike The Emperor, The Hierophant has seen a significant change over the years. He was once The Pope, and looked just as you would expect a Pope to look. In esoteric decks, however, he became a sort of generic religious figure, surrounded by suggestions of both Christian ritual and esoteric symbolism. He was renamed the "Hierophant," meaning "revealer of sacred things," after the title of the chief priest of the Eleusinian mysteries. The Eleusinian mysteries were late Greek initiatory rites organized around the symbolism of corn, emblem of Demeter/Isis, and this reference provides an esoteric connection between The High Priestess and The Hierophant.

So who portrays the Hierophant in the Russian Tarot of St. Petersburg? Remember that our High Priestess, Olga, was the first ruler to convert to Christianity. She was unable, however, to convert others, and even her son was unmoved by her attempts. *His* son, therefore, was born a pagan (in 956), and lived a pagan life until 988. Having overrun his brother princes and taken control, for practical purposes, of Kievan Russia, Prince Vladimir realized that in order to unify his people and improve relations with his neighbors, it would be useful to adopt a monotheistic religion. Vladimir sent out investigative teams to evaluate various religions, and in the end, was persuaded by the beauty of the Greek Orthodox churches and liturgies to adopt his grandmother's faith.

Having found his Christian mission, Vladimir took it seriously. He ordered compulsory mass baptisms, built churches, imported icons, and generally got the new religion off to a speedy start. Not only that, he discovered a personal zeal for good deeds and became known for his charity as Vladimir the Good. In fact, in the thirteenth century, he was made a saint. And so we find him, as the Hierophant, wearing the vestments of a patriarch, crowned with a bishop's miter, and hovered over by cherubim. On his chest is a pectoral icon representing the favorite Russian theme of Virgin and Child, and surrounding him, depicted by a red circle, is the aura of saintliness. Missing from the Russian Tarot of St. Petersburg image,

V

The Hierophant

however, are the two kneeling figures who are shown in many decks receiving the Pope's blessing.

Traditional attributes of The Pope or The Hierophant include wisdom, mercy, generosity, and patience. He is, obviously, a symbol of organized religion, and of the priesthood in general, including piety, self-discipline, and the way of devotion. He may also be related to teaching and knowledge in general. On the negative side, The Hierophant can be associated with rigidity, fanaticism, narrow-mindedness, or a destructive kind of too-goodness. In the archetypal cycle of the trumps, he represents the development of internal as opposed to external (Emperor!) sources of control. The Hierophant is the side of the animus which links conscious and unconscious will, just as the Pope (or *pontifex*, bridge) links humanity with God.

The choice of Saint Vladimir, Grand Prince of Kiev, to portray the Hierophant brings out the vital link in Russian culture between spiritual life and active participation in the world. In Old Russia, church and state were one, public and private behavior were indistinguishable, and life revolved around the observance of the Christian calendar—a constant flow of feasts, fasts, and masses. The life of Vladimir illustrates how political and religious interests may run together, but more importantly, how spiritual transformation may affect personal actions. Vladimir is noteworthy not only for his conscious rejection of pagan "disorder," but also for his genuine change through conversion, from a casual life to a considered one, from self-serving motives to charitable ones. In this way, the Russian Tarot of St. Petersburg image suggests how The Hierophant may inform and illuminate its male complement, The Emperor.

A note on the Hierophant's regalia: His robe is a mere suggestion of the extraordinary needlework done by Russian women in the service of the church. In reality, each pane on such a grand garment would contain a beautifully embroidered portrait of a saint, or a scene from the life of Christ, all created to reflect the glory of God.

The next pair of cards changes focus from family and society to personality. The Lovers card deals with the revelation of personality through intimacy. The Chariot considers the projection of personality through the formation of a public identity. Like the previous pairs, these two cards represent two aspects of a single topic. This pattern of pairs can be traced through the whole major arcana, but there are other patterns as well— groups of three cards and groups of seven cards (The Fool is not included in a group) are common divisions of the trumps.

VI The Lovers

The image of The Lovers has undergone quite a change through time. Early cards usually showed noble lovers, hovered over by Cupid with his arrow. But in the Waite deck, the courtly couple were replaced by Adam and Eve, and Cupid became an angel. This is one of the places where Waite's own interest in Christian mysticism most obviously affected his designs for the trumps, and it is not surprising that in the Russian Tarot of St. Petersburg, which emphasizes Christian imagery, The Lovers card is a bit more like Waite's card than like the traditional one.

Even so, the card is really quite distinctive from any of its predecessors. Like the couples in traditional designs, our Lovers wear clothes (Waite's are nude), but their costumes are very specifically Russian. She wears Russia's most familiar costume, the *sarafan,* and he is conventionally dressed in an embroidered overblouse of *krasny,* the "beautiful red," with full trousers tucked into his boots. They are quite young (he is beardless) and unmarried (she wears her hair in a single plait and does not cover her head). And they are overseen not by a simpering cupid, and not by Waite's enormous, anthropomorphic angel, but by a cherubim—second highest being in the celestial order, and a commonly used symbol in Russian ecclesiastical art. (Cupid was often portrayed in Renaissance art as a *putti,* or "cherub," but those fat little baby angels were an artistic conceit of the period. The *real* cherubim were majestic and mysterious, with four or six wings, folded so that their bodies could not be seen.)

Waite's design for the Lovers included the two trees of Eden mentioned in Genesis: the Tree of Life and the Tree of the Knowledge of Good and Evil. Curled around the latter tree (conventionally portrayed as an apple tree, though there is no biblical reason for the association) is the Serpent, symbolizing Satan's temptation of Eve. In the Russian Tarot of St. Petersburg, however, only one tree appears, complete with apples and snake. Added to the picture are personified Sun and Moon; these symbols, like the cherubim, were a common feature of the beautiful

embroidered altar cloths used in Russian Orthodox churches, and they were typically shown looking at Christ, signifying that all creation was focused on the son of God. On our Tarot card, the heavenly residents seem fascinated with the Lovers—who, in turn, seem fascinated with each other. The Lovers appear to be entirely absorbed in their approaching embrace, oblivious to the danger of the Serpent lurking behind them.

But also behind the couple is an entirely original addition to the cast of The Lovers: a lamb and a young goat. The man is holding a crooked staff, suggesting that he is a shepherd. But why should he be? Adam, of course, was said to have named the animals and ordered them. Still—why illustrate this point with a lamb and a kid, animals which are not especially associated with Russia? The only symbolic structure which seems to fit here is that taken from Matthew 25:31-46, in which Christ is described as being like a shepherd, who upon his second coming will separate the just from the unjust, as "the sheep from the goats." Then he will set the sheep on his right hand and the goats on his left, just as they would be in The Lovers if our shepherd turned to face them.

The Lovers card is usually interpreted in terms of romantic love, attraction, union, marriage, beauty, and choice; negative connotations include frivolousness and the triumph of passion over wisdom. In the archetypal cycle of the trumps, The Lovers usually represents the union of animus and anima, the male and female principles of the psyche which were explored in the previous four cards. But through the parable of the shepherd, the Russian Tarot of St. Petersburg image suggests an added dimension of meaning. Matthew concludes the parable with Christ's explanation of why the just were saved: "For I was hungry, and you gave me food, thirsty, and you gave me drink; I was a stranger, and you brought me home…" When the mystified souls ask how they had done these things, Christ replies, "Believe me, when you did it to one of the least of my brethren here, you did it to me."

This story reminds us that The Lovers represents not just one kind of love, but three: *eros* (romantic love), *agape* (love of friends and family), and *caritas* (the love of all being).

VII The Chariot

In the beginning, there was a Chariot, but no charioteer. The original Tarot card depicted a kind of parade element called a "triumphal chariot," on which a public figure rode in a procession, much as our current-day celebrities ride on floats in parades. The early Visconti-type card showed a woman riding on the Chariot, but the figure quickly became a man in armor, though still clearly involved in a parade rather than in a battle. With Wirth's Tarot, and then Waite's, new symbolism was added, including stars, moons, sphinxes, and even the sexual motifs of *lingam* and *yoni* (symbolic representations of male and female genitalia, found in the art of India). In almost all decks, however, the chariot itself remains closer to a platform than to a real vehicle, and it never seems to be moving.

The Russian Tarot of St. Petersburg's Chariot breaks from this static tradition, and introduces a chariot in motion, complete with prancing horses and flying reins. The charioteer is dressed for battle in medieval times, and his cape billows behind him. The horses—pulling in opposite directions, as they do in traditional Tarot cards—are gaily caparisoned, and boast the flowing manes and tails especially loved by Russians. (In fact, horses not naturally well-endowed in this department were sometimes given false hair pieces!) The chariot itself, meanwhile, features a decoratively carved wooden front, and a purple canopy trimmed with stars. Though the chariot is not one of the several common Russian styles (and there was never any noteworthy use of chariots in battle among the Russians), the Russians had so many types of carriages that this could easily be one of them; it does, however, look a bit more like a gypsy wagon than like a typical Russian carriage.

Among the interesting details of The Chariot are the artist's initials, "Y.S.", carved into the front panel of the chariot, and the charioteer's girdle (reminding us that this is the card of personal achievement). Look carefully at the girdle and you will see that it recalls almost exactly the winged disk and crest which adorn the front of the Chariot on the Rider-Waite card; even the lingam and yoni are included (get out your magnifying glass!). The star-studded light purple edge of the chariot's canopy recalls the starry crown and crescent moon epaulets worn by Waite's charioteer. Each of the two charioteers actually carries the same arrow-tipped scepter, and the shapes of their corselets and gauntlets are much the same as well.

The Chariot has traditionally been interpreted—with unusual consistency and simplicity—along the lines of triumph, conquest, victory, and/or success. It is generally considered to refer to public matters, such as politics or business, and is widely thought of as the "career" card. Negative interpretations of the card include the hollow or pyrrhic victory, dominating ambition, or reckless zeal. In the archetypal cycle of the trumps, The Chariot is associated with the development of a persona, a public personality which controls (and may even deny) the expression of the true self.

Perhaps The Chariot of the Russian Tarot of St. Petersburg suggests speed and drama (qualities frequently associated with The Chariot, but usually not shown in the design of the card) because the Russians embraced both so enthusiastically. The great writer Nikolai Gogol may have been telling us something about The Chariot when he mused, in his comic exploration of Russian life, *Dead Souls*, "What Russian does not like to drive fast? Which of us does not at times yearn to give his horses their heads and let them go crying, 'To Devil with the world!'?" Which of us, indeed—Russians or not.

The next pair, Strength and The Hermit, were not originally a pair at all. In old-style Tarots, card number 8 was not Strength but Justice. Waite reversed the places of the two cards for unexplained esoteric reasons. Ever since Court de Gébelin introduced the idea of an esoteric Tarot, there had been a great deal of debate over the "real" order of the cards; many Tarot theorists claimed that the cards would reveal their occult message only when the right order was known. Perhaps the best way to look at the matter is to look at all of the next four cards together. Strength and Justice, regardless of their placement, are qualities sought by the Hermit in the face of a complex and mysterious reality, represented by the Wheel of Fortune.

VIII Strength

In the earliest decks, Strength (or Fortitude) was sometimes represented by Hercules with a club, subduing a lion. Another type of card showed a woman seated near a pillar. At some point, the two designs must have coalesced, with the result that in Marseilles-type decks, the image of Strength is a woman opening the jaws of a lion. Waite used basically the same image, except that the woman is closing rather than opening the lion's jaws; she wears a profusion of flowers, and a lemniscate (as with The Magician, this feature was probably derived from the hat style worn by the Marseilles figures) floats above her head.

The Russian Tarot of St. Petersburg card pays homage to Waite by adorning the lady with a garland of flowers and placing a rose in her hand. But here she has a different relationship with the lion than is depicted in most cards. She is not doing anything to the lion; rather, the two seem to be communing in some way. The lion's paw rests on her knee and she appears to be stroking its mane. In the background is a windmill of the Dutch style, just like those which can be seen in pictures of Old Russia, dotting the vast, flat plains.

The lion was, of course, used as a heraldic symbol in Russia, as it was in most European countries. Though lions once roamed throughout Europe and Asia, they were long gone by the Middle Ages, and they came to be known as symbols rather than as real animals. The lion was, and still is, seen as emblematic of strength, majesty, courage, and fortitude, so it became associated with royalty. But the lion has also long been viewed as an animal unusually close to human beings; tales of lions and humans exchanging favors abounded throughout Europe, and part of the lion's nobility was believed to be his generosity. Lions were purported to release their prey if beseeched, and were reputed to be especially gentle in the company of virgins.

One of the most famous stories concerning lions and humans, known as early as ancient Greece, is that of the good person who removes a thorn from the lion's paw, illustrating the triumph of gentleness over the wild power of nature. This story was told of St.

Jerome, and it was said the lion thereafter became his devoted companion. St. Jerome was among the saints especially loved by Russians, even though he never visited there, and in a beautiful sixteenth-century icon, the saint is shown aiding the lion. Behind the two figures in the icon is the opening of a hermit's cave—very similar to the one shown in the next of the Russian Tarot of St. Petersburg trumps, The Hermit.

Lions are widely associated with the sun, which is the ruling planet of Leo, the astrological sign symbolized by the lion. One widely accepted interpretation of the image on the Strength card is the union of Leo and Virgo, represented by the lion and the young woman. (In the Russian Tarot of St. Petersburg, we can see by her single plait and her uncovered head that the woman is unmarried.) Typically, the card is considered to represent strength, fortitude, and courage, particularly when these qualities are seen from a spiritual perspective. It is also connected with mercy and with purity on the positive side, and, on the negative side, with obstinacy and overbearingness. In the archetypal cycle of the trumps, Strength represents the coherence of personality that comes from the union of ego (The Chariot) and self (The Hermit).

The windmill in the card is a very interesting addition to the traditional symbolism of the image, one which points out an alternative to the conventional interpretation of the card. Windmills are man's way of harnessing the power of the winds, or *drawing strength from nature.* Looking afresh at the girl and the lion, we see she is not subduing the lion, but, through their physical contact, actually taking strength and courage from the lion. This interpretation is very much in keeping with the Russian love of the wild and closeness with nature, and it adds a wonderful new dimension to a card which has traditionally been viewed in perhaps a rather simplistic way.

IX The Hermit

The Hermit was originally an old man with an hourglass, signifying the passage—and the ravages—of time. It seems likely that the cloaked and bent figure of the old man was later interpreted as a robed monk or hermit, and the hourglass was metamorphosed into a lantern (recalling the lamp with which the Greek philosopher Diogenes was supposed to have gone seeking the truth). The card has traditionally been interpreted along these later lines, carrying the sense of retreat from the world, philosophy, meditation, and spiritual inquiry on the positive side; isolation and over-prudence on the negative. The Hermit has often been equated with the "wise man," and in the Golden Dawn system, The Hermit, The Magician, and The Hierophant were considered to represent the three Magi. In the archetypal cycle of the trumps, The Hermit represents the development of inner depth through introspection or self-analysis.

Although the six-pointed star, or hexagram, in the Hermit's lantern is taken from the Waite's design, in every other respect, the Russian Tarot of St. Petersburg gives a notably Russian style to The Hermit. He wears the traditional bast shoes and a simple robe edged with peasant embroidery, covered by a cowled cape; he carries a crooked staff like that of the "shepherd Adam" in The Lovers. Behind him is a hole in a rock, signifying a cave of the type used by desert-dwelling ascetics, and matching almost exactly the symbolism found in icons of hermit-saints such as Jerome. The Byzantine church, from which Russian Orthodoxy drew so much of its inspiration, was famous for its monasteries, and for its tradition of asceticism. In Turkey, Greece, and Syria, especially, spiritual aspirants took advantage of natural rock formations for simple shelter, while they lived a life of prayer and self-denial. Kievan Russia had its own Monastery of the Caves, a honeycomb affair of monk's cells in the soft stone of the Dnieper's banks.

The visual reference to this tradition introduces the special meaning of the Russian Tarot's Hermit. In Russian culture, from the fourteenth through the early seventeenth centuries, a distinctive religious theme developed, in which wandering ascetics called "holy fools" came to be revered for their prophetic utterances. These *skitalets* were learned and widely traveled men who renounced the flesh "for Christ's sake," and by this means were thought to acquire powers of special knowledge. Their powerful role in Russian culture came about because their prophecies and practices reinforced the general apocalyptic emphasis of medieval Russian religion. The calendar of the old Orthodox Church extended only to the year 1492, and it was widely believed during the fourteenth and fifteenth centuries (as it had been in the first several centuries after Christ) that the end of the world was near at hand. This idea fueled the already strong emphasis of Russian religious thought on the sacredness of suffering, and increased the veneration of the holy fools, who imitated Christ's mission of suffering. Through the rigors of their spiritual practices, the ascetics sought to gain a glimpse of the divine light or "energy" of God. (Compare the Russian words *svet*, light, and *svyatoy*, blessed.)

The whole Russian monastic tradition was heavily influenced by an Eastern Orthodox mystical movement known as Hesychasm. (This same movement was deemed heretical in the Western church.) Hesychasm taught that man could achieve direct personal contact with God through the "inner calm" developed by such practices as remaining in darkness, fasting, controlling the breath, and continuous prayer. In the Russian church, monasticism was very loosely organized, and there were many different varieties of these practices carried on by individuals and small groups, as well as by larger monastic communities. Monasteries were believed to be sites for the accumulation of spiritual energies, which, like a magnetic field, would attract all sorts of loose elements and also radiate invisible spiritual power into the surrounding areas. This was an important concept, because part of the Russian ideology was an expectation that nature itself would be transformed through redemption, and the closeness of the hermit-saints and the holy fools to nature was part of their special value.

From this point of view, the Tarot Hermit can be seen not just as a card of personal spiritual pursuit, but as an image connected with prophecy, redemption and mystical clairvoyance.

X Wheel of Fortune

The "old" and "new" images of the Wheel of Fortune are practically two different cards, though fundamental aspects of their interpretation remain the same. In early cards, and in the Marseilles-type decks, the Wheel was portrayed as a type of carnival ride, on which figures (at first humans wearing animal ears to signify their folly, and later, animals representing humans) rise to the top of the wheel and then fall—or fall off. Originally, legends written on the cards marked the various positions on the wheel: "I shall reign," "I reign," "I reigned," "I am without reign." Later the legends were dropped, and then when the esoteric interpretation of the Tarot emerged, the image, and the message, of the card were changed completely.

Waite's design for the Wheel of Fortune changed the wheel itself from a carnival ride to a flat circle, embellished with a variety of occult symbols and figures: the Hebrew letters Yod, Heh, Vau, Heh (that is, Jahweh or Jehovah, the unnamed name of God, also known as the Tetragrammaton); the alchemical symbols for mercury, sulfur, salt, and water; the Four Beasts of the Apocalypse (evangelists Matthew, Mark, Luke and John, represented by their winged emblems); and the Egyptian figures Typhon (descending), Anubis (rising), and a sphinx, sword drawn, atop the wheel. In this profusion of symbolism, Waite was following the ideas of the French occultist Eliphas Lévi, and Waite explains that "the symbolic picture stands for the perpetual motion of a fluidic universe and for the flux of human life." Another feature of the design—the letters "T," "A," "R," and "O," (read as both "Taro" and "Rota" or "wheel")—is intended to show that "Providence is implied through all."

The Russian Tarot of St. Petersburg trumps have so far been closer, in most cases, to traditional designs than to esoteric ones; frequently, the cards have combined aspects of both, and added further meaning through allusions to Russian history and religion, as we have already seen. It comes as a surprise, then, to see the Wheel of Fortune taken seemingly whole from the Waite deck. But with the application of a little Russian history, this card is transformed into a wonderfully different and informative view of the traditional trump. The word *rota* has a special meaning in Russian history, and one which sheds light on the nature of fortune.

From 1036-1054, Jaroslav I, The Wise, reigned over Kievan Russia at its height. But he realized that the traditional way of handing down power, which had little logic and less stability, was destroying order in the country. In an effort to avoid another chaotic succession, Jaroslav devised a system of inheritance called the "rota." According to this plan, his five sons were to rule over the five principal cities, the richest city to the eldest son and so on down the line. When the eldest son died, the next would move up to the richest city, and the younger sons would move up accordingly; the fifth city would then go to the eldest son of the just-deceased eldest son.

Needless to say, the rota system broke down quickly, for the sons did not die in the proper order. Within a few generations, there were too many princes, most of them selfish and warlike, and their continual strife made the Russian state not only crippled within, but also vulnerable to attack by nomadic warriors. The problematic rota system was partly responsible for the decline of Kiev, and for the conquest of Russia by the Tatars in the thirteenth century. But viewed in the context of the Wheel of Fortune, rota offers a valuable message, which can be summarized in the old axiom, "The best-laid plans of mice and men often go astray."

The Wheel of Fortune reminds us that security is an illusion, and that attempts to control destiny most often backfire. There are no "positive" and "negative" poles of interpretation for this card, because the core meaning—fate, chance, luck, destiny—always combines the two poles within itself. In the archetypal cycle of the trumps, Wheel of Fortune signifies the achievement of harmony with the cyclical nature of life and experience.

An entertaining note: Get out your magnifying glass again, and look at the face of the sphinx. It appears to be Peter the Great, identifiable by his signature mustache. Peter, who was nearly seven feet tall in real life, was often cartooned as a cat because of his mustache, and he is portrayed satirically here as a tiny face on a lion's body.

XI Justice

Justice has remained among the most stable of all the Tarot trumps. From the earliest images until the present day, Justice has been, in most decks, a seated female figure, holding in one hand scales (for weighing the truth), in the other a sword (for enforcing the law). She is usually linked with Themis, the Greek goddess of laws, and with Maat, the Egyptian goddess who personified "Truth" or "Justice." In Greek mythology, Themis, who was one of the Titans (the original twelve children of Heaven and Earth), was the mother of the three Fates (the Moirae). Both Themis and Maat represented not only justice and law in the context of civil order, but more importantly, they symbolized, as goddesses of creation, the principle of order in the universe.

The Russian Tarot of St. Petersburg follows the traditional imagery of the Justice card, with one exception. Here the woman is standing, rather than sitting. Her dress of royal purple is traced with a delicate gold pattern and trimmed with jewels, and her traditional fur-trimmed Russian crown is worn over a long veil of the "beautiful red," and topped with an eight-pointed star. Behind her is a carved wooden arch.

The arch is a very interesting feature of this card, because it has no Christian symbolism. In fact, there is no Christian symbolism on the whole card. Since there are so many Christian references in the Russian Tarot of St. Petersburg, it seems noteworthy that there are none here. In fact, the arch is not only not Christian, it is rather specifically pagan. The two pillars of the arch, each topped with four faces, are interestingly similar to an ancient Slavic idol discovered over a hundred years ago in a Polish river. (Throughout the areas now known as Russia and Eastern Europe, "drowning" was the usual fate of the old idols after the introduction of Christianity.) This unique square-formed obelisk, nearly nine feet tall, is thought to represent the war god Svantevit, whose four faces atop the stone look in all directions. Although little is known of where and when specific gods were worshiped by the Slavs, it is probable that

Svantevit had cults in early Russia, and it is certain that Perun, the thunder god, was well known there.

Archaeological excavations of cult sites in Russia have revealed that carved wooden pillars were often used to mark out the *temenos* or sacred space used for the cultic rites. So it is interesting that our Justice card uses two pillars, topped by an arch representing the heavens, to enclose the space of the goddess. The connections between the pillars and the arch are guarded by twin dragons, and at the top of the arch, over a field of stars, is the sun, recalling that the earliest Slavic cults were solar. The preeminent sun god seems to have evolved into the god described by Procopius in the sixth century, when he wrote that the Slavs "in fact regard one god, the creator of lightning, as the master of the world." Even so, the Slavs also worshiped numerous nature deities, such as spirits of trees and water. The oak tree was especially revered for its sacred power.

The Slavs, of course, were not the only sources of gods and cults in early Russia; the Scythians had left their mark, and there was Turkish influence as well. But Russian paganism in general was closely linked to the importance of the sun, which is not surprising in so forbidding a land. The arch over the goddess of Justice, then, recalls many themes of pre-Christian Russia, and gives a distinctive imprint to the card. We are reminded that "justice" is not a simple matter of laws, but rather a delicate system for maintaining the right balance of heaven and earth, humanity and nature. The earliest codification of Russian law (carried out under the same Jaroslav the Wise who created the "rota" system) was called the *Russkaya Pravda, pravda* meaning in Russian both "truth" and "justice."

The Russian Tarot of St. Petersburg image of Justice seems to emphasize one of the several traditional meanings of the card: equilibrium. Justice is often viewed as the opposing card to Wheel of Fortune, contrasting purposeful order with random chance, and is also linked with deliberation, reason, and right. Negative interpretations include vengeance and injustice. In the archetypal cycle of the trumps, Justice may be related to the achievement of a sense of one's place in the order of the universe, from which is derived moral integrity.

The next card, The Hanged Man, has long been considered the most mysterious of the Tarot trumps, though as we shall see, the mystery may be more imagined than real. Nevertheless, it is a powerful card, and though it does make a pair with Death, the card following, it is also—like The Fool—a card which may be seen as standing apart from all the others. The sequence of the trumps can be seen as dividing the major arcana in half, so that all the previous cards lead up to The Hanged Man, and all the subsequent cards lead away from it. It is, in a sense, the "balance point" of the major arcana.

XII The Hanged Man

The Hanged Man is another card which has remained quite stable throughout the history of the Tarot. It began and continued as the image of a male figure, hanging by one foot from a wooden frame, looking pensive but not particularly uncomfortable. Waite changed the U-shaped frame to a cross-shape (a Tau cross, often associated with the Old Testament, rather than the typical "Christian" cross of the New Testament), and placed a radiance around the head of the man. In most decks, the man's free leg is crossed to form a figure 4, which some feel links this card back to The Emperor.

Two questions have generated the mystery of The Hanged Man. First, why is he hanging there? And second, why does his expression seem so detached? The first question may be illuminated, historically at least, by the fact that hanging upside down (though not necessarily by one foot) was the prescribed punishment for treason in Italy at the time when the Tarot trumps seem to have been developed. It was then common practice to shame the families of traitors by publicly displaying paintings of the traitors, hanging in their telltale positions, and that custom seems likely to have been the origin of The Hanged Man. In fact, the early version of the card was called The Traitor. But as with so many other features of the Tarot trumps, when the historical context was removed and the image had to be evaluated from the standpoint of symbolism alone, the resourceful imaginations of the occultists produced some very inventive new interpretations.

The Hanged Man has generally been interpreted according to one of two major themes. One is sacrifice or service, the other is suspension of will, transition, or initiation. The negative aspect is paralysis or limbo. In the archetypal cycle of the trumps, the card represents "the dark night of the soul," a period of doubt or confusion leading to profound life change.

In the Russian Tarot of St. Petersburg, an interesting fairy-tale framework is added to The Hanged Man. The tree from which he hangs is still living (like the tree in Waite's image of The Hanged Man), and it is growing apples so profusely that they tumble from the branches. Atop the tree is the legendary Firebird, a phoenix-like creature of exquisite plumage, with a particular appetite for apples. The Firebird appears in numerous Russian folk tales, along with characters such as Maryushka, the modest maiden whose beautiful needlework is beyond price; the evil sorcerer Kaschei; and the good Ivan Tsarevich. Ivan is the purest and usually the youngest of the tsar's sons, and there are many stories of his faithfulness. In one, he is set to mind his father's apple orchards, which are ravaged nightly by the Firebird. Because he keeps watch faithfully, he is able to pluck a feather from the Firebird's tail, and with it he not only vanquishes Kashei, but obtains his heart's desire.

In Latin, the word *malum* means both "apple" and "evil." This coalescence probably derives from the ancient relationship between the Great Goddess and the apple; as Goddess worship declined (or, in many cases, was suppressed), various aspects of the Goddess came to be considered threatening. The source of both the positive and negative associations of the apple probably originated with the apple itself, for when it is cut transversely, the outline of the core forms the shape of a pentacle. The concealment of the apple's life-giving seeds inside the pentacle associated the fruit with the virgin goddess Kore, who lived inside her mother Demeter, Mother Earth. But by the Middle Ages, the apple—once a symbol of immortality—had become associated with sin and was assumed to be the fruit with which the serpent led Eve astray.

All this notwithstanding, the apple is perhaps the best-loved fruit of Russia. It is widely cultivated and served in every conceivable way. Apples, "fresh and of all kinds, some sweet as pears, others scrunchy as winter," were a special feature of Christmas feasts in Old Russia, according to the *Folk Encyclopedia of 1845*, and apple fairs are still popular events. But the Hanged Man, his hands tied behind his back as Tarot tradition dictates, cannot reach the apples. Is the Firebird plucking at the ropes that bind him to the tree? Will he be released, and take the apples of the Great Goddess? Is the Hanged Man suspended between mortality and immortality?

The Russian Tarot of St. Petersburg brings new mystery to The Hanged Man. Like the preceding card, this one refers not to the well-known Christian Russia, but to the pagan roots of myth and folklore which long continued to shape Russian culture.

XIII

Death

XIII Death

The first thing that is always said about the trump Death is that the card *does not* represent physical death, but rather profound or extreme change. It seems likely, however, that the card did originally refer to physical death. The central figure of the skeleton or grim reaper was the same figure associated elsewhere with literal death. Moreover, one early card shows the words *Son fine* ("I am the end") issuing from the mouth of the skeleton, which seems plain enough in its meaning. The later development of the Death trump consisted principally in adding severed heads and limbs to the picture, and in Waite's deck, extra symbols such as a flag bearing a white rose on a black field. In some images, Death is on foot; in others, he is riding a horse. He is sometimes cloaked, and in the Waite design, he wears armor.

The Death card is one of the few instances in which the Russian Tarot of St. Petersburg departs substantially from both old and new trump designs. Here we see a barren landscape, littered with the apparent debris of battle: a slain body, a quiver of broken arrows, a skull, an abandoned shield, and two swords. A newly severed head and a scythe are also shown, along with a perched crow and other carrion birds circling overhead. This scene of desolation is presided over by a huge, helmeted skull, its chin resting on a similarly large sword. In an eerie bit of detail, skin still covers the lower part of the skull, preserving the mustache and even a cleft in the chin.

In its way, this card is far more mysterious than its companion, The Hanged Man. *Whose is the skull?* Were it not for the mustache, we would probably dismiss the looming skull as a generic symbol, its size reminding us—as the Death card has historically done—that death overcomes all. But that personal detail suggests an identity. The clues are slight, but, accumulated, they point to perhaps the best (and least) known of all Russian historical figures, Ivan IV— better known as Ivan the Terrible. The wax figure of Ivan in the Kremlin wears a helmet similar to the one on our skull; Ivan wore the same sort of droopy mustache, and in an icon-portrait, he was shown with reddish hair, much the color of the mustache here.

Furthermore, Ivan, who is certainly among the most important of Russian monarchs, is not shown elsewhere in the trumps, though we have already encountered the great princes St. Vladimir and Ivan III, as well as Peter the Great.

The word which we translate as "terrible" means, in Russian, something more like "awesome." Although Ivan IV was notorious for his unpredictable temper and for his fits of cruelty, he was in reality not more extreme in his behavior than many other despots of his own and earlier times. And on the other side of the coin, he was devoutly religious, reputedly suffering torments of guilt over his temperamental acts (one of which was the accidental murder of his own son). It was, in fact, Ivan IV who carried the identity of church and state to its completion, and he conceived of himself as the head of a monolithic religious civilization, rather than as a military or political leader.

Ivan IV presided, often personally, over much death during his half-century reign, and that connection alone might make him an appropriate figure for the Death card. Death, in the Russian Tarot of St. Petersburg, is given the same sort of relentless grimness which characterized the card in early decks, when its symbolism was closely connected with the Black Death that swept through Europe in the fourteenth century, decimating the population. Here, the towering skull, with its lingering mustache, seems to remind us of the vanity of power and the inevitability of death.

Traditional meanings of the Death card, however, focus not on these sobering messages, but rather on profound change, transformation, passage, and the cycle of destruction and renewal. From a negative standpoint, the card may signify stagnation or destructive change. In the archetypal cycle of the trumps, the Death card symbolizes the "death" of the ego, which results in the rebirth of the spirit.

It may be worthwhile to consider that transformation, though it may sound picturesque, is not necessarily a less overwhelming idea than literal death. The very seriousness of the Russian Tarot of St. Petersburg image reminds us that profound change is profoundly difficult.

The next two cards form an almost perfect pair, representing two poles of behavior: Temperance (moderation) and The Devil (excess). They are the first of four pairs which turn our attention away from the local and temporal toward the cosmic and eternal.

XIV

Temperance

XIV Temperance

Temperance is another card which has seen little change. The basic card image is a figure pouring liquid from one vessel into another. In the earliest cards, the figure was a woman, but in the Marseilles-type decks, it became an angel. Then, in Waite's deck and in many subsequent esoteric designs, a pool or stream was added, and the angel was depicted dipping the toes of one foot in the water.

The Russian Tarot of St. Petersburg follows tradition, but adds a subtle reference which broadens and strengthens the meaning of the card. In other decks, the angel is generic, but in the Russian Tarot of St. Petersburg, the angel is given a specific identity: it is Raphael, the archangel who was often identified in Renaissance art by the straps crossed over its chest. The straps are part of a "wallet" or knapsack worn by Raphael in the persona of "guardian spirit," protector of pilgrims and other travelers. (This reputation came from the Book of Tobit, in which a stranger accompanied the youth Tobias on a journey, and at the end, revealed itself as the angel Raphael.) However, equal importance has always been accorded to Raphael's connection with healing, symbolized in the name: *Rapha,* the Hebrew word for "healer," attached to *-el* (the typical suffix of angelic names), meaning "shining one."

Traditionally, Temperance has been among both the easiest and the most difficult cards to interpret. The basic idea is a simple one; the action of pouring from one vessel to another may represent either dilution (for example, cutting wine with water) or conservation (spilling nothing). These interpretations connect up with the concept of temperance as moderation. Other suggested meanings of the card are combination, purification, patience, and rhythm on the positive side; and on the negative, the lack of these characteristics. Yet no commentator has been really satisfied with these explanations of the card image, which seems somehow weaker and less focused than the other trumps.

The choice of Raphael as the Angel of Temperance is of special interest, then, because it offers a new but very appropriate connection for the card. The inspiration for this may have come from the angel's toes in the water, for one of the most important attributes of Raphael is a connection with the Pool of Bethesda. It was said (John 5:1-15) that an angel (traditionally thought to be Raphael, but unnamed in the Bible) would periodically stir the waters of this healing pool, and that the first person to enter it afterwards would be healed. The presence of Raphael in the Temperance image of the Russian Tarot of St. Petersburg seems to suggest a healing aspect to the card, bringing connotations of physical, as well as spiritual, health derived from the qualities of moderation, purification, patience, and so on.

This interpretation also fits very well into the archetypal cycle of the trumps. Remember that the last two cards, The Hanged Man and Death, have taken us through, first, a spiritual crisis (the "dark night of the soul"), and then a profound change, symbolized by the death of the ego. Temperance, then, offers a period of healing and a return to balance. This period of balance would prove to be especially important, coming as it does before the temptations and tribulations symbolized in the next two trumps, The Devil and The Falling Tower.

The presence of the angel Raphael may have one other meaning in the Russian Tarot of St. Petersburg. The Italian Renaissance painter named Raphael was a great artistic inspiration for Russian romanticism in the nineteenth century. The Russian artistic tradition had always elevated the Madonna above all other subjects, and when Raphael's Madonnas were "discovered" by Russians, the paintings were widely considered to be perfect expressions of beauty. Most revered was the Sistine Madonna. Many Russian artists and intellectuals made pilgrimages to see the painting in Dresden, and the poet Zhukovsky, a frequent visitor, wrote of it:

> *Ah, not in our world dwells*
> *The Genius of pure beauty:*
> *Only for a time it visits us*
> *From the heights of heaven.*

Raphael, as both angel and inspired painter, reminds us that temperance—in the form of distillation, combination, and creation—is at the heart of beauty. That is perhaps the reason why Crowley, in his Thoth deck, renamed the Temperance card "Art."

XV The Devil

The Devil is missing from the very earliest decks. Later, in both the Marseilles and the Waite decks, he is shown standing on a pedestal with two yoked demons. Although the Devil himself is variously represented in the Tarot tradition (frequently as part-animal, part human, sometimes as a hermaphrodite, and usually with horns), the two other figures on the cards are typically demonic. In a few decks, however, they are human beings threatened or trampled by the Devil.

The Russian Tarot of St. Petersburg follows the traditional configuration, but departs from convention by making the two subservient figures humans rather than demons. In Waite's design the two figures are recognizably a man and a woman, nude, but they have horns and tails; in the Russian Tarot of St. Petersburg they are a human couple in traditional Russian dress. The purpose of this symbolism becomes abundantly clear as soon as one recognizes the identity of the "Devil": Joseph Stalin.

This is the only overt reference to recent Russian history in the Russian Tarot of St. Petersburg, which makes the card particularly effective. The image operates on two levels: on the first level, the choice of Stalin uses historical reference to bring the concept of evil into the realm of human behavior. On the second level, the portrayal of Stalin—tattooed, bat-winged, horned and wearing the pentacle—creates a detailed allusion to the nature of evil itself. When all the parts of the picture are put together, the result is a symbolic summary of Stalin and his rule, a period in which millions of Russians died in purges or starved in planned famines.

Those who were not killed outright by the Stalinist regime became virtual slaves of the state; as suggested in the image of The Devil, Stalin held the people in chains. The huge Communist apparatus towered over the individual, just as the Devil dwarfs the man and woman beneath him. The KGB, Stalin's secret police, spied on everyone in the country, just as the tattooed eyes on the Devil's chest ceaselessly watch. In the end, Stalinism sucked the lifeblood from Russia in the same way a vampire might drain his victim, so it is fitting that the Devil Stalin bears the symbolic bat-

like wings. (Vampires have a long history in the folklore of Russia and Eastern Europe.) It's appropriate, also, that Stalin, the so-called "strong man" of Communist Russia, is shown here as very heavily muscled and bristling with coarse hair.

The tattoos add to the general appearance of coarseness, but they also have specific meanings. It is difficult to read them precisely, but I believe that on the right hand are Stalin's initials (in the Cyrillic alphabet) and on the left arm is the number "34," presumably referring to the year 1934, when Stalin began the great purge which wiped out virtually everyone in Russian political and intellectual life who did not agree with him. A Russian interpreter speculates that the lettering on the right arm signifies the expression "For Homeland," and on the left arm, "For Party."

There is a snake-entwined sword on Stalin's right arm, and on his left, a book (possibly representing the *Communist Manifesto* or Marx's *Das Kapital*). The eyes on his chest, as already suggested, seem to symbolize the watchfulness of the Stalinist state—but perhaps something more as well. If the eyes, as ancient wisdom has it, are the windows of the soul, then here, the soul (or consciousness) has become embedded in the flesh.

This interpretation fits the traditional meaning of The Devil, which is domination of the material, base instincts, lower consciousness, lust, and excess in general. In the sense that this card can be thought of as having both positive and negative aspects, the positive connotations are animal or instinctual nature in its better form, while the negative meaning can be seen as evil in the most profound sense. In the archetypal cycle of the trumps, The Devil represents what Jung called "the shadow," the unconscious region of unexplored impulses and ideas. The Russian Tarot of St. Petersburg version of The Devil certainly focuses attention on the card's most unattractive aspects, but it still preserves the sense of human strength and goodness in the gesture of the man and woman reaching out their hands to each other.

The Devil forms a similar, or sympathetic, pair with the next card, the Falling Tower; both deal with difficult and painful aspects of reality, and in the Russian Tarot of St. Petersburg, both cards use metaphors from the twentieth-century upheaval of Russia. But the Falling Tower also looks forward to its complementary pairing with the Star. After the terrors of captivity and the sterility of materialism depicted in the Devil, and the constant threat of disruption and disaster revealed in the Falling Tower, the Star—a card of hope and aspiration—promises new beginnings.

XVI The Falling Tower

The sixteenth trump has been variously called "The House of God," "The Falling Tower," "The Lightning-Struck Tower," and simply, "The Tower." It has long been considered as mysterious as The Hanged Man, but whereas we now know the fairly simple origin of the Hanged Man image, we still have no idea what The Tower may initially have been meant to represent. Among the many suggested possibilities are the Tower of Babel, the destruction of Sodom and Gomorrah, the Second Coming, and the Castle of the Grail King. Traditionally, The Tower image has contained a brick or stone edifice, its top blown open by a lightning bolt; two figures tumbling from the tower; and large circular drops falling from the sky.

Although there are many different ideas about the original meaning of The Tower, they all seem to lend themselves to an obvious central theme: sudden disaster, destruction, ruin. This card is also interpreted as a shock or disruption of any kind, and in the opposite aspect, as a cleansing or renewal. In the archetypal cycle of the trumps, The Tower is associated with the breakdown of psychic structures and defenses (sometimes through experiences of mystic insight or consciousness expansion; sometimes through traumatic destabilization of the personality).

The Russian Tarot of St. Petersburg, as we have come to expect, adds another level of meaning to The Tower. This card, like the previous one, refers to recent events, though less obviously. Here the Tower is clearly a Russian bell tower, and it appears not to have been struck by lightning at all, but to have exploded from within. The unexplained blobs falling from the sky in other card designs have been replaced with objects, apparently flung from the tower. The objects—all symbols of traditional Russian culture, religion, and government—include the Imperial crown, the Russian Orthodox cross, the chalice and censor used in religious rites, and a shower of gold coins. Another of the objects is a *kvosh,* the distinctive Russian drinking vessel which looks rather like a gravy boat.

It seems clear that the Russian Tarot of St. Petersburg Tower refers to the Bolshevik Revolution of 1917, which brought about

the destruction of the Imperial regime and of the Orthodox Church. In fact, all religion was eventually banned under Communist rule, a fact we are reminded of by the inclusion of a Roman cross among the falling objects in The Tower. The two figures, of course, represent the destruction of the traditional Russian way of life.

The Russian Tarot of St. Petersburg Devil, as we have seen, examines one of the dreadful consequences of Communist rule in Russia, suggesting the violence and oppression of Stalin's rule. The Falling Tower reminds us of another consequence: the dehumanization of Russian life. The culture of Old Russia—as depicted throughout the deck—was filled with color, symbolism, and ceremony; although great inequity and unfairness existed, at the same time, there was for centuries a sense of meaningfulness and continuity. Unfortunately, the Bolshevik Revolution did not really end injustice, but to a great extent it *did* end the richness of Russian culture. For decades, everything which most Russians had loved and believed in was ruthlessly suppressed, and the sense of family and community (called *sobornost)* which had sustained the Russian people through so much tribulation was entirely subverted.

It is significant that the type of building chosen for The Falling Tower is a bell tower. Nowhere else on earth were bells so beloved as in Old Russia, where, from the tenth century on, a whole language of bells told of disasters and holidays, funerals and festivals. By the sixteenth century, bells were so much a part of Russian religious life that they were considered sacred instruments of worship, and were cast in every size and every metal, from tiny silver bells to the world's largest bell (twenty-six feet tall and sixty-six feet around). The bell tower, a symbol of beauty and permanence, is destroyed in the Falling Tower, reminding us that everything in life is more fragile than we realize. The essential message of this card is, perhaps, the inevitability—and the poignancy—of loss.

XVII The Star

The Star was originally so called (presumably) because its central figure, a robed woman, held a star in her hand. But the imagery of this card was changed significantly in the Marseilles-type deck, where the central figure became a nude woman, kneeling by a stream and pouring liquid from two vessels. The later imagery is obviously connected with that of the Temperance card: both figures pour liquid from two vessels; both are by the water (in Waite-type decks, both have one foot on land, one in the water); and both are seen beneath star-filled skies. But it is unclear why they should have taken on this similarity. Perhaps the simplest explanation is based on their order in the sequence of the trumps, for these two gentle, ethereal cards flank the two most disturbing images in the deck, The Devil and The Falling Tower.

The figure in The Star is a mortal woman, not an angel, and instead of conserving liquid by pouring back and forth between the two vessels, she pours the liquid *out*; with one hand she pours into the water, with the other onto the land. This symbolism has been interpreted as representing the order and continuity of being (in the symbolic circular flow of water through heaven and earth), and thus has been connected with The Star's traditional meaning of hope. Other positive interpretations of The Star include faith, immortality, and inner light, while negative suggestions are dreaminess, disappointment, and pessimism. In the archetypal cycle of the trumps, The Star represents the new vision of reality which comes out of the breakdown associated with The Tower.

As discussed in the general remarks on the major arcana, the Russian Tarot of St. Petersburg changes certain aspects of The Star's symbolism, and adds specific references to Russian history and culture. The bird that traditionally represents the soul in this Tarot image has been replaced by a butterfly, associated with resurrection. The empty costume on the bank suggests the ephemeral nature of the body, from which the resurrected soul has been released. The woman, wearing traditional Russian costume, represents the soul clothed, or embodied—reinforcing the symbolism of continuity

XVII

The Star

and the "cycling" of the soul through many stages, just as water is cycled through many states of being in its journey from rain to flowing stream and back to rain again.

In the background of The Star, tents resembling those used by Napoleon's armies offer a reminder of the Russian people's triumph over a seemingly hopeless situation. The singleness of purpose and the magnificent courage of the Russian people in the face of Napoleon's vastly superior forces greatly impressed the rest of Europe. (Napoleon himself later wrote that the unyielding tactics of the Russians had "no precedent in the history of civilization." "What savage determination!" he continued. "What a people! What a people!") The effect on the Russians themselves was hardly less dramatic, for it reinforced their belief in both the sacredness of suffering and the special providence which God reserved for the Russian people.

These aspects of Russian belief may offer a more specific understanding of The Star. The interpretation of this card has become rather vague today, because we tend now to think of hope as a kind of wishfulness, rather than as faith or belief, which were the older—and more profound—meanings of the term. The Russian Tarot of St. Petersburg seems to suggest, through its imagery and allusion, that the hopefulness symbolized in The Star is not merely a kind of optimism or aspiration, as it is so often supposed, but in fact the *certainty of renewal,* whether through salvation and resurrection, or through rebirth. The emphasis of the card on the relationship between body and soul also reinforces the old association between stars and souls, which has expressed itself in many cultures as a belief that falling stars represent the descent of new souls to be born on earth, and that departing souls are carried by angelic beings to their new lives as shining stars in the heavens.

Interesting note: By tradition, there are seven small stars and one large star on this card. The large star is thought by some to be Sirius, the brightest star seen from Earth, and by others to symbolize the Star of Bethlehem.

The next two cards, The Moon and The Sun, are an obvious pair: night and day, unconscious and conscious, intuition and reason, feminine and masculine. Note, however, that this pair is also part of a trio (including The Star) of references to heavenly bodies. This celestial trio relates to the final trump, The World, by means of Judgment, representing divine oversight of human affairs. Thus, these last five cards form their own group, dealing with the large-scale structures of reality.

The images of the sun and the moon in the two cards bearing their names are done in a style which was used in the ornately embroidered altar cloths of Old Russia, as well as in the lacquerware designs of Palekh and—especially—Kholuy.

XVIII The Moon

In The Moon, more than in any other single card, the inventiveness of the Russian Tarot of St. Petersburg is revealed. The image combines aspects of the whole Tarot tradition with entirely new elements that greatly enliven this enigmatic trump.

The earliest Moon cards were considerably different from the one we have come to know. In the Visconti-type decks, the card was quite simple, showing only a girl holding a crescent moon. In another fifteenth-century deck, and in some later ones, The Moon depicted two scholars or astronomers with scientific instruments, apparently observing the moon. But Marseilles-type decks show the familiar stone towers, baying dogs, and crawling lobster (sometimes a crab or crayfish). The original intent behind this image is unknown, but the effect is quite clearly one of mystery, darkness, and depth, suggestive of primordial, instinctual life. Waite-type decks use the same image, which almost certainly replaced its predecessors because it expresses the "strangeness" commonly associated with the moon and its influence.

One of the most interesting things about the Russian Tarot of St. Petersburg Moon is that it uses the well-known imagery of towers, dog, and lobster, but also refers back to the earlier card design by placing a telescope on the roof of one of the towers. The telescope, of course, was unknown at the beginning of the Tarot tradition, and highly controversial for many years after its invention early in the seventeenth century. The telescope proved the undoing of the Catholic Church's effort to suppress the idea that the Earth revolved around the Sun, so this instrument of observation became a symbol of the triumph of science over religion. But in the Russian Tarot of St. Petersburg image, this triumph is overturned, for the telescope (which is quite a large one when seen in proportion to the size of the tower) is in the *background* of the picture, while the foreground depicts a richly mythic world.

Perhaps this juxtaposition is a reference to the fact that Old Russia lagged far behind the rest of Europe in its embrace of science. Although Peter the Great enthusiastically introduced his country to

European ideas about science and education, the vast majority of Russians continued to believe in an imaginative universe which combined folklore and Orthodox Christianity, rejecting—if they had heard of them at all—scientific ideas about the Earth and its place in the cosmos. Scientists, and indeed, all "intellectuals," were regarded with deep suspicion by the people. It was not until well after the Communist revolution that science and technology became high priorities in Russia, and then the emphasis was on practical (and tactical) advantage rather than on inquiry for its own sake.

It's amusing to note that in the Russian Tarot of St. Petersburg card, the telescope and the Moon appear to be glaring at one another, while down below, a character from Greek mythology glides along the river. The boatman is Charon, the ferryman who took the souls of the dead across the river Styx. But the river in the picture appears to be the Volga; its shore, like the banks of the Volga, is lined with fir trees, and the carved wooden boat is reminiscent of of the famous Volga riverboats. An English traveler in the 1850's wrote of these craft, "Native barks glided calmly past us, strange-looking things…some were in the form of a serpent, others in that of a fish, a griffin, or some other fabulous creature."

Traditionally, The Moon card has represented the soul, the unconscious, the intuition, dreams, emotions, and instinctual life. Negative connotations include deception, delusion, and darkness. In the archetypal cycle of the trumps, the Moon symbolizes the exploration of psychic depths. But beyond these familiar associations, the Russian Tarot of St. Petersburg offers a reminder that we all, in part, still live in a mythic world. The human imagination has an innate inclination to endow reality with meaning, and then to create stories, songs, and images which express that meaning. Although the *details* of mythologies are different in different cultures, the *patterns* are to a great extent the same—and that is why Charon, in his chiton, looks right at home on the river Volga.

XIX The Sun

Traditionally, The Sun is a card of joy and triumph, representing the victory of light over darkness. It's associated with earthly happiness, but also with enlightenment and spiritual power, and it is often interpreted as intelligence (in distinction from intuition, as symbolized by The Moon). It is such a positive card, brimming with energy and abundance, that there are few negative aspects, but it can indicate arrogance or over-rationalization. In the archetypal cycle of the trumps, The Sun represents the emergence of the positive ego, now enriched by its journey into the psychic depths represented in the Moon.

The earliest images of The Sun, like The Star and The Moon, were little more than symbolic representations of the astronomical body; in the Marseilles-type decks, the Sun was pictured shining on two children. The Waite deck kept one of the children, now astride a horse, and added a riot of sunflowers. This basic Waite image is used in the Russian Tarot of St. Petersburg, but the garden wall typically shown in Waite-type cards is replaced by the wall of a fortified city. The child shown now carries a red ("beautiful") banner, and the sunflowers are as tall as trees, towering over horse and rider.

The Sun is the trump perhaps most closely connected with the symbolic traditions of Russia. As the preeminent expert on Russian culture, James Billington, writes, "If the high culture of Russia from the early tenth to the early twentieth century was largely dedicated to the Christian God and controlled by a deified Christian prince, the pre-Christian sun god stands behind both of these figures;" Sun worship was intrinsic to the Scythian, Persian, and Slavic backgrounds of Russian culture, and its remnants were found throughout Russian folk life. The symbolism of the sun was an integral part of many folk designs, and the changing of the seasons, especially the summer and winter solstices, was the most important aspect of the folk rituals which persisted in the Russian countryside almost until modern times.

Given this background, it is not surprising that a kind of pagan energy infuses the Russian Tarot of St. Petersburg's Sun. The smiling golden sun, closely resembling the symbolic suns depicted in icons and altar embroideries, beams dramatically in a black sky, while the horse prances in a blooming meadow. The color and lushness of early summer dominate The Sun, and provide a contrast to the wintry look of The Moon. But the most striking objects in the picture are the sunflowers.

The hardy sunflower, which grows as tall as ten feet, thrives on the prairie and in waste places, springing up unbidden where no one might have troubled to plant a flower. In Russia and elsewhere, the sunflower, so called because it turns to follow the source of light, is a symbol of resilience and steadfastness. A Russian Orthodox metropolitan used the analogy of the sunflower when he spoke to the Siberian pioneers of the seventeenth century, summing up both the religious emphasis of Russian culture, and the characteristic Russian patience with hardship and suffering. "Even in darkest days, the sunflower completes its circular course, following the sun by unchangeable love and natural inclination… May our love to our sun, the will of God, be strong enough to draw us inseparably to it in days of misfortune and sorrow, even as the sunflower in dark days continues without faltering."

In the Rider-Waite design for The Sun, the sunflowers grow profusely behind a wall, offering a cheerful background for the happy child at the center of the picture. In the Russian Tarot of St. Petersburg's Sun, however, the sunflowers, with their peculiarly Russian message, nearly dominate the card. In this way, we are reminded that joy and abundance are seldom unshadowed, and that they are rarely constant.

XX

Judgment

XX Judgment

Judgment is among those trumps which have changed very little in the various versions of the Tarot. From the earliest images, Judgment has been represented by one or more angels blowing trumpets, while below them, the dead rise from their graves. The obvious reference is to Judgment Day as depicted in the Bible, the time following the end of the world as we know it when all souls will be judged and either condemned to Hell or raised to Heaven.

Traditionally, however, the interpretation of this card is concerned less with the theological "endtime," than with personal resolution and renewal. Judgment is often associated with transition from one state of being to another, and with the conclusion or closure of events. All of these meanings are potentially either positive or negative, depending on the nature of the passages they are concerned with. In the archetypal cycle of the trumps, Judgment represents the recognition of the self, that is, the dawning realization of who one really is.

The Russian Tarot of St. Petersburg follows the conventional design of the Judgment card very closely, but (as usual) with a few added touches. The angel is depicted in the familiar manner of the Russian icon, with stylized curls, tiara and halo, flowing cape and folded wings. The banner fluttering from the angel's trumpet, like the one in the Waite deck, is adorned with a Greek cross, symbol of the church victorious. But an interesting Russian sidelight of this image is that the Greek cross, rarely used by the Orthodox Church, was emblazoned on the banners of the militant Streltsy, traditional challengers of the Czar's power. The crosses on the gravestones below are in the typical Russian style. But in addition to the crosses, atop one of these markers is a small stone angel, which appears on close examination to look very like the real angel above; this interesting touch suggests the ways in which our earthly symbols participate in some higher level of meaning. The uniformly gray headstones give the impression that our worldly lives are, in a similar way, mere colorless copies of the spirit life of that awaits us.

There are two especially interesting features contained in the Judgment card. The first and most immediately noticeable is the fact that vines seem to be growing on the man, woman, and child arisen from their coffins. On one level, this image symbolizes the decay of the body in the grave; on another, it reminds us that our bodies are intimately interconnected with the organic life of the planet. Vines, because they insinuate themselves wherever there is opportunity, have long been associated with themes of fecundity and tenacity, and they are closely related in many cultures with worship of the mother goddess. Russian folklore is filled with the symbolism of "mother earth," and with nature spirits such as the Vili and the Rusalka who have the power to affect the lives and destinies of human beings.

The other striking feature of the card is the crescent upon which the angel stands. It is a deep crescent, suggesting that it is part of an egg-shape rather than a circle, and its translucent blueness immediately attracts the eye. But most unusual is the fact that the woman in the picture is actually touching—or perhaps even holding—the crescent. Once we see that, the scale of the whole picture is changed; the angel no longer seems to be a vision in the sky, but rather a real and intimate part of the family scene below. Here again, as with the little stone angel, there seems to be a reminder that we here below are more closely connected with what exists above than we characteristically realize.

This interweaving of the angelic, the human, and the earthly lends an extra dimension of meaning to the Judgment card. It suggests that transformation, whether viewed as redemption or as renewal, is not a single, instantaneous event. Rather, it is a continuous process of which we are only intermittently aware.

An interesting note regarding the angel of Judgment Day: Although the trumpet is popularly associated with the angel Gabriel, and Gabriel is generally thought of as the angel who will announce the final judgment, there is no Biblical evidence for this notion. The idea of Gabriel—one of only four archangels actually named in the Bible—as "annunciator" probably developed from the fact that Gabriel brought Mary the news that she would give birth to Jesus. Angelologists, however, believe the angel of Judgment day is in fact Remael, the "shining one of God."

XXI The World

Perhaps fittingly, the final trump has possibly the most confusing history of all the cards. Early hand-painted cards depict The World as a scene from familiar medieval life. In one early example, two putti hold aloft a sphere containing a miniature village; while in another, a regal woman appears above a wonderfully detailed picture encompassing rivers, castles, knights, and even a lighthouse. In these cards, the "world" was clearly not the planet (then unknown) or some abstract theological concept of creation, but rather the way of living familiar to the people of the time. An alternate title for those first cards might have been simply "Life."

In the early *printed* cards, however, a different convention appeared, seeming to represent Christ in a mandorla (the pointed oval shape formed when portions of two circles are overlapped). He is surrounded by the symbolic representations of the four Evangelists taken from the Book of Revelations: Matthew as the man, Mark as the lion, Luke as the bull, and John as the eagle. The Christ figure was shown in these cards wearing a cape and holding a stick in his hand, just as he was described in Matthew when the soldiers mocked him before the crucifixion. However, in subsequent deck designs, the figure of Christ seemed to evolve first into an androgynous figure and then into a woman, encircled by an oval wreath recalling the mandorla. Like the earlier Christ, the woman wears a cape and holds one or two batons, but she is standing on one foot, and as the figure becomes more carefully drawn in later decks, she seems to be dancing. The Evangelists were still shown in the corners of the card, but their presence became somewhat mysterious when the central figure was no longer Christ.

There is no clear reason why the evolution from Christ at the crucifixion to dancing woman (pagan goddess?) took place. However, the later female figure fit into esoteric interpretations of the card, and so she remained the central image in Waite's deck and the others derived from it. Typically, The World has been interpreted as completion, attainment, and perfection; it may also be seen as harmony, unity, or wholeness. Because everything is fulfilled in the World, the

positive and negative aspects cannot be separated: all is one. In the archetypal cycle of the trumps, The World represents the synthesis of the personality, in which all elements are integrated into the self. Interestingly, this sense of The World card is naturally captured in the Russian word for "world"—which is the same as the word for "peace."

The Russian Tarot of St. Petersburg's World follows the traditional image of the Waite-type World in most respects, but with a few of the Russian themes which have been carried throughout the deck. The dancing woman wears the familiar kokoshnik headdress, and her drapery is of a patterned fabric like those used so often in Russian folk dress. In an interesting convergence, the wreath which traditionally encircles the dancer on The World is here replaced by the elliptical frame used for all the cards in the deck, reminiscent of the wrought metal frames used on icons, or the little oval doors of Fabergé Easter eggs, opening to reveal a whole miniature world inside.

The most interesting and distinctive aspect of The World card, however, is its depiction of the "world" as the planet Earth. This image is the Earth as seen from space, complete with continents, oceans, and swirling clouds—an image completely unknown to us until the first orbital satellite, Sputnik, was launched by the Soviet Union in 1958. The Russians, for so long a country that lagged far behind in the scientific revolution, became in the twentieth century highly competitive in the race for greater power through science. Communist materialism created a new Russian universe, stripped of the old religious mystery, and revealed the earth as "nothing more" than a ball of matter. But in the Russian Tarot of St. Petersburg card, the symbols of the evangelists float in space around the planet, reminding us that the region beyond the sky has turned out not to be the location of Heaven after all.

Indeed, with all our knowledge of matter, the true mystery only deepens. We know more about the planet, the atom, and space and time than ever before. But as our knowledge increases, so does our realization of how much we have yet to learn. At the very same time that the Communist vision of life has been collapsing, the "unscientific" values of imagination, beauty, and belief that sustained Old Russia have been reasserting themselves around the world. But so too have fear, irrationality, violence, and all the burdens of history returned to haunt us in Eastern Europe, while famine and pestilence, the horrors promised in Revelations, seem almost to circle the globe.

Perhaps the dancing woman of the Tarot World, with her entourage of Evangelists and her curiously evolved symbolism, bespeaks the strangeness, wonderful and terrible, that surrounds our planet at this moment in its long history. Her dance may be the ineffable expression of grace, hovering just beyond our reach but present in every place we look.

THE MINOR ARCANA

The twenty-two trumps of the major arcana have always been considered more powerful, more mystical, more archetypal than the fifty-six minor arcana cards. As already mentioned, many believe that the trumps were constituted separately, perhaps by a religious sect or secret society, and later joined with the four-suited portion of the deck for purposes of gaming. Since no one knows where either set of cards came from, there is no way to tell whether or when the two were brought together. Nor do we know exactly when or why they were *un*joined, but whatever happened, the suited deck came down to the modern day in a slightly altered form which we call "playing cards." The suit signs were changed (Cups became Hearts; Swords, Spades; Coins, Diamonds; Batons or Rods, Clubs) and the fourth court card, The Page, was dropped from the deck. Only The Fool remained from the trumps, in the form of the Joker.

Full Tarot decks of seventy-eight cards have been in continuous use since they appeared in the fifteenth century, but they have waxed and waned in popularity. Interestingly enough, playing card decks, which have no images except for the court figures, have been used for divination at least as much and probably more than Tarot decks, demonstrating that the numbers and suits alone can give a great deal of information when properly interpreted. In fact, there were no images at all on the Tarot minor arcana cards until the creation of Arthur Edward Waite's deck in the early twentieth century. (One early deck, the fifteenth-century Sola-Busca, included pictures on the pip cards, but no other card makers followed this lead, presumably because of the huge increase in labor required to illustrate all the cards.)

Although Waite created a scene for each of the pip cards, he never explained the meanings of the scenes, or how the scenes were linked to the number and suit assignments of the cards. In the absence of such explanations, interpreters have taken the traditional divinatory meanings of the cards and analyzed the pictures as if they were illustrations of those meanings. Generally, the pictures on the pip cards can be thought of as memory aids; the people, objects and events depicted in the scenes can be used to form symbolic associations. These associations will help the reader not only to remember specific divinatory meanings of the cards, but also to form an impression of the real-life people, objects and events which may be associated with the cards in the reading.

Since Waite set the pattern for pip illustrations, there are no differing traditions for these images. Most twentieth-century decks either follow the Waite designs or leave the number cards unillustrated. A few modern decks use illustrations which are completely different from Waite's, but since each of these decks is unique in its approach, there's really no pattern or theme for the pips other than that established by Waite. The Russian Tarot of St. Petersburg pips follow Waite exactly, but as with the major arcana illustrations, these pictures contain some added elements which link them with Russian history and culture.

Even though illustrated pips can be a significant help in working with the Tarot cards, the most important aspect of utilizing the minor arcana is understanding the meaning structures represented by the suits and the numbers. The minor arcana is divided into four suits, which correspond with the four elements (earth, air, fire, and water). This basic correspondence provides the pattern for a whole system of relationships built on division into four parts. The twelve signs of the zodiac, for example, are divided into four groups that correspond with the four elements, and so the Tarot suits can also be related to astrological signs through this connection. The suit of Cups relates to the element of water and so also to the signs of Cancer, Scorpio, and Pisces.

Many cultures utilize this "quaternary" pattern in their belief systems. Native Americans, for example, organize sacred reality according to the four directions, and Tibetan Buddhism describes the gateways to mind practice as the Four Ordinary Foundations. The universality of these quaternaries suggests that all the different structures created in this way can be seen as aspects of a fundamental or primary structure which underlies our experience of the phenomenal world. Almost throughout the history of magical practice, these correspondences have been considered very important. Medieval alchemists, Renaissance magi, and secret societies such as the Rosicrucians and the Hermetic Order of the Golden Dawn all worked with the correspondences and developed them in great detail. In our own time, as we discover new ideas and information, the quaternary structure has continued to grow. Contemporary physics, for example, recognizes four basic "forces" (the electromagnetic force, the strong nuclear force, the weak nuclear force, and the force of gravity), and Jungian psychology tells us there are four basic personality functions (feeling, thinking, intuiting, and sensing).

After being divided into four, each segment of the minor arcana is then divided into two parts, the court cards and the pips. The court cards, which represent persons by gender, rank, and type, again divide into four positions (King, Queen, Knight, and Page). The pips, which represent what are called "mundane" events, those which take place in real time on the physical plane, divide into ten positions, Ace (or one) through Ten. Each of these numbers has its own metaphysical significance. The number One, for example, is the number of both beginning and wholeness; Four the number of stability; Ten the number of completion and renewal.

To understand each card, then, it is necessary to understand the nature of its suit and of its number or personality, so first we will look at these general properties of the minor arcana, and see the special way each has been developed in the Russian Tarot of St. Petersburg.

The Suits and their Tokens

The four suits of the minor arcana use four objects to symbolize their individual natures. Each object serves as a token of its suit, and is displayed on every card in the suit. The four objects are a cup, a sword, a coin (occasionally, just a round disk), and a "stick" of some kind, variously shown as a rod, club, wand, or baton. Taken together, the four suit tokens represent aspects and organizations of human life. In late Medieval Europe, where the Tarot was given the form we are now familiar with, society was organized into a hierarchical structure which is summarized in the four suits: the warrior/noble class is represented by Swords;, the priestly class by Cups, the merchant class by Coins, and the peasant class by Rods or Clubs. From a modern point of view, the four suits can be seen as describing the four levels of psychological life: the Freudian super-ego or conscience (Swords); conscious, material life (Coins); the personal unconscious or emotional/intuitive level (Cups); and the Jungian collective unconscious or archetypal realm (Rods or Clubs).

SWORDS

The suit of Swords is connected with thought, judgment, and communication. Its element is air, the element of mental life. Although the sword is commonly perceived as a fighting tool, and many of the Waite designs for the Sword cards seem to carry out this theme, the Tarot sword actually represents any kind of cutting instrument. Its basic symbolism is that of "cutting through" or "cutting away." In this sense, the sword is connected with logic and rational powers. To remember the basic nature of Swords, think of the sword cutting and slashing through the air, its native element. The astrological complements of the Swords suit are Gemini, Libra, and Aquarius, the air signs.

Swords are also found widely in myths, especially in stories of heroes. The young Arthur must retrieve the magical sword Excalibur in order to gain his future as king; Siegfried must reforge the broken sword Balmunga before he can slay the dragon, discover the ring, and win Brunhilde. The sword is often a symbol of strength and triumph, but it is also associated with physical death or dismemberment, and so may symbolize detachment from the body. Whereas Cups represent the watery soul, or (in Greek) *psyche*, Swords represent the airy spirit, or *pneuma* (the Greek word for both "spirit" and "breath"). In mythic terms, the process of "soul-making" is often described as a journey into the depths (as when Orpheus descended into the underworld in search of Eurydice) while the process of "spirit-making" usually shows the protagonist moving upward and outward, exploring frontiers, founding cities, and vanquishing enemies.

The symbolism of the sword is so potent that even though the sword has long since become obsolete as a weapon of real combat, it continues its role as a ceremonial weapon even today; our own Marines still wear a sword as part of their dress uniform. Fencing is a favored sport of Jean-Luc Picard (captain of the Enterprise in *Star Trek: The Next Generation*), perhaps because this artistic form of sword-play denotes grace, precision, and control.

Historically, there are two large categories of swords: the long swords and the short swords. Long swords are divided into four families, the most basic and widely used of these families being the "Bastard" style, with two edges and a point. The Bastard is a broadsword, which means that it has a fairly wide and almost rectangular blade, as opposed to its more romantic cousin from the Rapier family, which features a thin, tapering blade. Also called a "Hand and a Half," the Bastard was an early improvement—lighter and more maneuverable—on the two-handed "great sword" which had been in wide use through the fifteenth century. When the European Bastard was introduced, around 1500, it was very simple in form, with a hilt composed of a knobbed pommel, a plain grip, and straight quillons (the cross-pieces at the base of the hilt). Within a few years, however, the hilt began to be made more complex, with curved guards, swirled pommels, and so on.

The type of sword used as a token for the Swords suit in the Russian Tarot of St. Petersburg is a Bastard of the plainest and earliest sort. Its hilt is so short that the sword would actually be quite difficult to fight with effectively, and the jewels which adorn the hilt suggest that this sword is more ceremonial than functional in nature. In this way, we are reminded that the Swords suit is not really associated with physical conflict, but rather with mental activity. The crucial aspects of the sword, as far as Tarot symbolism is concerned, are its tempering (similar to the process of developing and strengthening an idea), its pointedness (useful for establishing a direction and clarifying an argument), and its association with skill. The proper use of a sword is very hard to learn, just as the proper use of the mind is difficult to master.

COINS

The suit of Coins represents physical life, commerce, and community. Its element is earth, the element of material life, and its astrological complements are the suits of Taurus, Virgo, and Capricorn. Whatever belongs to the body, to the senses, or to the realm of values is connected with earth. In the Waite deck, the token of this suit is the pentacle, a five-pointed star which symbolizes the five senses and serves in magical practice to create a "ground" or connection with the earth. However, the more traditional coin tokens offer a rich metaphor for our involvement not only with matter, but with our fellow human beings.

Coins are among the most interesting products of civilization because, like alphabets, they are one of the few explicitly agreed-upon symbolic systems used in a community. After all, money is of value only as long as everyone who uses it *agrees* on its value, and so a monetary system represents a consensus of the group that uses it. In earliest times, trade was carried out "in kind"; that is, goods were exchanged for other goods of like value. But this system was inherently limiting and inconvenient, since it required finding a match between people who wanted each other's goods. So a neutral method of exchange was created, by means of "commodity money." For a long time, most coins were commodity money, meaning that their value for trade was equal to the value of their materials—gold, silver, copper, etc. (A little more money lore: paper money is necessarily "credit money," equal to something other than the value of its own materials. When either coins or paper money become equivalent to a value set by the government, rather than being redeemable in some product such as gold, they become "fiat money," and that is the type of most money today.)

In keeping with their purpose as a symbolic medium of exchange, coins were used in most societies as a vehicle for other kinds of symbolism. They were typically decorated with religious and political images, such as crosses and portraits of rulers or historical figures. Even today we still have symbolically charged images on our coins, though most of us rarely stop and think about them. There are, however, a great many coin collectors who study art, history, and society through the medium of coins.

The earliest coins were struck in the eighth century B.C., in Lydia, but the real era of coinage began a few centuries later, when the Greeks began to decorate their coins. The first significant gold coinage was produced by Philip II of Macedonia in the third century B.C. Philip's successor, Alexander the Great, issued coins bearing pictures of the god Zeus and the mythic hero Heracles. From that point on, coins became more and more elaborate. Exceptionally beautiful coins were created by the Byzantine Empire, usually bearing a portrait of the reigning emperor on one side, and an image of Christ on the other.

But in spite of its Byzantine heritage, Russia did not have a regular monetary system until the time of Peter the Great. Prior to Peter's innovative reign, the Russians used a very primitive system of exchange, based on a simple silver coin called a *grivna*. (Interestingly, the word *grivna* originally meant "amulet," reminding us that in early times everywhere, coins of monetary value were closely related to amulets and talismans of magical value.) The earliest Russian coins were minted in Kiev during the tenth century, and after that, coins of various values were issued at various times, with little relationship to each other or to any particular value. Finally, the ever-inventive Peter set up a system of coinage based on the English model, with several related denominations and values close to the real weights of their metals.

The coin used as a suit token in the Russian Tarot of St. Petersburg does not appear to resemble any real historical coin of Russia. In fact, it does not really look so much like a coin as like a shield; the raised lip and rivet-heads around the edge are all quite impractical for a coin, but very useful for a shield. Further, the emblem of St. George in the center of the cross is a pattern commonly found on shields. So it may be that the coin is actually a commemorative type instead of a monetary coin. Here again, the suit token seems to suggest a symbolic rather than a literal interpretation. The coin is shown not so much as a convenient means of commerce, but rather as a symbol of solidity and security. This interpretation reinforces the physical and traditional nature of the suit of Coins.

CUPS

The suit of Cups is connected with emotions, relationships, and the unconscious. Its element is water, the element of psychic and emotional life, which is symbolically associated with the soul. A cup can be any kind of vessel, and its nature is to hold or enclose anything that is liquid or fluid. Similarly, our self-awareness gives form to the fluidity of emotional and intuitive life. So it is fairly easy to remember the association of Cups with the realm of feeling. The astrological signs complementary to Cups are Cancer, Scorpio, and Pisces, the water signs.

The "cup" is actually found frequently in mythic lore, representing a magical receptacle of great wisdom and power. In Celtic mythology, for example, the "cup" is a cauldron, and in Christianity, the "cup" is a chalice, the Holy Grail. These tokens were frequently the objects of epic quests, such as the legendary search for the Grail which has inspired songs, stories, and poems right up to our own day, when Grail lore has been dramatized in popular forms such as the musical play *Camelot* and the movie *Indiana Jones and the Last Crusade*.

The Russian Tarot of St. Petersburg uses a quintessentially Russian form of the cup as its suit token. The special shape of the

Cups token is that of the *bratina,* which looks like a loving-cup without handles. Bratinas were created in many different styles and materials, but they were always globular in shape, with a flat bandlike lip. A bratina was usually inscribed, in decorative Slavonic lettering, with a Russian saying such as "True love is a golden cup, which can never be broken; the soul alone can change it." Bratini were used as toasting cups, and were passed from person to person, symbolically uniting the drinkers in eternal brotherhood. Persons of high rank commonly had personalized bratini made just for this purpose.

The golden bratina on the cards is comparatively rich in design, decorated with gem-studded four-petaled florettes, and beading around the traditional flat lip. However, it is not designed in the ornate style of Imperial Russia, but rather has the more down-to-earth appearance of something from an earlier time. The choice of the bratina, for many centuries a symbol of Russian community, as the Cups suit token emphasizes that this suit is concerned not only with personal feelings, but also with communication and relationship within a world of shared feelings, beliefs and traditions.

CLUBS

This suit is unique because it can be represented by so many different types of "sticks"—rods, batons, clubs, and wands. The basic image behind all this variety is the branch, a symbol of living growth which is often shown in art and myth as the opposite or complement to the sword. In many early Tarot decks, the token for this suit was represented as a club or rod made of living wood, often with leaves still growing from it; but in other decks, the token was shown in the form of a ceremonial instrument such as a mace or baton. These latter objects are actually relatives of the original "war-club," which was no more than a slightly shaped tree limb. Later, a stone might have been lashed to the end of the limb; and later still, more sophisticated versions evolved in which a club-head of iron was attached to a wooden haft. Finally, this simple weapon was transformed into the handsomely wrought steel mace of the Renaissance.

From earliest times, the club or mace was considered not only a weapon, but a symbol of rank. Egyptian mace-heads were artfully carved from alabaster and obsidian, and were frequently shown being carried by dignitaries in ceremonial contexts. In the late European Renaissance, when the mace had outlived its usefulness as a weapon, it became an important ceremonial object and was always part of royal regalia. Even today, we see mayors and judges use its modern counterpart, the gavel.

Whatever its form, the general aura of the mace or club is one of power and prestige. On the other hand, the staff and the rod—two of the other tokens used for this suit—are associated with physical labor, and so with the working class or peasantry. Still other symbolic siblings of the mace or club include the baton—wielded by orchestra conductors and drum majors—and the wand, quintessential tool of the magician. These variations on the basic form are suggestive of creativity. But although these types are all different, underlying their variety is the common theme of *energy*: creative energy (wands), directive energy (batons), combative energy (clubs), and active energy (rods).

Since rods, clubs, batons, and wands all have different connotations, the particular style of "stick" chosen for use in a deck offers a general framework of interpretation for the suit. And given the martial character of Russian history, it's not surprising that the Russian Tarot of St. Petersburg uses the imagery of the club (combative energy) to designate this suit. But that choice doesn't necessarily limit the way the suit should be interpreted. All the forms of energy are present in the suit token, even though only one is directly symbolized.

The suit of Clubs is associated with fire, the element of active life. Its astrological complements are the signs of Aries, Leo, and Sagittarius. The basic ideas of the suit include doing, making, and moving. In the Russian Tarot of St. Petersburg, the Club token is long and graceful—indeed, too long to use effectively in battle. So like the Sword token, the symbolic rather than the literal meaning of the suit sign is emphasized. The long line of the Club, together with its studded head, suggests direction and effectiveness, energy put to a purpose.

The Court: General Observations

The court cards were part of the Tarot deck from its earliest appearance, but there is no way of knowing exactly why this particular group of cards was included in the deck's structure. Obviously, these royal figures were important in the world of the nobility, probably the first users of the cards. But royalty was also a very large symbolic factor in the lives of people at every social level. Kings, queens, and their courtiers (such as knights and pages) represented order, tradition, stability, and beauty. Although we now think of aristocracies as unjust because they are unequal, to the Europeans of the fifteenth century, a hierarchical social structure was the natural state of affairs. In fact, the idea of a society *without* fixed roles and strong leadership would have seemed in those days not merely ridiculous but quite frightening!

It is important, from the standpoint of understanding the Tarot, to see that kings and queens are not some vanished species. At first, the court cards may seem like an anachronism, leftover symbols of a long-past way of life. But royalty is not by any means absent today from our own lives or imaginations. Although we now elect our political leaders, they still live in such a different and distant world, wielding so much power, that it often seems they might just as well be hereditary nobles. And we are as fascinated today with our celebrities—movie stars, tycoons, astronauts, athletes, musicians, and many others—as any society ever was with its kings and queens.

Our celebrities, like the royalty of old, provide a point of reference common to everyone. Once upon a time, all the people of Russia, no matter how far apart they were economically or geographically, were united because they all had the same tsar. Today, each of *us* is connected with people across our own nation and around the world because we all recognize certain symbols—Madonna, Luciano Pavarotti, Batman!

The Tarot court cards, then, are about symbolic positions in society. The King is the founder/leader/father; the Queen is the consort/mother/teacher; the Knight is the son/heir/hero; and the

Page is the aspirant, eager to prove his worth by service. No matter how these characters are portrayed, their essential social meaning is the same. In the Russian Tarot of St. Petersburg, the court figures are naturally depicted as creatures of the old nobility, with full formal regalia and palatial settings. In fact, these are some of the most striking cards in the deck; the backgrounds of these cards offer glimpses of the richness of Russian royal life, and each of the court figures has a real personality, visible in his or her stance and expression. Since Americans have no tradition of monarchy to use for imagining these symbols, they have difficulty relating to the court cards, especially in a reading situation. If so, we can substitute other structures: for example, the chairman of the board, the CEO, the supervisor, and the employee; or the President, the First Lady, the Vice-President, and the Press Secretary; even Kirk, Spock, Bones, and Scotty.

Traditionally, court cards have been interpreted in readings as symbolizing real people in the querent's life. For example, the King of Cups might be seen as an older man whose personality fits the water traits. The court figures are also frequently associated with specific positions (King of Cups as husband, King of Coins as boss, and so on). Many readers today, however, take considerable latitude with the court cards, treating them as representations of basic psychological structures. From this point of view, the King of Cups might be the masculine side of emotional life or the highest degree of affective experience.

The Court: Card by Card

The Pages usually represent one of the following: a young person (boy or girl); a message (such as a letter or phone call); unexpected news or events; a beginner in any enterprise. All of the Pages may be read in these ways, but the Page of each suit also has specific divinatory meanings, as shown in the following descriptions.

Page of Swords

A youth stands on a rocky outcropping, examining the sword he holds aloft. Behind him we glimpse the tower and walls of a small city. In addition to the general meanings of the Page, the Page of Swords may represent a spy or rival.

Page of Cups

A young man kneels upon a stone hillock. He is looking at a fish encircled by a glowing aura or halo, which arises from a cup held in his hands. A city is seen in the distance. The fish is a traditional symbol of Christ, and serves here as a reminder of the relationship between the Tarot Cup token and the Holy Grail. In addition to the general meanings of the Page, the Page of Cups may represent a marriage proposal or a birth.

Page of Clubs

A young man is dressed in military garb and seems to stand at attention on the steps of a palace balustrade. In his hand is a viewing glass, suggesting that he is a guardian. In addition to the general meanings of the Page, the Page of Clubs can represent courage and fidelity.

Page of Coins

A richly dressed young man reads a scroll by candlelight. The carved facade behind him, and the parquet floor, suggest he is in a noble house, or perhaps a chapel. In addition to the general meanings of the Page, the Page of Coins may represent a student or disciple.

The Knights are usually associated with men (and sometimes women) in early adulthood (twenties and thirties). However, they may also represent, more generally, action in the sphere symbolized by the suit; for example, the Knight of Cups might represent action in an emotional or romantic matter.

Knight of Swords

Even as the Knight wields his sword, cape flying, his steed is rushing off the edge of a precipice. The Knight of Swords is dashing, brave, impetuous. This card may also represent cleverness and subtlety.

Knight of Cups

The Knight astride his prancing horse (fancifully colored gray with a strawberry mane and tail) reaches into the cup he holds. This card traditionally suggests arrival or approach. The Knight of Cups frequently represents a lover, or sometimes a dreamer.

Knight of Clubs

Knight of Clubs

This Knight is riding swiftly away from his city, along a rocky ledge. He carries a club upraised over his shoulder, as if he is prepared to meet trouble. The expression and demeanor of the Knight reinforces the traditional meaning of this card, which is associated with departure or flight.

Knight of Coins

A mounted Knight bears a bright standard, emblazoned with a sunburst. He carries a coin as his shield, and his armor suggests he is going to or returning from battle. The Knight of Coins symbolizes reliability and usefulness. A person represented by this card is usually trustworthy.

The Queen is the only female court card in the traditional Tarot deck, so it has generally been used to represent women of all ages. However, the Queen may be seen more specifically as a mature or experienced woman, with the Page considered to represent an immature or inexperienced woman. The Queen of each suit may also be thought of as representing the feminine aspects of the suit's nature. For example, the Queen of Cups might symbolize the feminine structures of emotional life, such as nurturing and receptiveness.

Queen of Swords

The Queen of Swords appears regal and fearsome as she stands on the palace balcony. She holds a sword pointing downward, and behind her, the walls and spires of the city can be seen. The Queen of Swords may represent a woman of power and intelligence, and/or a woman who has known sorrow and trouble. Widows are traditionally represented by this card.

Queen of Cups

The Queen of Cups appears wonderfully exotic. Her clothing is richly patterned and she seems to be almost dancing on the beautiful carpet as she holds aloft a cup containing two roses. Behind her, seen through the carved portal of wood and adamantine, a table with pitcher and fruit looks almost like a still life. This setting perfectly fits the poetic, imaginative and wise Queen of Cups.

Queen of Clubs

The Queen of Clubs is engaged in needlework, one of the Russian woman's most revered activities. Seated outdoors near a gazebo, she appears to be enjoying great peace and pleasure. Traditionally, the Queen of Clubs is a skillful woman—magnetically attractive, and frequently associated with both home and countryside.

Queen of Coins

The Queen of Coins, like the Queen of Cups, is presented in front of a table with fruit and a pitcher. But the two scenes are very different. The Queen of Coins is mature, relaxed, comfortable in her palatial surroundings. This card traditionally represents a prosperous woman: generous, intelligent, and helpful to others.

The Kings are figures of maturity and power. They frequently represent husbands, fathers, bosses, and other authority figures such as doctors, lawyers, statesmen and military leaders. The King of each suit may also be thought of as symbolizing the masculine aspects of the suit's nature. For example, the King of Cups might suggest masculine aspects of feeling and emotional life, such as competitiveness, outward focus, or future orientation.

King of Swords

Sitting uncrowned before an ornate window, the King of Swords seems to be caught in a moment of thought. The sword at his side leans casually against his leg. This card traditionally represents a man of authority and/or mental cleverness (a boss, a general, a judge or lawyer), and may also refer to suspicion or mistrust.

King of Cups

The King of Cups looks almost like an Eastern pasha, seated on a plump pillow with a colorful cloth wrapped about his legs. The fancifully carved bench on which he sits is so tall that his feet must rest on a footstool, and his cup is raised as if he were about to make a toast. The King of Cups is traditionally a good man, creative and kind, often involved with the arts or sciences.

King of Clubs

The King of Clubs appears to be holding an audience. He is gesturing toward someone unseen, his ceremonial club in one hand, the other hand upraised as if to express his authority. The King of Clubs is traditionally noted for his nobility; he is passionate, swift, and strong.

King of Coins

Rich and regal, the King of Coins is seated before a spectral view of the flags and crosses atop his city's spires. His position—feet planted solidly, gaze strong and straight ahead—expresses his nature: practical and dependable, skillful in business, and successful in life.

The Aces: General Observations

The Ace is the beginning of the numerical progression from one through ten. The name "ace" is taken from the word *as*, meaning whole or one. Unlike many words, *as* has an almost completely consistent form through Greek, Latin, and Middle English, and it is clear that in all of these languages, the import of the term is unity (wholeness, oneness) rather than singularity. Accordingly, the Tarot Ace can be seen as the totality of its suit, from which all the pip cards unfold.

In card games, the ace can frequently be used either as a one or as a card which beats ten. Tarot, similarly, treats the Ace as both beginning and end of the pip sequence (rather like the Fool in the major arcana). Tarot Aces have a special meaning, different and more comprehensive than the types of meanings assigned to the pip cards. Aces have the general sense of beginning or opening, and the Ace of each suit represents new possibilities in the realm to which the suit refers. So the Ace of Cups suggests new levels or areas of emotional/psychic experience, while the Ace of Coins brings the sense of open horizons and new energy in financial/material affairs.

This interpretation of the Tarot Ace is related to a traditional design for the card, which shows a hand reaching out of a cloud to present or hold forth the suit token. According to Cirlot's *Dictionary of Symbols*, "a hand emerging from a cloud is the most common symbol of Divine Omnipotence"—an interpretation which enriches the association of the Tarot Aces with gifts of fate. The hand/cloud design is found in Marseilles-type decks, and was adopted by Waite for the Aces in his influential deck, but the earliest Tarot decks showed only a single suit token (often worked into a geometric design) on the Ace.

Three of the Aces in the Russian Tarot of St. Petersburg follow the later style, while one—the Ace of Cups—is of the earlier type. The Ace of Cups was created by Yury Shakov, and we can speculate that he may have intended to follow a similar pattern with the other Aces. But in an interesting departure from both traditions, he has added a character to the card, a Russian horseman. Since Shakov's intentions for illuminating the remaining Aces were unknown, the second artist completed the sequence in the more familiar hand/cloud style.

The Aces: Card by Card

Ace of Swords

Ace of Swords

Atop the upthrust sword is a brilliant crown and a leafy, berry-laden branch, signifying the traditional association of this card with triumph, initiative, and strength.

Ace of Cups

The glowing aura which surrounds the cup in this card suggests the richness of spirit, while the horseman expresses the power of love and joy.

Ace of Clubs

The living, fruitful tree and the hilltop city which accompany the traditional uplifted club remind us of the creative and spiritual energy associated with this suit.

Ace of Coins

The Firebird, the symbol of fantastic and elusive desires, is seen perched lightly on the rim of the coin. The coin, poised between the church above and the city below, symbolizes the realm of earthly human experience.

The Pips: General Observations

Cards two through ten, which complete the sequence of number cards for each suit, are often called "pip cards." The term *pip* refers to the spots on a die or playing card; for example, each of the seven diamonds on the seven of diamonds card is a pip. Considered the least metaphysically significant of the Tarot cards, the pip cards are nevertheless very important in readings because they deal with the many matters which make up our everyday lives. Friendship and love, money and work, secrets and struggles are all part of the minor arcana world detailed in the pip cards.

Because there are so many pip cards in the Tarot deck, it is difficult to memorize an extensive list of meanings for each card. To make it easier to work with the pips, they can be generally interpreted by the combination of their numerical value and their suit designation. Using this "shorthand" will help you recognize the general character of each card more quickly. Then you can add additional levels of meaning as you become more familiar with the cards.

So as part of understanding a particular pip, you need to know both the meaning of its suit and the significance of its number. Two, for example, is the number of duality and equilibrium, so the Two of Cups is related to emotional equilibrium (the union of opposites) and the Two of Swords to mental duality (ambivalence or indecision). The pictorial images of the Waite-type decks don't always seem to fit these interpretive principles at first glance, but a general understanding of the inherent nature of the numbers will usually add illumination to the meanings of the pip cards.

The study of numbers and their mystical/magical meanings is quite complex, but most commentators would agree that the following basic correlations are valid.

Zero	Formlessness.
One	Unity, wholeness.
Two	Duality, tension.
Three	Synthesis, resolution.
Four	Stability, rationality.
Five	Variety, contention, the quintessence.

Six	Equilibrium.
Seven	Complexity.
Eight	Continuity.
Nine	Completeness.

These ten numerical elements are combined in various ways to form the higher numbers. The higher numbers can be looked at as a combination of their numerical elements; twelve, for example, contains a one (unity) and a two (duality), which is one of the reasons it is considered such a powerful number. Higher numbers can also be viewed in terms of their multiplication factors. From this point of view, twelve is three (synthesis) times four (stability) or two (duality) times six (equilibrium). Finally, higher numbers can be reduced by adding their digits together. By this method, twelve is reduced to three and takes on the properties of synthesis and resolution.

In addition to the number/suit approach, another helpful method of working with the pip cards is the use of a key word or phrase for each card. Each of the card descriptions that follow will begin with a key word or phrase chosen from among the wide variety of traditional interpretations to best fit the image depicted in the Russian Tarot of St. Petersburg. These keys can be used as a starting point for learning about each card.

A good way to discover the special significance embedded in each of the Russian Tarot of St. Petersburg pip images is to compare it with the corresponding Waite image on which it is based. By looking at elements that are changed or added in this deck, we can see more clearly how the Russian references enhance the pip cards and give them new areas of depth and meaning.

The Pips: Card by Card

SUIT OF SWORDS

Two of Swords

Key: Ambiguity

A woman in traditional Russian dress wearing a sarafan, kokoshnik, and fata holds a sword in each hand, pointing upward. She stands in front of a carved archway, apparently outdoors.

In the traditional Waite design, the woman is blindfolded and holds the swords crossed across her breast, characteristics suggesting indecision or ambivalence. In the Russian Tarot of St. Petersburg design, however, the woman appears strong and purposeful in her balancing of the two swords. Instead of being seated by the water, as in the Waite card, she is standing firmly on land. This card indicates that two forces, perhaps opposed or perhaps complementary, are being held in balance.

Two of Swords

Three of Swords

Three of Swords

Key: Sorrow

The Three of Swords is one of the only two designs in the Waite minor arcana which does not include a person. (The other is the Eight of Wands.) In that deck, the image, which shows three swords piercing a heart, is a very painful one. Rain is falling in the background, heightening the unhappy feeling of the card.

The Russian Tarot of St. Petersburg shows the swords in front of the heart, but here they are not piercing it. In the background are three bells, hung from arches, and covered—as were many of Russia's lovingly made bells—with a delicate tracery of heart-shaped and floral patterns. The heart itself, traditional centerpiece of this card, is covered with the same beautiful scrollwork, and flanked by two columns which echo the archway shown in the Two of Swords. Though the image expresses a certain melancholy, we are reminded by the bells— rung in Russia on every meaningful occasion, whether sad or joyous— that in Russia, suffering itself is believed to be a creative experience.

Four of Swords

Key: Rest

In the Waite deck, the figure resting in the Four of Swords is a knight. He looks like a medieval effigy, lying on a stone bier below a stained glass window. Three swords hang over his head, pointing straight toward him, while one is displayed beneath his resting place. This image supports such traditional interpretations of the Four of Swords as illness or retreat from strife.

But here again, the Russian Tarot of St. Petersburg offers a less harsh version of the image. The long hair, caftan, and youthful face of the resting figure make it difficult to tell whether it is male or female, but we can see that he/she appears snug and relaxed among a pile of furs and pillows. Above the sleeper, an open window reveals a blue sky and the burnished gold of a church dome; the beautiful tilework which adorns the sleeper's resting place is a reminder of the skill and diversity of Russia's craftworks. Here, the four swords suspended overhead slant away from the sleeper, maintaining the peaceful feeling of the image, which resonates with another traditional interpretation for the Four of Swords: rest and restoration.

Four of Swords

Five of Swords

Five of Swords

Key: Treachery

The Russian Tarot of St. Petersburg offers a much more dramatic version of the Waite image for the Five of Swords. In the distance, a walled city is burning, recalling the many battles and sieges of Russian history. Two warriors in the foreground stand on rocky promontories. One brandishes two swords, the other clutches his cape, gazing into the distance where a third figure kneels as if in despair.

In both the Waite and the Russian Tarot of St. Petersburg versions of the card, one figure appears to be smiling surreptitiously at the suffering of the others. This tableau suggests the traditional interpretations of treachery, dishonor, and infamy. But even so, the rich colors and textures of the warriors' costumes and the vivid distant flames give the Russian Tarot of St. Petersburg image a grandeur that is in keeping with the scope of Russia's panoramic past. Perhaps this is a reminder that right and wrong are not always easy to distinguish.

Six of Swords

Key: Escape

The basic elements of the Waite design for this card include a female figure with bowed head, seen from the back as if leaving in a boat, and a ferryman, also seen from the back, steering the simple boat with a pole. Both figures are present in the Russian Tarot of St. Petersburg card, but there are subtle differences. Here, the male figure steering the boat is seen from the front, looking steady and purposeful. The boat is sumptuously carved, with a beautifully decorated sail. Both figures are richly dressed. And perhaps most significant, the child shown huddled next to the woman in the Waite deck is absent in this image.

As a result of these differences, the Russian Tarot of St. Petersburg card gives the impression that the occupants of the boat are not fleeing, but are perhaps engaged in a private voyage. Though their demeanor suggests problems may be present, they don't seem to be downtrodden refugees. So here again, the feeling of the card is less grim, more open to a variety of interpretations.

Six of Swords

Seven of Swords

Seven of Swords

Key: Design

A warrior kneels outside a walled city. He holds several swords, and others are arrayed around him. In the background, wisps of smoke are seen from an encampment of tents. The man looks thoughtful, staring intently at one of the swords.

This card differs significantly from the Waite version, in which the sword-bearer appears to be running away from the battlefield. The contemplative look of the figure in the Russian Tarot of St. Petersburg image fits in well with the traditional interpretation of this card as related to planning and design. He seems to be considering a strategy, or perhaps reflecting on the situation in which he finds himself.

Eight of Swords

Key: Captivity

A woman is tied up with ropes and surrounded by swords. Clearly, she is in an unpleasant situation—yet in the Russian Tarot of St. Petersburg image, she is much better off than in the Waite image. The Waite card shows this woman blindfolded (like the damsel in the Two of Swords), but here she is able to see. And whereas the Waite card has all the swords embedded in the ground around her, the Russian Tarot of St. Petersburg deck leaves one sword suspended in mid-air, as if it were about to cut the ropes and free her.

Behind the woman is a church, the symbol of salvation, and beside her is a living tree, another suggestion of hope. Her long, beautiful hair, the most prized possession of a Russian woman, plays in a gentle breeze. While she is clearly captive, her plight appears less threatening here than in the Waite card. This image is more clearly suggestive of Waite's own description of the Eight of Swords: "It is rather a card of temporary durance than of irretrievable bondage."

Eight of Swords

Nine of Swords

Nine of Swords

Key: Despair

The image of the weeping woman on the Nine of Swords is perhaps the most poignant of all the Tarot cards. She is clearly inconsolable, the victim not of some passing sadness, but of true grief. Deep night reigns outside her window, and the candles burn down. The points of the nine swords curve around her body, almost touching her.

If anything, this image is even more evocative of deep despair than the corresponding Waite image. In the Waite card, the figure is sitting up in bed, as if she has awakened from a nightmare. But in the Russian Tarot of St. Petersburg, she kneels on a stone ledge, almost in the fetal position. There is certainly no softening of this image, which reminds us that real pain and the "dark night of the soul" are inevitable parts of life.

Ten of Swords

Key: Ruin

In this card, too, the image is more rather than less dreadful than its Waite counterpart. The knight lies pierced through the heart, his cape swirled beneath him, a fan of swords opening out from his wounds. We see his face, peaceful in death, and his own sword lies beside him, as if dropped from his hand in the last moment. An arc of clouds completes the powerful and telling composition of the picture.

Perhaps this card is especially striking because its rich colors and elegantly arranged shapes contrast so sharply with its deathly subject. In the Waite card, the figure lies face down, struck through the back with all ten swords in a neat row. He is anonymous. But in the Russian Tarot of St. Petersburg, the figure seems real; we see his face. Although this card is traditionally not associated with death or violence, but rather with loss and desolation, the image reminds us that everything can change, vanish, in a moment's time. The Ten card sums up the suit of Swords in both its orientations: the completion of mental life is physical death, and the fulfillment of strife is ruin.

Ten of Swords

Two of Cups

SUIT OF CUPS

Two of Cups

Key: Union

This card follows the Waite card very closely: a man and a woman face one another, each holding a cup. They symbolize union, friendship, sympathy, and/or romantic love. Waite's card observes the tradition which aligns the masculine with the right (conventionally, the "strong" and "rational" side), the feminine with the left (the "weak" and "irrational"), but in the Russian Tarot of St. Petersburg, the positions of the two figures is reversed. This change may reflect the deep reverence of the Russians for the feminine.

The card also follows Waite in incorporating a curious emblem. Above the cups of the lovers is what Waite describes as "the Caduceus of Hermes, between the great wings of which there appears a lion's head." The caduceus, a wand twined about by two serpents and surmounted by a pair of wings, is a very old symbol, associated with balance, wisdom, and right conduct, as well as with the kundalini energy. The winged lion is a symbol of St. Mark.

Three of Cups

Key: Celebration

Three gaily costumed women are gathered together. Each holds a cup, and one waves aloft a garland of flowers. Their finery suggests that they may be participants in one of Russia's many festivals. Not only were numerous feast days celebrated by the Church, Russia also preserved a wide array of its pre-Christian holidays, celebrating the harvest, the change of seasons, and other aspects of the rich connection between life and earth. In the countryside, the belief in spirits who inhabited woods, waters, and fields persisted almost until modern times, and ritual celebrations were held to acknowledge the power of the unseen world.

The traditional meanings of the Three of Cups include celebration, friendship, and gladness. But the card may also suggest excessive merrymaking, in the form of drunkenness, and can even signify addiction.

Three of Cups

Four of Cups

Four of Cups

Key: Concentration

The young man in this image focuses his attention on three cups set in front of him. A hand emerging from a cloud holds out to him a fourth cup, but he fails to notice.

The Four of Cups is traditionally associated with discontent in the form of weariness or satiety, signified by the young man's bored contemplation of the cups before him. The unseen fourth cup suggests that other values and opportunities are being ignored. But there is an additional element added to the Russian Tarot of St. Petersburg card. Here, the man holds a gem in his left hand, and he looks with interest at the cups before him, as if trying to decide which of them should receive the stone. His expression is eager rather than bored, and the message of the card seems to be about misplaced attention—the focus on material rather than spiritual values.

Five of Cups

Key: Loss

Three overturned cups and two upright ones make up the five cups of this card. The overturned cups have spilled their contents upon the ground, and a man sits over them, contemplating a loss.

Here again, the Russian Tarot of St. Petersburg presents the man on this card as a real individual, rather than an anonymous figure. In the Waite deck, the man is seen only as a cloaked silhouette, his back turned. But the Russian Tarot of St. Petersburg image shows us a man, mature and richly dressed, whose sadness is evident. Behind him is a Russian city, reminding us of the many sorrows that have befallen Russia. The man's empty scabbard suggests he has lost his power; perhaps he is the ruler of the city, which has been lost to invaders. His demeanor reinforces the traditional associations of this card: disappointment, sorrow, and loss. The upright cups, however, suggest that something remains.

Five of Cups

Six of Cups

Six of Cups

Key: Memory

This is the only Cups card which makes a considerable departure from the Waite pattern. The Waite card features two young children in a cottage garden, surrounded by cups filled with flowers. The Russian Tarot of St. Petersburg image retains the flower-filled cups, but places them on a mysterious tier of stone tables. The young people—who are quite a bit older than the Waite children—are working together on arranging a cup of flowers, which reminds us of the Russian love affair with flowers. ("Flowers! wrote the visiting Theophile Gautier. "There really is a Russian luxury! The houses are stuffed with them!") Not only did flowers grow wild about the countryside, gardens were carefully cultivated; and in the cities, flower markets provided a profusion of blooms.

One traditional meaning for the Six of Cups is nostalgia for a better past, such as the world of childhood. But other meanings, which seem better suited to the Russian Tarot of St. Petersburg card, are associated with pleasurable memories and with sexual fulfillment—in general, the recollection of sensual riches.

Seven of Cups

Key: Fantasy

While the Six of Cups focuses on memory, the Seven of Cups turns to imagination—things not remembered, but dreamed of. The Waite card shows a silhouetted figure gesturing in awe at seven cups from which tumble all manner of fantasy objects: coins, gems, serpents, even whole cities.

In the Russian Tarot of St. Petersburg, the silhouette becomes the figure of a poor peasant in patched clothing. Holding a staff and clutching a shawl about his neck, he gazes at the cups with a bemused expression, as if wondering who they could belong to. Through this personalization, the card evokes our awareness of the extreme disparity between rich and poor throughout Russian history, as well as reinforcing the theme that imagination and fantasy play an important role in all our lives. Desire and illusion, in both their positive and negative senses, are also traditional associations for this card.

Seven of Cups

Eight of Cups

Eight of Cups

Key: Letting go

This card shows a man walking away from eight cups. Perhaps he is a wandering holy man, as suggested by his bare feet and his staff. He walks beside a stream, with the moon overlooking his journey.

Traditionally, the Eight of Cups suggests the abandonment of emotional entanglements or unhappy situations. It is also related to the theme of leaving behind worldly success in search of higher meaning. The Russian Tarot of St. Petersburg card reinforces this theme through its depiction of the wanderer, who looks as if he might be the same figure shown in the Seven of Cups; the two cards form a little story, in which the man, rejecting material desires, may have left behind his cloak and shoes to set off in search of spiritual life. Such "holy fools," whose lives were entirely given over to the will of God, were widely admired in Old Russia for their prophecies and for their denunciations of injustice. Among the most famous of these men was St. Basil, namesake of the great cathedral on Red Square.

Nine of Cups

Key: Satisfaction

The Nine of Cups shows a brightly dressed fellow, wearing the cap and carrying the staff of a countryman. He is much younger than the men in the previous two cards. Before him are arranged nine cups.

The interpretation of this card is among the least disputed in all the minor arcana. It is sometimes called the "heart's desire" card because it represents the fulfillment of all wishes: material well-being and emotional satisfaction. But the Russian Tarot of St. Petersburg card adds an extra and most interesting note to the traditional simplicity of this card. Interspersed among the cups are two small glasses of the type used for drinking vodka in Russia. Although the overuse of vodka in Russia is notorious, the drink has complex associations in the Russian culture. When introduced to Russia in the seventeenth century, vodka was thought by some to be the alchemists' "elixir of life," and the drink was appreciated for its quality of inducing spiritual reverie. The two vodka glasses in this image may suggest that reality alone cannot bring complete satisfaction.

Nine of Cups

Ten of Cups

Ten of Cups

Key: Complete contentment

The Ten of Cups, like the Tens of all the suits, represents the completion of the nature of the suit—here, the completion of emotional life. It's also important to note that the *completion* of emotional life lies beyond the satisfactions of one's personal desires (pictured in the Nine of Cups). The necessary additional ingredient is companionship and community.

Once again, the figures in this card face toward us, where the figures in the Waite card face away. Throughout this suit in the Russian Tarot of St. Petersburg, the personal element has been paramount. A happy couple is shown, their children playing safely behind them, their town seen in the distance. Overhead, an array of cups forms a rainbow, the symbol of earthly joy. Here are all the elements of a happy life that contribute to the stability and continuity of the community. In this way, the image reflects the traditional association of the Ten of Cups with both home life and home land: the place of one's birth, the country of one's allegiance. Since this theme has always been so richly a part of Russian feeling, it is fitting that the Russian Tarot of St. Petersburg card is depicted with such joy and vividness.

SUIT OF CLUBS

Two of Clubs

Key: Influence

In this card, a well-dressed man stands firmly planted on a rich carpet, a club in either hand. Behind him is an intricately carved frieze, and windows looking out on the towers and spires of a city.

By his costume and bearing, the man appears to be a boyar. The boyars, a powerful group made up of land owners and wealthy merchants, wielded great influence on Russian affairs. From early times, the boyar families consolidated their power through marriage (princes and tsars frequently selected their brides from among the boyars' daughters) and through control of the *Duma,* or council of advisors. The collective will of the boyars often deter-mined how government affairs were conducted, and even who would be tsar. The boyar is the perfect Russian symbol for the Two of Clubs, a card which traditionally suggests dominion, influence, and wealth.

Two of Clubs

Three of Clubs

Three of Clubs

Key: Enterprise

The Three of Clubs features another boyar, more magnificently dressed than the first. He stands on a balustrade, overlooking a river or harbor. Close at hand are church spires, and in the distance, a wooden ship with a brightly painted sail. The sunburst emblazoned upon it signifies activity and heroism.

Russia's great river system was among the key factors which led to her success as a commercial power. Boats and barges criss-crossed the vast Russian land, connecting its peoples, and carrying goods—furs, timber, food, and a huge variety of other commodities—to the bustling seaports for export. Thus the ship on the Three of Clubs summarizes the traditional interpretation of this card, which deals with enterprise, trade, and commerce. More personal meanings can include initiative and pride.

Four of Clubs

Key: Perfected work

Partnership, beauty, accomplishment, and harmony are all represented in this card, which shows a couple standing before their home. The man holds in his hand the laurel wreath of victory, and at their feet is the rainbow. A golden sun reflects its light on the clouds.

The house in this picture is typical of the intricately carved and brightly decorated wooden homes loved by the Russians. Beside it is an apple tree, symbol of earthly desires. Fruits of all kinds abounded in Old Russia, but the apple was best-loved; an amazing variety of apples were cultivated, and in legend, the apple was the favored food of the fabulous Firebird. All of these associations point to an essential meaning of the Four of Clubs, which deals not just with the perfection of work, but with the achievement of civilization and culture. This card is frequently related to the idea of harvest, as well as to the richness of homelife.

Four of Clubs

Five of Clubs

Five of Clubs

Key: Strife

Five men with upraised clubs are seen in a swirl of capes, as if quarreling. Yet the colors and patterns of their garments and the attentive expressions on their faces suggest there is strength and beauty in their conflict. This picture is a reminder that strife can be creative.

The swooping capes which make this design so striking reflect an element of the icon-painting tradition. The icons of early Novgorod, which were the first to offer a distinctive Russian (rather than Byzantine) style, frequently featured saints in flowing capes, arranged in large, bright swaths of color. The lush colors of this card also recall the brilliance of Russian folk art, while the oval shape of its tight composition is reminiscent of the famous Russian Easter eggs. All in all, the striking design pulls together many aspects of Russian art, and focuses attention on the creative relationship between art and conflict. But this card can also carry the meaning of competition, opposition, and scattered energies.

Six of Clubs

Key: Victory

In this traditional image, a laurel-crowned horseman leads a procession. With clubs held aloft and pennant flying, the parade bespeaks victory.

This is another card about which there is little dispute. It has the sense of difficulties overcome, the achievement of stability, and the resolution of strife. Together, the Five and Six of Clubs describe a path from conflict and disarray to order and accomplishment. In this rendering, once again, color and line make a bold statement, reminding us of the scope of Russian history, with its oscillation between great beauty and great turmoil.

Six of Clubs

Seven of Clubs

Seven of Clubs

Key: Valor

A lone man stands on a precipice, wielding a club as if to assure himself of his own strength. Overhead, a dove soars.

This is the only one of the Russian Tarot of St. Petersburg Clubs which makes a significant departure from the Waite model. The addition of the dove suggests that peace has been achieved. Why, then, does the solitary warrior stand on the very edge of the abyss, alone with his weapon? Perhaps the important message of this image is the personal, interior nature of courage. The man alone tests himself against himself, in the spirit not of warfare but of peace through strength.

Eight of Clubs

Key: Swiftness

This is the other (in addition to the Three of Swords) minor arcana card which does not have a human figure. In the Waite deck, the eight clubs (wands) are shown pointing downward across the card, with just the hint of a landscape below. The Russian Tarot of St. Petersburg, by contrast, shows the clubs pointing *upward,* as if being launched from Earth toward heaven; below a city is depicted in detail. Again, as in the Four of Clubs, the sun gilds the underside of the clouds.

This card traditionally means that events are unfolding quickly, or that speedy action is indicated. It may indicate energy or communication as well. By providing a realistic and sunlit landscape for the card image, the deck reinforces the positive sense of this card. The upward path of the clubs also suggests that events are open to development and possibility, rather than drawing to a conclusion.

Nine of Clubs

Nine of Clubs

Key: Position of strength

A young man stands amidst a group of clubs, looking warily around him. This card traditionally carries the meaning of protection or defense, so the man may be seen as standing against outside threats to preserve his own safety and that of the community. With his back to the trees, and his weapons ready to hand, he occupies a position of strength; any attack will be visible, and he is ready to meet every possibility.

The defensive posture was common to Russia throughout its history. Because there were few natural barriers provided by the Russian landscape, Russia was subject to attack from many directions and was often forced to fend off invaders. The epitome of Russia's traditional protectionism was seen in the vast defensive buildup of the Communist state. But a more positive interpretation of the Nine of Clubs focuses on preparedness, suggesting that stored energy can be productively utilized to meet challenges.

Ten of Clubs

Key: Burden

As always, the Ten reveals the completion of the suit. Here, the activist, energetic bent of the Clubs culminates in great burden and even oppression. In the Waite deck, a man is seen struggling under the weight of ten clubs, but in the Russian Tarot of St. Petersburg image, a warrior with many clubs seems to be attacking a walled city. The sense of this image is more active, and it suggests responsibility rather than oppression.

In the Russian Tarot of St. Petersburg, the sequence of pips in the Clubs suit seems to focus on the well-loved Russian values of independent action and communal connection. Although these values may seem on the surface to run counter to one another, in Russian culture they were inseparable. In Old Russia, self-sufficiency was the ideal of manhood (the typical Russian prided himself on being a "jack-of-all-trades") yet communities were cooperative and interdependent. The images of the Russian Tarot of St. Petersburg Clubs show the many phases of personal endeavor (influence, enterprise, accomplishment, conflict, victory, valor, action, protection, and responsibility), set in the larger context of social structures and values.

Ten of Clubs

Two of Coins

SUIT OF COINS

Two of Coins

Key: Changefulness

In the Waite design, the young man on this card appears to be juggling two coins as he dances near the sea. In the Russian Tarot of St. Petersburg, however, the young man stands on a precipice, the coins hovering over the abyss at his feet. Hands open, he looks down at the coins, almost as if he had dropped them.

The traditional meaning of this card is concerned with activity and change. The character in the Russian Tarot card looks as if he is poised on the brink of something, about to take action. The coins look as if they may be out of his safe reach, which suggests additional meanings sometimes given to this card: obstacles (especially monetary ones) and instability. Behind the young man, the sea can be glimpsed, painted in the traditional icon style which makes the waves look like solid scrolls of bright blue.

Three of Coins

Key: Skill

This card portrays a master craftsman at his work. In the Waite deck, the craftsman in the image is a stonemason, but in this deck, he is a musician. As he plays, a richly dressed man (probably his patron) looks on. The observer carries a ring of keys, suggesting that he is the master of a great house.

The floor and column which provide the setting for this little scene are decorated with the bright colors and gay designs of Russian folk art, enhancing the card's emphasis on aesthetic values. The musician plays the triangular balalaika, best-loved of Russian instruments. Its strings are plucked to produce a distinctive sound, suited to the ebullient yet often melancholy music of the Russian countryside. Traditional associations of this card include all forms of workmanship, as well as skill in any area of endeavor.

Three of Coins

Four of Coins

Four of Coins

Key: Possessiveness

In general, this card is related to earthly power, that which is conveyed by material possessions. But it also has a shadowy undercurrent of greed and acquisitiveness. In the image, a plump man smiles possessively over a casket of jewels, clutching a coin in his hand. Another coin, atop the treasure trove, is surrounded by a mysterious glow.

The dark, unadorned walls of the room shown here create an environment devoid of beauty or meaning. Only the horde is illuminated, and the man pays attention to nothing else. This vignette conveys a foreboding sense of the power which possessions may gain over our lives and spirits. Yet there is also another side to this card, which may also mean pleasure and satisfaction—the enjoyment of what is given to one in life. The Four of Coins begins a series of three cards which focus on various aspects of material life.

Five of Coins

Key: Loss

While the miser admires his treasure in the Four of Coins, people go without in the Five of Coins. Here we see a man and woman, barefoot, their clothes tattered and mended. They seem to be on a journey through a barren landscape. Heads drooping, the two are obviously tired and in despair.

The Waite card shows two beggars, one on crutches, trudging through the snow. But while the Waite image is certainly pathetic, the Russian Tarot of St. Petersburg may be more realistically moving. It is remindful of the hardships suffered by so many of the poor in the vast Russian land. The couple in the picture appears to be resting before moving on, in search of some better life. Perhaps they are peasants leaving behind a village where there is not enough land to go around, or they may be escaping from forced service in the army. But whatever their story, they seem to embody not only the principle meaning of this card (want, material need), but also a second traditional association with love (sometimes illicit love).

Five of Coins

Six of Coins

Six of Coins

Key: Generosity

The third card in this trio depicts charity—the opposite of the Four of Coins, and the antidote to the Five of Coins. A wealthy man (notice his fur-trimmed hat and luxuriously embroidered boots) is seen giving coins to a poor man. Behind them is the city, a reminder that generosity is one of the cornerstones of a civil society. This card may be associated with gifts of all kinds, as well as with the positive aspects of prosperity.

The traditions of charity and gift-giving were very important in Old Russia, where hospitality was legendary. Rich and poor alike kept an almost perpetual "open house," and social relations were very similar to family relations. (Indeed, peasants habitually addressed their equals as "Brother" and "Sister" and their elders or superiors—including the tsar—as "Father" or "Mother.") The obligations of nobility were widely preached, if not always practiced; the young tsar Alexander II, for example, when he did his lessons well, received a gift of money—which he was then expected to give to charity!

Seven of Coins

Key: Apprenticeship

In the Seven and Eight of Coins, the theme shifts from relationships with money to relationships with work. The Seven traditionally represents work that is not yet completed or not highly rewarded, such as that of an apprentice or student. The Waite illustration shows a man leaning thoughtfully on a gardening implement, apparently taking a break from his labor.

The Russian Tarot of St. Petersburg offers a much richer image: a woodworker with his ax. Skill with wood was among the most important attributes of the Russian man, for almost everything in early times was made from the trees which covered the north of the country. Not only homes, such as the fancifully carved house in the background of this card, but virtually every article of daily life could be made of wood. The depiction of a woodworker on this card thus reminds us that much of human labor is done not for personal glory, but to make life more comfortable and beautiful. In the house behind him can be glimpsed a stove, the heart of every Russian household. The stove was the usual home of the *domovoy* or "house spirit," as well as the center of all activities during the cold Russian winter.

Seven of Coins

Eight of Coins

Eight of Coins

Key: Achievement

In this card, the apprentice of the Seven becomes a journeyman—an artisan of great skill—and the Russian Tarot of St. Petersburg card accordingly depicts a blacksmith at his trade. Metalwork of all kinds was practiced as high art in Old Russia, but no metalworker was more crucial to Russian society than the humble blacksmith. Because of the vast expanse of the Russian countryside (and the urban gentry's aversion to walking), transportation by horse-drawn wagon or sleigh was a vital necessity; therefore, the blacksmith's role of horseshoer was highly valued. But in addition, the blacksmith created and mended many of the tools used by other workmen, including the all-important ax.

The burly smith shown in this card symbolizes the importance of labor in all its forms, including physical strength as well as artistry and expertise. On the wall behind him is a horseshoe, an emblem of good fortune which reinforces another meaning of this card: prudence.

Nine of Coins

Key: Security

This card, too, is associated with prudence and with achievement. It shows a woman in a serene garden, suggesting wealth and luxury. Because the woman is alone, there is also a feeling of privacy. Her surroundings and appearance suggest she is well cared for, both by herself and by others.

The woman shown in the Russian Tarot of St. Petersburg image is not as slender and youthful as most of the female characters depicted in the deck. She seems to be a mature woman, beautifully but not lavishly dressed. Behind her is a palatial home, and around her grow delicate and carefully kept trees. Everything about the image suggests the security and comfort that riches can bring, but like her counterpart in the Waite deck, the woman appears more reflective than delighted. Her pose and expression remind us that wealth may be an isolation and a burden, as well as a liberation.

Nine of Coins

Ten of Coins

Ten of Coins

Key: Prosperity

As always, the final card in the pip sequence takes the nature of the suit to its fullest measure. Here, an older man is surrounded by children and grandchildren, symbolizing the riches of a life well-lived. In token of care and regard, the young woman hands her elder a wrap.

In traditional Russian life, age was valued and respected. Households were typically made up of extended families, among whom the eldest members exercised great influence. The average Russian family placed great value on the treasured possessions which were passed from generation to generation—icons, embroideries, intricately carved gingerbread molds. But these material possessions were valued much more for their meaning and history than for their monetary value. Thus the real definition of wealth was the love and respect of family and friends, the accumulation of wisdom, and the creation of a good life. This definition is equally fitting for the Ten of Coins, which symbolizes the fulfillment of all material needs and desires, as well as the richness of home and family.

Chapter 5

Divination with the Russian Tarot of St. Petersburg

*D*ivination is a time-honored way of getting in touch with the many aspects of people and situations which aren't immediately apparent to our conscious attention. Putting yourself in a receptive frame of mind—for example, by concentrating on the imagery of the Tarot cards—helps you to become more aware of the many subtle influences which shaped the past and create the future.

The process of using the Tarot cards for divination is called "reading" because when you become very familiar with the card images, they can actually tell a story or explain an idea, just like words on a page. Through a process of shuffling the cards and then laying them out according to a specific model called a "spread," the card images can be used to form connections and sequences that are rather like sentences or paragraphs. Once you know how to interpret the Tarot images and discover the patterns that are revealed in a spread, you can gather information from the cards and relate that information to real people and events, either in your own life or in someone else's.

To use the Russian Tarot of St. Petersburg as an introduction to Tarot reading, you should begin at the beginning, with a simple and straightforward approach. Here is a very basic ten-step guide for the beginning reader. It assumes that you are reading for another person, but most of the process is the same if you are reading for yourself. If you are reading for another person, be sure and let them know that you just learning the process of reading and hope to have their cooperation and support as you work with the cards. (Try not to read for someone who seems negative or fearful.) Rather than having the person ask a specific question, just invite them to relax and explore the cards with you.

A TEN-STEP TAROT GUIDE FOR BEGINNERS

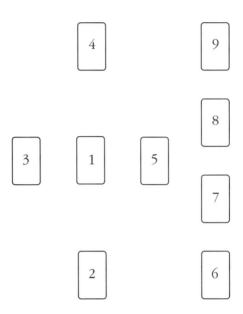

The Celtic Cross Spread

1. Shuffle the cards very thoroughly. Some readers prefer to shuffle themselves, using the process to focus their concentration. Others like to have the cards shuffled by the other person, often called the "querent." Whoever shuffles the cards should stop either when the cards seem to indicate a stopping place (by buckling or refusing to meld, for example) or when you have a feeling that it's time to quit.

2. Lay the cards out in the selected spread. The most widely used traditional spread is called the "Celtic Cross," and it's a good one for beginners. To form the Celtic Cross, take the first card off the top of the deck and lay it face up in the center of a clear space at least two feet square. (Place each card face up and right-side up as you continue.) This is Card 1 (present situation).

Next, place another card (Card 2, unconscious knowledge) directly beneath the first card. Then place the following cards around the center card, in order: directly to the left (Card 3, past influences); directly above (Card 4, conscious knowledge), and directly to the right (Card 5, future events). Now you've created the cross pattern.

Last, place a vertical column of four cards to the right of the cross. The first card, at the bottom of the column, is Card 6 (querent's view). Next up the column is Card 7 (view of others), then Card 8 (hopes and fears), and finally, Card 9 (future direction) at the top of the column.

3. Look over the whole spread of cards to get a general idea of the reading. *First,* check to see how many major arcana cards are in the spread; two or three major arcana cards is average for a nine-card spread. The higher the number of major arcana cards, the more power and energy there is in the reading. Also, a high proportion of major arcana cards usually indicates that forces outside the querent's control are affecting his or her life. *Second,* see if one or two suits dominate the minor arcana cards; if so, the reading is probably focused on that aspect of the querent's life. (For example, if there are lots of Cups, the reading may be especially informative about the querent's emotional life and relationships.)

4. Look at the images on the cards and see if they prompt any immediate ideas or insights. If so, you might want to express your thoughts out loud (using a small tape recorder is helpful to many people in reading) or make written notes.

5. Look up the remarks in this book for each one of the cards in the spread. These remarks are very general, but they will help stimulate and organize your own imagination. Keep talking or making notes as you do this.

6. Look at each card in relationship to its position in the spread.
Each of the specific places in the spread has a particular meaning.
The first card (1, present situation) you laid down represents the
essential circumstance affecting the querent in the present. The card
to the left of it (3, past events) represents something in the querent's
past experience which is influencing the present situation. The card
above it (4, conscious knowledge) represents something the querent
is presently aware of, while the card below it (2, unconscious
knowledge) represents unconscious perceptions influencing the
situation. The card to the right of the central card (5, future events)
represents something which is likely to happen in the future.

In the vertical column, the bottom card (6, querent's view)
represents the querent's own understanding of the situation, while
the next card (7, other's view) represents the influence or
perceptions of other people, as they see the situation. The third card
in this column (8, hopes and fears) represents a fundamental wish
or anxiety of the querent's, and the card at the top (9, future
direction) represents the probable outcome of the situation if
present trends prevail.

**7. Think about the cards in the spread as if they were telling a
story**. A sample story might go like this:
    "Once upon a time, something happened (Card 3, past
    events). So later, (Card 1, present situation). The central
    character (querent) believed (Card 4, conscious
    knowledge), but didn't realize that (Card 2, unconscious
    knowledge). He/she perceived (Card 6, querent's view),
    but everyone else thought (Card 7, other's view). Then,
    unexpectedly, (Card 5, future events). The central
    character didn't know what to do because he/she was very
    afraid/hopeful that (Card 8, hopes and fears). If nothing
    changed, it seemed certain that (Card 9, future
    outcome)."
Here's an example of what the story might sound like with real
cards. (You may find it helpful to actually lay out the cards
mentioned and follow the images as you read the story.)

"Once upon a time, there was a person, Sharon, who was so *preoccupied* (Card 3, Four of Cups) with one thing that she didn't notice something else important was happening. So later on, Sharon felt confused and *ambivalent* (Card 1, Two of Swords). She thought the problem was *stress* (Card 4, Five of Swords), but didn't realize that *childhood memories* (Card 2, Six of Cups) were upsetting her. Sharon felt she was actually being very careful and *prudent* (Card 6, Temperance), but everyone else thought that she was being *tricked* (Card 7, the Magician) and manipulated by a business associate. Unexpectedly, a powerfully attractive *woman* (Card 5, Queen of Clubs) came into Sharon's life. Sharon didn't know how to deal with this new influence because she was fearful of *changes* (Card 8, the Falling Tower). If nothing is done to alter this course of events, it seems certain that Sharon will become even more *worried* (Card 9, Nine of Swords)."

This sample story is told very simply, but that is the best way to start. As you become more experienced with the cards and the reading process, you can recognize and describe more complicated situations, with deeper characterizations and more lines of future development.

8. Share the story with the person you are reading for. If the story seems very clear to you, tell the whole thing and then discuss whether any of it might apply to the querent's life. If you don't see the story very clearly, tell the querent about the events or people you do see, and ask if they fit into the querent's life in any way. Through the discussion process, you can gain further insight into what the cards may be saying to the querent by filling in the generalizations of the story with real people and events.

9. Conclude the reading by summarizing for the querent your mutual discussion of the cards. Don't try to give advice or make predictions. If you see alternatives that the querent hasn't considered, you can point them out in a neutral way, without seeming to suggest a particular point of view or specific course of action.

10. Put your cards away in a quiet, safe place. (You don't have to have a special box or wrapping for your Tarot cards unless you want to, but don't just leave them lying around.) Make some notes about what you learned during the reading, and think about what you would like to work on or perhaps do differently in future readings.

    This basic approach will help you get started. You may have noticed that in this simple method, all the cards are read upright. Traditionally, reversed cards were given negative interpretations, and since contemporary Tarot reading focuses on growth and insight, rather than on fate and doom, many readers today do not use reverses. There are, after all, plenty of cards in the Tarot deck which represent problematic aspects of life! If you are unsure whether to interpret a card in a positive way or in a more problematic way, consider the position it occupies and the other cards in the spread.

    Once you are comfortable with the simple form of the Celtic Cross spread described here, you can increase the amount of information in the spread by adding more cards. Begin by doubling the spread—just go around the cross a second time so that you have a pair of cards in each position. Then read each pair as if the two cards in the pair were "talking to" or modifying each other.

    The basics of Tarot reading are the same no matter what deck you may be using. But the deck you choose can set a special mood for the reading, or yield particular kinds of insights by virtue of its style and imaginative appeal. The Russian Tarot of St. Petersburg offers several special qualities for reading. Its vibrant colors are visually stimulating, its flowing shapes inspire creative associations, and its exotic designs evoke a rich world of human emotion and activity. To gain the most from reading with these unusual cards, just open up to the drama and mystery they impart not only to the Tarot enigmas, but also to the intimate scenery of everyday life.

THE RUSSIAN ICON SPREAD

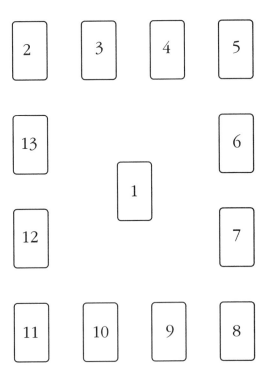

Although the Celtic Cross described above is an excellent all-purpose spread, different spreads (like different decks) can offer different kinds of information. There are many specialized spreads which can be found in a variety of Tarot books. But it can also be interesting to make up your own layouts, perhaps letting a particular deck inspire a special spread. I have created a new layout called the "Russian Icon" spread especially for the Russian Tarot of St. Petersburg, and you may enjoy trying it with the deck. It is based on a distinctive type of Russian icon known technically as a "hagiographic" icon, which is used to depict the life of a saint.

Hagiographic icons represent the saint in the middle, surrounded by squares or rectangles, each containing a painted scene from the saint's life. When I first saw one of these icons, I immediately thought it looked like a Tarot spread. When I wanted to create a Tarot layout that would be especially suitable for the Russian Tarot of St. Petersburg, I used the hagiographic icon as a model. The spread I devised can be used to review a querent's life and to discover some of the key events, people, and experiences that have shaped it. (These key items do not always turn out to be what the querent might have expected, by the way!)

To lay out the Russian Icon spread, first select a card to represent the querent. This can be done in a variety of ways: 1. You can have the querent select a card visually. Just ask him or her to look at the card images one at a time until they feel a strong identification with one of them. (You may want to limit the cards to trumps and/or court cards.) 2. You can have the querent select a card "at random" from a shuffled pile or stack. 3. You can choose a card based on the querent's sex, age, temperament, appearance, and/or astrological sign.

Next, place the querent card in the middle of a clear space at least two feet square. Then lay down the first card above and to the left of the querent card. Take another card from the top of the well-shuffled deck, and place it face-up and upright. Continue to lay down cards in this way, moving clockwise, and placing four cards on each side of the square. There will be twelve cards in the "frame," for a total of thirteen cards (including the querent card).

Traditionally, a hagiographic icon depicts the major events in a saint's life, beginning with his or her birth in the upper left-hand corner of the frame. Therefore, the upper left-hand card in the Russian Icon spread should be interpreted in terms of the circumstances and influences of the querent's birth, and that is a good point at which to begin the reading. The timeframe of the events depicted in a particular reading will, of course, depend on the age of the querent. (That is, ten or twelve important events in the life of a twenty-five-year-old will probably take place much closer together than the same number of events in the life of a fifty-year-old.) Generally speaking, however, the top row of the frame should relate to the querent's childhood and adolescence; the right-hand column to maturity; the bottom row to the querent's present situation; and the left-hand column to the future.

In reading the Celtic Cross, the Russian Icon spread, or any other layout of cards with the Russian Tarot of St. Petersburg, remember that the images themselves will stimulate insights. Don't rely too much on fixed meanings for the cards; instead, open yourself to the vivid colors, and the rich scenes which portray the traditional Tarot images in the light of a very old and immensely fascinating way of life. When you look through the oval frames of the Russian Tarot of St. Petersburg cards, it is as if you were gazing into another world—one which is vastly different from our own and, at the same time, very much a part of our shared human enterprise. Let that distant world offer you insight into the events and people that pass through your own life.

The Russian Tarot of St. Petersburg will enhance any Tarot collection, and will be a pleasure to every Tarot reader. Enjoy it for its rare charm, and remember that it depicts not only Russia's great spiritual and creative past, but also the qualities of hope, grace, and care which can enrich all our lives.

Bibliography

Alpatov, M. W. *Art Treasures of Russia.* New York: N.D. Harry N. Abrams, Inc.

Andrews, Peter. *Treasures of the World: The Rulers of Russia.* New York: Stonehenge Press Inc., 1983.

Ascher, Abraham. "The Kremlin," Newsweek, New York, 1972.

Billington, James. *The Icon and the Axe.* New York: N.D.

Blinoff, Marthe. *Life and Thought in Old Russia.* University Park, PA: The Pennsylvania State University Press, 1961.

Cross, Anthony, ed., *Russia Under Western Eyes 1517-1825.* New York: St. Martin's Press, 1971.

Downing, Charles. *Russian Tales and Legends.* New York: Henry Z. Walck, Inc., 1956.

Duncan, David Douglas. *Great Treasures of The Kremlin.* New York, N.D. Harry N. Abrams, Inc., Publishers,

Ferguson, George. *Signs and Symbols in Christian Art.* New York: Oxford University Press,1959.

Godwin, Malcolm. *Angels: An Endangered Species.* New York: Simon and Schuster, 1990.

Guliayev, Vladimir. *The Fine Art of Russian Lacquered Miniatures.* San Francisco: Chronicle Books, 1989.

Hall, James. *Dictionary of Subjects and Symbols in Art.* New York: Harper & Row, Publishers, 1974.

Hare, Richard. *The Art and Artists of Russia.* Greenwich, CT: New York Graphic Society, 1965.

Harrold, Robert. *Folk Costumes of the World.* London: Blandford Press, 1988.

Higonnet-Schnopper, Janet. *Tales from Atop a Russian Stove.* Chicago: Albert Whitman & Company, 1973.

Horizon Magazine Editors. *The Horizon History of Russia.* New York: American Heritage Publishing Co., Inc., 1970.

Horizon Magazine Editors. *The Horizon Book of the Arts of Russia.* New York: American Heritage Publishing Co., Inc., 1970.

Huth, Hans. *Lacquer of the West.* Chicago: The University of Chicago Press, 1971.

Kaganovich, Abraham L. *Splendours of Leningrad.* New York: Cowles Book Company, Inc., 1969.

Lehner, Ernst and Johanna. *Folklore and Symbolism of Flowers, Plants and Trees.* New York: Tudor Publishing Company, 1960.

Martin, John Stuart. *A Picture History of Russia.* New York: Bonanza Books, 1968.

Massie, Suzanne. *Land of the Firebird: The Beauty of Old Russia.* New York: Simon & Schuster, 1980.

Maxym, Lucy. *Russian Lacquer, Legends and Fairy Tales, Vol. II.* Lucy Maxym, 1986.

Voyce, Arthur. *The Art and Architecture of Medieval Russia.* Norman, OK: University of Oklahoma Press, 1967.

Wallace, Robert. *Rise of Russia.* New York: Time-Life Books, 1967.

Wilcox, R. Turner. *Folk and Festival Costume of the World.* New York: Charles Scribner's Sons, 1965.

Notes

Notes

Notes

Notes

Notes